DATE DUE

Coal, capital and culture

What has the closure of the pits done to coal-mining communities? How has the miners' strike of 1984–5 influenced the self-image of the working class? This book is based upon research into four coal-mining communities in the West Riding of Yorkshire. Acute, well observed and informative, it alters our understanding of these communities in the 1990s as dramatically as the classic study *Coal is Our Life*, by Dennis, Henriques and Slaughter, did in the 1950s.

'The strength of the book lies in the way that it has attempted to use a thorough-going sociology of mining communities to assess historical and contemporary change in mining districts. It will add considerably to our knowledge of this significant area of British society.'
Huw Beynon, *Professor of Sociology, Manchester University*

Dennis Warwick is a Retired Senior Lecturer, now Life Fellow, at the University of Leeds and **Gary Littlejohn** is Reader in Comparative Sociology at the University of Bradford.

Coal, capital and culture

A sociological analysis of mining
communities in West Yorkshire

Dennis Warwick and Gary Littlejohn

London and New York

First published in 1992
by Routledge
11 New Fetter Lane, London EC4P 4EE

Simultaneously published in the USA and Canada
by Routledge
a division of Routledge, Chapman and Hall, Inc.
29 West 35th Street, New York, NY 10001

Typeset in 10/12 Garamond by
Falcon Typographic Art Ltd, Edinburgh
Printed and bound in Great Britain by
Biddles Ltd, Guildford and King's Lynn

British Library Cataloguing in Publication Data
A catalogue record for this book is available from the British Library.

Library of Congress Cataloging in Publication Data
Warwick, Dennis.
  Coal, capital, and culture: a sociological analysis of mining
  communities in West Yorkshire / Dennis Warwick and Gary Littlejohn.
  p. cm.
  Includes bibliographical references and index.
  1. West Yorkshire (England) – Social conditions – Case studies.
  2. Mining districts – England – West Yorkshire – History – Case studies.
  3. Miners – England – West Yorkshire – Social conditions – Case studies.
  I. Littlejohn, Gary. II. Title.
  HN398.E5W37   1992
  306'.09428'1 – dc20   91–23173   CIP

ISBN 0–415–05015–4

Contents

Illustrations

PLATES

FIGURES

TABLES

Preface

The decline of coal mining, consequent on policies of pit closure, changes in energy policy, the sterilisation of coal resources through the withdrawal of capital investment, as well as the depletion of coal seams, is eroding an industrial culture in West Yorkshire. Former busy mining localities are changing and with few firm plans for new capital investment, the skills, knowledge and sentiments of a century of development are being put to a severe test. The book will explore the social and cultural dimensions of the changes, by drawing upon several sets of data collected in the last decade in four mining localities within the Wakefield Metropolitan District.

Our approach will parallel that of recent sociological work which has stressed, despite predictions of their demise under the impact of social change, the continuity of traditional social networks – based in kinship, friendship and neighbourliness in household and community settings. Repeatedly our data point to the significance of such networks as bases of continuity and as resources to be drawn upon in a period of change. In addition, we think that such resources form such an important feature of these industrial localities that it can be defined as a kind of capital, local cultural capital, which is, like economic capital, unequally distributed and has an effective role in differentiating between households and localities.

Our book is to some extent an attempt to replicate a classic study of mining localities undertaken in the 1950s by Norman Dennis, Fernando Henriques and Cliff Slaughter. Our localities were chosen so as to cover the same geographical area. We begin, therefore, with a summary of the literature on community studies, with particular reference to coal mining localities, and, in the second chapter, will discuss the classic study, *Coal is Our Life*, (Dennis, Henriques and Slaughter, 1956), in the light of our theoretical framework. This is drawn from sociological work on contemporary social change and conflict, and includes reference to Alain Touraine, Pierre Bourdieu, Manuel Castells and Raymond Murphy. We shall be concerned therefore with the role of the state, social classes, the force of social movements, particularly the labour movement, and questions of social and cultural reproduction and social closure.

Following these chapters, we will present an outline of the development of the mining industry and the towns and villages of West Yorkshire, as a backdrop to the question of continuity and change in our four localities. We shall use data from census and other sources, local and national, to emphasise the relation between coal mining and the labour movement, and the development of a local culture, which has tended to support particular divisions of labour. This will lead to our discussion in later chapters of household and community relations, with reference to the domestic division of labour, women's paid employment, education and other social conditions.

The final question will be the future of such localities, and in order to answer this we wish to discuss the effect of the miners' strike of 1984/5 and its implications, in the context of current tendencies in industrial (post-industrial?) societies.

Acknowledgements

This book has become possible through the help of many friends and colleagues, but above all from the men and women in four West Yorkshire towns who answered so many questions in our interviews and conversations. We would like to thank the Economic and Social Research Council for funding the research in 1986 and 1987 on which much of the analysis in the final three chapters is based (Grant Number G1325005), the University of Leeds Research Fund, which supported the collection of information in 1984, and the Department of External Studies, Leeds University, and the Workers' Educational Association, Wakefield Area, which sponsored the Tutorial Classes in the Featherstone and Hemsworth areas. It was the members of these classes who collected and classified data from the 1871 and 1881 Censuses and from local sources, which is used in Chapter Three. They were Lesley Berry, Linda Dickinson, John Gatecliffe, Elaine Lennox, Tony Lumb, Alwyn Midgley, Jeanette Meek, Linda Oldfield, Ann Portas, Frank Waude, Ralph Waude, Dorothy Williams, Elsie Williams, Jim Williams and Mary Wilson in Featherstone (see Berry and Williams, 1986). The Hemsworth class was Joyce Fieldsend, Stanley Hatton, Lorraine Lowe, Bill McQuade, Stuart Precious, Louise Price, Michael Price, John Radford, Joyce Roy, Mavis Ryan, Geoffrey Sugden, Gladys Vaughan-Birch and Joyce Wimpenny. Margaret Warwick assisted as tutor with both WEA classes.

The 1986 and 1987 surveys were carried out within the ESRC Social Change and Economic Life Initiative, coordinated by Duncan Gallie of Nuffield College, Oxford. Special thanks are due to Professor Sheila Allen, who co-directed our part of that research, and to Claire Peterson (of Nashville, USA), who spent the academic year 1985/6 researching with us and helped considerably in the initial phases of it. Val Carroll was our Research Assistant for the whole of that project and it was her skills and good humour that kept the research going through many difficulties. Chris Limb contributed many hours of secretarial work and we received much help latterly, in interviewing and technical assistance, from Caroline Welsh. Jill Calvert, Margaret Gee, Pat Graham, Margaret Heathcote, and Gillian Smith gave valuable advice, technical help and/or acted as interviewers. Without them and a number of other helpers like Ruth Gothelf, the surveys could not have been completed.

In earlier parts of the work Zygmunt Bauman, Griff Griffiths, John Williams, Chris Hunt, Patricia Morris and Ellen Renton gave advice and/or considerable time to interviewing, and participating in and recording local events. We also received help and encouragement from members of the Wakefield Metropolitan District Council, its Economic Development Unit, from John Goodchild and members of the Wakefield District Library and Archives, from local library staff, particularly Simon Rice and Christine Williams-Brown, and from the West Yorkshire Archives Department. Michael Peake, Steve Scholey and other members of the staff of the Pontefract General Infirmary Chest Unit assisted us generously in work connected with the 1987 and 1989 surveys of our localities.

As we will point out in the first chapter, there is a lively upsurge of locality and community studies in Britain, but we also want to record our appreciation of advice and encouragement given by colleagues in a number of universities around the world. In particular we thank members of the Departments of Sociology at Vanderbilt University, Nashville, Tennessee, at La Trobe University, Melbourne, Australia and at Canterbury, Christchurch, New Zealand. At the last named, Bob Hall and David Thorns have been particularly helpful in formulating issues and concepts in contemporary studies of communities, which we have used. Finally we would like to thank members of staff in our two University Departments, the Department of Social Policy and Sociology at Leeds University and the Department of Social and Economic Studies at Bradford University. We also acknowledge the work done on our photographs by the Photography section of the Audio Visual Service at the University of Leeds.

Chapter 1

Introduction

A framework for the analysis of community and social networks

COMMUNITY AS A SOCIAL IDEAL

The miners' strike of 1984 and 1985 was largely a conflict over the restructuring of, and redirection of capital from, the coal industry and the loss of jobs which that entailed. The location of mining has generally been outside urban areas and has often meant the transformation of former farming villages into larger settlements created around productive units requiring a labour force of anything from a few hundreds up to two thousand. Closure of a local pit, which makes up much if not all of the local labour market, almost certainly deprives a mining town or village of its chief source of income. It will also have several knock-on effects in the whole local economy, in the infrastructural provision of goods and services to the mining enterprise and in the distributive and service trades linked to the mining locality. One of the women's group organisers, whom we interviewed in October 1986, said:

> 'This strike was different. Before they've all been about money. They usually got what they wanted in the end when the strike was about money . . . the women used to push them back to work. This was totally different – it was about jobs and communities. . .'

It is not surprising that one of the most widely used slogans of the 1984/5 strike was 'Close a Pit: Close a Community'.

This slogan was clearly intended to appeal to those who saw 'community' as an ideal. The strikers and their supporters aimed to force their opponents, the Coal Board, the government and others, to accept that closing pits was not just an economic or political decision, but one which hit at the moral roots of human society. As Kamenka (1982) says

> In the nineteenth century, as a part of the great social changes first dramatized by the French Revolution and the Industrial Revolution, the concept of community acquired new content and a new urgency. It came increasingly to be contrasted, for better or for worse, with the individualism, the atomization, and the alienation that accompanied the

emphasis on private property, progress, enterprise, and capacity for innovation and change characteristic of the new, industrial–commercial society. By the twentieth century, the contrast between 'community' and 'society' as technical concepts or ideal types had become central in sociology, presupposed by much of the theory concerning the conflict between traditional society and the demands of 'modernization'. In the last two decades, the concept of community has become even more central to a wide-spread atmosphere and movement in western society – a revolt against progress and modernization, a rejection of individualism and of economic growth as alienating, a longing for the warmth, comfort and humanity of a *real* community.

(Kamenka, 1982: vii–viii)

While it is not self-evident that 'community' is or ever was the social force around which political or industrial activism could be generated and goals achieved, Kamenka is right, nevertheless, to draw attention to the potency of the concept in social and political thought. It is the main objective of this book to examine how far the sense and reality of 'community' did play a vital part in the year-long miners' strike and, as the grounding of that examination, to provide some contemporary evidence about localities which illustrate the realities of the social processes and institutions to which the concept of 'community' might be applied.

BACKGROUND TO OUR STUDY OF MINING LOCALITIES

The research began some ten years ago, not only with a wish to replicate the study of 'Ashton' (or Featherstone in West Yorkshire), which figured prominently in *Coal is Our Life*, but also to enter into the major debates within the sociology of communities, which formed a continuing link with the earlier study. Dennis, Henriques and Slaughter saw their study as a contribution to social anthropology, but one that was critical of the functionalist assumptions of some anthropological community studies applied to 'primitive' and to peasant societies. In such a study the field-worker

> was expected to provide a full and clear account of at least the main lines of economy, social structure, political organisation, ritual and ideology . . . [and] . . . the consistent functional interrelations of all these aspects of a society's culture.

(Dennis et al., 1969: 246)

Their own study was based in the thesis that internal consistencies could be explained not by functional imperatives, but by social forces which are external to the community. In particular they suggested the significance of the capitalist economy in which 'the social relations of work in the coal-mining industry in Ashton' (ibid.: 247) were located. It is recognisably Marxist in orientation as Bell and Newby suggest (1971: 169). The book is light on theory, however, and there was no attempt to express this idea overtly as a Marxist critique of functionalism. Furthermore, though it presents evidence of internal segregation and conflict in 'Ashton', as well as of solidarity and consistencies, the authors do not present these in terms of the contradiction between modern capitalism, with its alienating class divisions and conflict, and the social conditions which will allow the development of the full resources of humanity in communities. Thus there is no overt argument similar to that of Mahowald (1972), who claims that there are in Marxian texts the outlines of the *Gesellschaft* (society) and *Gemeinschaft* (community) oppositions, later to be taken up by Tönnies and Weber.

They were, of course, working in a discipline which had not yet been caught up in the issues of modernisation theory, and possibly saw the main theoretical issue simply in terms of a debate between the Gluckman 'conflict' approach (the authors acknowledge Gluckman in the text) and the 'functionalist' school of Malinowski. While we do not intend to discuss the relationship between social anthropology and sociology in studies of communities, a very interesting discussion, citing *Coal is Our Life*, can be found in the context of a discussion of Australian sociology (Austin, 1984). This broadly suggests the futility of inter-disciplinary blindness, since, while '[t]he subject matters of the two "disciplines" have been different, the logics of their theoretical development [are] very much the same' (ibid., 1984: 129). It is perhaps unfortunate, but Dennis, Henriques and Slaughter do not either consider their concept of 'community' worthy of much discussion (even taking account of the Introduction to the 1969 edition of the book), or note the contemporary debates based in 'the decline of community' thesis.

These two issues form our theoretical starting point. As we see it, the main thrust of our research in mining localities is based in questions both of internal structures and processes and of development and change at a much wider level. We shall not attempt to provide a full analysis of the development of locality and community studies to date. In any case there are good accounts by Bell and Newby (1971) and Wild (1981) which provide a cross-cultural perspective. Frankenberg (1966) provides an excellent summary of the British community studies tradition suggesting that stark dichotomies between rural communities and urban neighbourhoods, and, by implication, the 'decline of community' thesis, are unfounded. Simpson (1965), Havighurst and Jansen (1967) and Effrat (1974) have written key articles which provide overlapping attempts to categorise existing community studies, and to indicate possibilities for future research. One common prediction, which seems to link with Kamenka's (1982) assessment of the past two decades, was the likelihood of community-based action in urban societies.

There was a wide diversity of community-based action in the 1970s and 1980s. It was linked with sensed injustice over economic restructuring, the provision of state social services, and the loss of citizenship rights, and brought together groups variously solidifying around class, gender and ethnic characteristics. A new generation of community studies has emerged in consequence. Central to these has been Castells' study, *The City and the Grassroots* (1983), which examines the formation and development of community-based social movements. Others are the work of Redclift and Mingione (1985) and Pahl (1984) which somewhat more narrowly focus on the crucial significance of local social networks in responses to unemployment and economic change. Morris (1988) has summarised this development. Urban sociologists, often working with social geographers, have also contributed much to this reassessment of local social networks and local cultures. Cooke (1989), Duncan (1989) and Mellor (1989) provide very useful discussions of both empirical and theoretical considerations in this new work. Generally the question being asked by recent studies is how far 'localities can act as a viable base for social mobilization and exert influence on outside forces which help shape their destiny' (Cooke, 1989: 3). Common to them all, however, is a refutation of the 'decline of community' thesis.

THE 'DECLINE OF COMMUNITY' THESIS

It is, perhaps, as A.P. Cohen (1985: 25) points out, to the Chicago urban sociologists of the 1920s and 1930s (Park, Burgess, Wirth and others) that we owe the general hypothesis about 'the decline of community'. Their view was that 'modernity' consists in the replacement of close and widely diffused social bonds based in traditional small communities by the fragmented and situationally specific relationships of large, heterogeneous urban neighbourhoods. Their related 'melting pot' thesis suggested that urban America was experiencing a dynamic change in which people's identities and values were no longer based primarily in a number of traditional ethnic and rural social networks, but in a mass society, marked nevertheless by a detailed division of labour and life chances, and some rough equality of opportunity based in effort and achievement. They possibly overstressed the 'traditional' and 'modern' distinction, and read too much into the *gemeinschaft* and *gesellschaft* or the 'mechanical' and 'organic solidarity' dichotomies of the Weberian and Durkheimian schools, from which they drew their concepts.

In any case, the Chicago school is, as Bell and Newby (1971) indicate, more closely associated with what came to be known as the ecological approach. Their work consisted in empirical studies of what were seen as 'natural areas' where segregated groups of city dwellers tended to be located. Burgess's famous 'Zone' theory, suggesting where the different urban classes will be located, and how they might replace each other as conditions change, with influxes of migrants to the city, is an elaboration of the ecological idea. It was Stein (1964) who made the 'decline of community' thesis explicit, in his attempt to provide a basis for giving coherence to community studies. As Wild (1981) says, 'perhaps the commonest criticisms of community studies

are that they are non-cumulative and idiosyncratic . . . and (quoting Bell
and Newby, 1971) "they contribute little to each other"' (1981: 179). Stein
selects from the Chicago studies, as well as a number of other American cases,
to hypothesise that urbanisation, industrialisation and bureaucratisation are
eroding the sense of community. Wild, pre-figuring Cohen's later analysis,
points out that there are many weaknesses in the hypothesis, including the
view that

> Stein does not see that community as tradition, communion as sentiment
> and society as rationality are interacting and vying for supremacy in a
> cyclical or spiral process of social change.
>
> (Wild, 1981: 181)

Where Wild differs from Cohen is in the interpretation of the meaning of
the ideal–typical distinction between *gemeinschaft* and *gesellschaft* and the
categorical differences between 'mechanical' and 'organic solidarity'. Wild
sees the classical authors of these concepts as intending a sharp dichotomy
to emphasise the shift from traditional to modern society. Stein, and the
members of the Chicago school, committed the same error he says (ibid).

Cohen strongly suggests, however, that it would be more in keeping
with a reading of Weber and Durkheim to see their 'ideal types' or
'categories' as interpenetrating dualities. While there were some clear
distinctions between the social networks of villages and those of large
industrial localities, the claim that mass society would be a product of
industrial capitalism, and that social networks would take on new and
more homogeneous forms and ideologies, was only part of the story.
Reality is more complex. In contemporary society, old institutions have
adapted, rather than disappeared. New styles may have been imported and
'become new vehicles for the expression of indigenous meanings' (Cohen,
1985: 37). Rather than proposing, as mid-twentieth-century sociologists did,
that 'community is in decline', Cohen asserts that 'we confront an empirical
phenomenon: peoples' attachment to community' (ibid: 38).

THE ATTACHMENT TO, AND THE ASSERTION OF, 'COMMUNITY'

Castells' work (1983) is a discussion of urban social movements, communities
and social change. It is based in the premise that

> to understand cities, to unveil their connection to social change, we must
> determine mechanisms through which spatial structures are transformed
> and urban meanings redefined.
>
> (Castells, 1983: 301)

For Castells, structures are transformed and urban meanings are redefined
when dominant forces in a society are challenged by other competing forces.

The outcome is determined by the successful pursuit of tactics and strategies by opposed groups using whatever power they can muster. The players in the power game are not individuals, though key members of the opposed groups may perform a decisive role at certain stages of the conflict. The opponents are collectivities, such as major corporations, bringing together business, professional and finance capital, states, both central and local, using political and bureaucratic or technocratic power, and what we may term components of civil society, such as trade unions, community groups and social movements.

Cities, and neighbourhoods within cities, are transformed both structurally and culturally when, for example, housing provision is determined by the needs of the homeless rather than the demand for a return on private or corporation capital investment; when neighbourhoods are provided with social facilities which recognise the cultural preferences of minority groups rather than being bulldozed for new highways or shopping precincts, which serve out of town commuters; or when decisions are made by participating citizens rather than by distant and unrepresentative bureaucracies.

Castells is asserting that major social change only occurs when the dominant cultural orientations shift, say from individualism to collectivism, in response to a transformed balance of power between opposed corporations, state authorities, social groups and movements. As a former Marxist, he now no longer sees a historical necessity for a shift from capitalism to socialism, or from 'society' to 'community', but argues that history is open. Locally-based power may be as able to exert a decisive influence on social transformations as large corporations or state agencies.

This approach to social change is based, as Castells tells us, on the social action theory of the French sociologist Touraine. Empirically, the latter is concerned with social movements and struggles at the level of societies, whereas Castells deals with urban movements in the 1970s, struggling over housing (Housing Action Groups in Paris), community control (Black and Gay Rights in San Francisco) and democratic participation and citizenship (Citizens' Movement in Madrid). In all of the case studies, Castells fruitfully suggests the significance in the struggles of the assertion of 'community'. He may be accused of over-optimism in his assessment of the potential of locality-based movements to influence the change of urban meanings, and he may have biassed his analysis by choosing case studies which suggest that such movements tend to be oriented towards collectivist or socialist goals. Lowe (1986) presents such criticisms of Castells, with his analysis of British urban movements, including squatters and tenants' associations, and shows that we can neither be optimistic about outcomes, nor be sure of their socialist direction. There can be no disagreement, however, about the continuing significance of 'community' in contemporary social processes.

Morris (1988) also summarises recent British studies which have examined the relationships between households, employment and social networks. The latter have always played a crucial role as an indicator of the existence of 'community'. With reference to the early work of Bott (1957) and more recent studies such as Bell and McKee (1985), Redclift and Mingione (1985) and Pahl (1984), Morris notes that

> networks not only carry information and influence in connection with employment but also provide a source of support, both moral and material, in unemployment ... Support networks can provide the childcare or domestic services which free many married women to take up employment, although they act as a means of sanctioning and policing gender roles, thus constraining the sexual division of labour for many households...
>
> (Morris, 1988: 397–8)

Morris notes, too, that the socio-economic position of households in a locality can have an influence on such networks.

> The disadvantageous position of some households in declining local labour markets will have implications for access to work, socialization into different attitudes towards work, and the development of supportive networks.
>
> (ibid.: 401)

Networks provide resources, but also may create constraints, for households in particular localities. Such resources may be characterised, as we will argue later, as 'local cultural capital' (local ideologies, the knowledge, skills and influence contained in local social networks). Together these points seem to establish the continuing attachment of individuals and groups to forms of 'community'. They show how people are caught up in social processes at a number of levels, the dynamics of which we now turn to analyse.

THE SOCIAL DYNAMICS OF 'COMMUNITY' PROCESSES

Essentially the currently dominant conceptual apparatus for discussing these social dynamics of 'community' processes draws from the work of Weber. Neuwirth (1969) was possibly first to draw attention to the Weberian concept of 'social closure' and its application to empirical studies of community. Murphy (1988) has recently argued, drawing more fully on the ideas of Weber, especially as these have been used by Frank Parkin (1974), that social closure is a fundamental process of human societies generally. It is the practice of monopolisation and exclusion in pursuit of power to control human and environmental resources. Social closure is guided by ideas about how best to control these resources, such as through capitalism or state socialism. It is essentially seen as a conflictual process, and is near to the conception of Touraine, who sees social processes and institutions in terms of a struggle between social movements over historicity. (Historicity is his term for the great cultural orientations which shape our history.)

To Weber has been attributed the view that ideas are the 'switchmen' of history. Weber's own statement (in translation) was:

Not ideas, but material and ideal interests, directly govern men's conduct.
Yet frequently the 'world images' that have been created by 'ideas' have,
like switchmen, determined the tracks along which action has been pushed
by the dynamic of interest.

(from Murphy, 1988: 1)

Weber also used the concept of social closure and Murphy argues that
the 'tracks' in the above statement are 'none other than codes of social
closure: formal or informal, overt or covert rules governing practices of
monopolization and exclusion' (ibid.: 1).
Such codes of closure include those of:

1 Capitalism – closure around private property and the market.
2 State Socialism – closure around the monopolisation of power by a socialist
  political party.
3 Meritocracy – closure around credentials for entry into bureaucracies.
4 Gerontocracy – closure around experience and seniority.
5 Apartheid – closure around racist ideas.
6 Patriarchy – closure around notions of male supremacy.
7 Nationalism – closure around the idea of the nation.

Other forms of closure may occur around kinship and lineages, slavery, rank
or castes and religious affiliation. As far as locality studies are concerned,
as Hall (1987) has shown, in Western capitalist societies communities may
form on the basis of closure around property, kinship and neighbouring (or
'propinquity' as Hall and his colleagues call it).

Then Murphy argues that it is important not to overlook the relationships between the rules or codes of closure and, in particular, the prior
power of property over the others in capitalist or market economies. He
asserts that

far from being a force promoting equality, market competition in the
context of laws guaranteeing private property is the principal basis of
monopolization in capitalist society, whereas status-group monopolies,
including those founded on educational credentials, are important, but
only secondary, bases of monopolization.

(Murphy, 1988: 69)

It is, therefore, necessary to propose, suggests Murphy, an ordered view of
codes of social closure, so that the differences between societies and levels
of community processes can be understood.

Murphy puts forward a three-fold classification of such codes, labelling
them principal, derivative and contingent. A principal form of exclusion
is one that is backed by the force of the state and its legal apparatus. It
determines 'access to, or exclusion from, power, resources and opportunities'
and 'class situation' (p. 70). Derivative forms could not operate effectively

without the principal codes. They include credentialism, racism, religious sectarianism, sexism, kinship and propinquity. They may be written into the law, but generally are not, since the propertied have the legal right to choose. Even if they are instituted with the force of law, the propertied tend to disregard the laws because of their dominance based in the power of ownership and the cultural values which surround that. Contingent codes are those which are based in skills or physical qualities of persons not directly controllable by the principal codes of social closure. Murphy seems to be referring to scarce skills and virtuosity, which may be credentialled, for example, in medicine and the arts, and to qualities which are to some extent biologically determined and socially sanctioned like beauty.

These classifications lead to a formulation of what Murphy sees as the real dynamic of society, conflicts of interest pursued by strategies of closure, creating exclusions and opposing attempts to break down, or usurp, the structures of closure created by those who have for the time being established control. Such oppositions may have merely 'inclusionary' aims, simply to create a fairer share of resources in the existing society, or they may be 'revolutionary', desiring to overthrow existing dominant groups. They are likely to be different where the principal forms of exclusion are different. This leads then to a consideration of social movements which provide the obvious examples of forms of opposition. Generally social movements arise among those whose only power, if any, lies in derivative or contingent forms of exclusion. Social classes formed out of exploitation by a dominant class whose power resides in a principal rule of exclusion, may be fragmented by the application of contingent or derivative rules, for example the working class in Northern Ireland, split by sectarianism, or in any industrial society, where it is split by patriarchy, racism or both. These fragments may well be the basis of separate social movements or, if they define themselves in terms particular localities, as separate 'communities'.

This notion of fragmentation becomes the basis of Murphy's critique of existing class theory. If we define societies and collectivities of societies in terms of a theory of social closure, then it is impossible to agree with the idea, as put forward by some neo-Marxists, that the formation of social classes is structurally determined, even behind the backs of and with no place for creative action by class opponents. Neither is it possible to agree with other neo-Marxists, who define class in terms of consciousness and organisation, and class formation as an act of will rather than a consequence of an objective situation.

Closure theory teaches us to focus on a whole web of structural relationships of monopolisation and exclusion and to examine particular social contexts or conjunctures, and the possibilities for and constraints on usurpatory action. It is reasonable to see in the whole web of exclusions, a set of people who have a similar structural position. Social class can be defined in such a global way, but it is unlikely that social classes, globally defined, will act in common. Understanding the dynamic of society and history, and how social change might occur, with a theory of social closure, implies the examination of class fragments, their composition, their experience of inclusion and exclusion, and the likelihood of collective usurpatory action in terms of interests defined by them. The theory would also hold that usurpatory action will arise from 'an excluded aggregate', a set of people identified by recognised forms of exclusion, a consciousness formed in an ideological struggle and at least elements of organisation, in a particular conjuncture.

> A conceptual framework for the analysis of the connection between the structure of exclusionary practices as experienced, and conscious collective usurpatory action as engaged in, can . . . be developed from the Weberian concepts of 'status group' and 'communal' and 'associational' relationships. This framework provides a set of concepts for the analysis of the creative action of the excluded and it points to certain regularities and tendencies. Whether the excluded form amorphous, associational or communal status groups, and whether they develop an individualistic, a reformist or a revolutionary consciousness depends on their own creative action and on the historical conjuncture.
>
> (Murphy, 1988: 127)

Thus Murphy provides us with both a theory of community formation, amid a much wider discussion of social processes, and some proposals for research. In a footnote that links him to the main objective of this book, he suggests that it will still be possible to find 'some rare class fractions that form communities' and cites miners as possible candidates (ibid.: 131).

Murphy's argument is a relatively sophisticated example of the Weberian approach to the analysis of communities, and avoids many of the pitfalls of earlier attempts at theorisation of such issues. Nevertheless, it does have certain weaknesses which need to be addressed. First, the concept of 'closure' (with its associated notions of 'monopolisation' and 'exclusion', as practices designed to control resources) is effectively akin to an untheorised juridical conception of resources as assets which can be exclusively owned. Overlapping rights and claims, and their social conditions, are consequently relegated to the background, since the main features of interest are the conditions of closure. As the juridical notion of exclusive control of assets is applied to non-legal situations, 'closure' runs the risk of simply becoming a convenient label to describe what may well be important lines of demarcation and inequality. Such a danger, if realised, may mean that 'closure' actually obscures the analytical issues. For example, to treat apartheid as closure round racist ideas is to suppress the distinction between apartheid and the earlier South African policy of segregation, which was also racist, and is to ignore the relation of apartheid legislation and practices to the particular form of migrant labour on which the South African economy has historically relied. These features make apartheid, as a form of closure around racist ideas quite different from, say, the situation in the deep south of the USA before the civil rights movement of the 1960s. The vagueness of the concept of 'closure' makes it very difficult to analyse these different racist practices and institutions. It is not enough, either, to utilise, as Murphy does, the idea of a 'dual' structure of exclusion, and say that South African society is marked by exclusion on the basis of both property and race.

The second weakness evidently derives from the first. This is the causal priority which he gives to property as a form of closure in capitalist economies. Clearly this is related to the fact that 'closure' is a 'juridical' metaphor, and works most plausibly in relation to capitalist private property. However, one needs a theoretical basis for saying one feature of a society has greater explanatory weight than other features (which usually include the former's conditions of existence). Marx failed to solve the problem and neither Weber nor Murphy have even addressed it. They have simply asserted it and are perhaps not challenged more frequently because it seems plausible in the case of property.

The third difficulty is also linked to the first and second. This is the three-fold classification of codes of social closure: a hierarchy of principal, derivative and contingent codes. Notice that a principal one is defined as being backed by the force of the state and legal apparatus: the primacy of the juridical again. Derivative codes are ineffective without the principal ones. Contingent ones are not directly controllable by the principal codes, but refer to what Weber would have regarded as monopolisable assets (such as scarce skills) even though what makes them akin to property may have little or nothing to do with legal conditions. The idea that there should be a hierarchy of codes is questionable, since it assumes (except with contingent ones) that a fair degree of consistency can be secured between the different kinds on account of the primacy of the principal codes. Since no legal system is entirely consistent internally, it is logically impossible for it to secure total consistency in governing other codes. Yet if the principal code is not totally consistent, then (a) it secures dominance over derivative codes by force (which can only be the case unless and until such force is successfully challenged) or by other non-ideological means of gaining compliance; and (b) it is impossible to equate, as Murphy does, codes of social closure with the Weberian conception of ideas as switchmen directing action along certain tracks. If a hierarchical set of ideas is supposed to govern action (directing it along some tracks rather than others), then the principal ideas must have a mechanism for ensuring that the secondary or lower level ideas do indeed direct action along the 'right' tracks. If the principal ideas are not themselves consistent, then there is no way that they can guarantee this.

The basic mistake in positing a three-fold classification of codes in this way is that a structural relation between sets of ideas can only be sustained theoretically if a mechanism securing the structural relation is specified. If this mechanism does not reside in the ideas themselves (and it cannot, except in cases of consistent sets of ideas) then it must be open to challenge. Yet if it is open to challenge, as Murphy allows by mentioning 'contingent codes' not dominated by principal ones, then the supposed causal primacy of some ideas can only be temporary, rather than inherent in the ideas themselves. In that case, why should ideas backed by the state be treated as 'principal codes'? This primacy of the law and politics is no better than Marxism's 'determination in the last instance' by the economy.

It should be clear from our account of Murphy that he is well aware of the possibility of different 'codes' producing cross-cutting cleavages, and of challenges to practices associated with the 'principal codes'. While this seems to undermine the conception of principal codes, such an approach, with its emphasis on possible fragmentation within and between communities, provides a focus on concerns which we would not wish to be ignored. It bears a certain similarity to the ideas of Castells, where inconsistencies of forms of action are not necessarily ordered by a hierarchy of determinant codes but are resolved in actual struggle, whether in social movements or localities. Struggle, competition or other forms of interaction between agents (whether individuals, organisations or social movements) are determined *inter alia* by forms of discourse (not the same as 'codes' acting as switchmen), by forms of organisation (which affect the kinds of agents in play) and by resources. The articulation of these three aspects of interaction can both provide some of the conditions of such interaction and be the object of struggle, competition or negotiation.

Communities might then be best considered as locally-based forms of interaction exhibiting a reasonably high density of social networks, but not necessarily a high degree of consensus. With these considerations in mind, we now turn to the issue of defining a community.

A DEFINITION OF COMMUNITY

For the purposes of our analysis, we will confine our definition to human groups which share a common local space. It is obviously possible to conceive of non-local communities, referring, for instance, to scattered ethnic groups, or professions, but which have created rules of inclusion and exclusion, and which may be involved in strategies of monopolisation and usurpation. Some authors in fact prefer to use the term 'locality' rather than 'community', because of the confusion of meanings and levels which are involved in the use of 'community' (Cooke, 1989). We use both, in terms of a more objective starting point or space, that is locality, and of a more subjective moment, that is community.

For our studies we have a framework that draws critically from Murphy as the most recent exponent of social closure theory, but, as we have said, in the field of community studies, Neuwirth twenty years ago suggested the value of such an approach, with particular reference to ethnic communities (Neuwirth, 1969). She pointed to community as a variable, depending on processes of formation and closure. Using her suggestion and the concepts raised by Murphy we can place the notion of community into a dynamic model that is open to empirical investigation.

The process of formation of human groups in one locality is affected by competition for scarce resources, whether these are based in economic capital, political power, social status or whatever. The historical forces which bring people together 'by the dynamic of interest' into some form of local competition are usually linked to processes of closure which demarcate boundaries and set up internal social relations and networks. Such forces may also cause human groups even if bonded together at the levels of nation states, regions or localities, in common citizenship, to separate and diverge. Social polarisation can occur just as much as community formation.

Localities which have an economy involving capital investment for some form of productive enterprise in which labour is a major requirement are likely to experience internal power struggles and attempts at 'monopolisation of control'. Property and capital ownership is likely then to be the principal form of closure. Those excluded from control in the local economy who come to sense disadvantage in their position, and they may well be in the majority, will probably form associations based either in a common work situation or in a shared residential status, to attempt some kind of usurpatory action, either with inclusionary aims or even more radical ones, seeking a shift in the balance of power and the values which determine the distribution of resources. Differentiation and closure may occur within the disadvantaged and excluded groups, because of variation in skills and qualifications, in ethnicity and in gender.

Over a period of time, assuming a continuation of the principal form of closure, it is likely that shared residential status will lead to the development of kinship networks. This is not to deny the possibility that kinship may have been one of the reasons for people moving to such a locality, sharing a common interest in developing an enterprise or gaining employment. The expectation is that kinship will have been or will become another basis for social closure. It is assumed that the locality will develop sources of communal bonding and differentiation as associations and cleavages on grounds of property, work, neighbourhood, kinship, ethnic and gender relations come to be strengthened by time and habitual recognition. As Neuwirth (1969) said,

> certain members of a community may effect closure which is directed against other community subgroups. Communities are not necessarily socially or economically homogeneous, but may develop their own internal stratification systems.

Taking community as a variable, we are assuming that at the formation stage there are a number of grounds for association, which may lead to contractual, even coercive, relationships and within which more affective bonds begin to develop. Social networks may thus take on traditional or habitual characteristics, and these may lead to the sharing of values and sentiments, which will inform decision-making and possibly further strategies of monopolisation and exclusion or inclusion. Thus we wish to propose a notion of community as process, which draws together the three-fold definition put forward by Lee and Newby (1983) and which is based in work carried out and reviewed by Bell and Newby during the 1970s (Lee and Newby, 1983: 57). For them community is indicated by people living in a locality, by the existence of local social relations or networks, and by a shared sense of belonging.

Community for us is the probability of the settlement of a number of persons within a locality leading to the formation of local social networks. These will be linkages between people, either as individuals or households, on grounds of common working conditions, kinship, neighbourliness (propinquity) and friendship. Further, individuals, households and social networks may through a lengthy period of interaction develop common traditions, common sentiments and values, which may be a basis for what Schmalenbach (1961) called 'communion'. In such a state, which is perhaps less permanent than local social networks might be, peoples' bonds take on the strength of close friendship, and become a basis for solidary action.

This probability of community remains a variable open to empirical investigation and should not be seen as unidirectional. There may be a shift from local social networks of workers or neighbours into a traditional community based in strong kinship ties. Either of these may move towards a sense of communion or solidarity, and there may be reverse shifts. At each stage the boundaries of the community will be affected by processes of social closure, which will effectively demarcate who is an 'insider' and who an 'outsider', who is a 'local' and who an 'incomer'.

There is a strong probability that with the development of clear lines of closure around a common work situation, propinquity or kinship, especially if these are overlapping, what Hall (1987) calls 'latent' community will become 'manifest' community. In Hall's account there is an attempt to use the notion of community only when referring to ties based in propinquity. He prefers to use the notion of communion as something that may become manifest in separate spheres of work and property (or class), of propinquity (community) and kinship (family), when sentiments are expressly shared. Since, however, these categories of class, community and family so often become involved in each other in locality studies, we are not sure that the analytical distinction need necessarily serve any useful purpose. Further, this does not seem to be the way that Schmalenbach (1961) intended the concept to be used, although Hall claims a direct link.

The transition from a latent to a manifest state of community is marked by the explicit sharing of knowledge, skills and values. There is a strong probability that such a collection of local skills, communication networks, social values, and shared prestige and status rankings becomes a kind of cultural capital, which will be distributed perhaps unevenly through a locality. Joint possession of this capital provides a basis for local status differences, and local cultural capital becomes a means of maintaining the distinctiveness of one locality from another. We are here drawing on and modifying a concept which Pierre Bourdieu (Bourdieu and Passeron, 1977) uses in his analysis of social and cultural reproduction. For Bourdieu, cultural capital refers to what some would call 'high culture', and which tends to be distributed among the dominant classes. We feel that the concept needs to be liberated and that cultural distinctiveness is a useful notion in regard to the variations which can be observed in locality studies.

Local cultural capital varies in relation to the local economy. Communities may grow and they may disappear, though if a local culture has developed, it may provide the basis for a 'historical community' despite a restructured economy, maybe even for a generation or so. We are not, however, simply looking for 'community' or 'local cultural capital'. We are not simply searching for survivals. We will leave that to idealists and archaeologists. As sociologists we are looking for social processes and the manner in which key processes like social closure and exclusion operate to serve human interests. This is what guided the authors of *Coal is Our Life*, and it is their work in particular to which we now turn in an analysis of mining communities.

Chapter 2

The sociology of mining communities

THE IMAGE OF A PIT VILLAGE

We started the first chapter with an assertion of community as an ideal, and of its destruction as an immoral act. In British mining localities during the 1984/5 strike, there was much evidence of similar expressions and of the strength of both traditional ties and emotional attachment to a locality, and of their historical basis.

> 'I think Red Hill is a good village to live, I've lived here all my life and so's Alf. I don't mean to look at, I can't see it would ever be in a picture book of photographs of beautiful England. There's lots of people would look at it and to them it'd just be a dark and dreary place, with nothing different to it from a hundred other pit villages. They'd say to themselves well what'd be lost if this village didn't have its pit no longer? Well, me, I'd answer that by saying what would be lost would be the heart and soul of all the people who live in it, and who've lived here for not just our generation or our parents' but from even before that . . . [i]f you've lived here all your life, this is your home, this is where you belong. When I go even to Peterlee on the bus shopping, I'm glad to come back here at the end of the afternoon: I wouldn't want to live there . . . I'm happy to think when I'm walking down that street there that's where my mam and dad walked, and their mam and dads in their day before them.'
>
> (Pauline Street, quoted in Parker, 1986: 119–20)

Red Hill is the fictitious name of a pit village in County Durham, where Parker interviewed twenty-five men and women at the time of the miners' strike of 1984/5. During the Second World War, as a conscientious objector, rather than do military service he had worked down a pit, to which the official tribunal directed him.

> For eighteen months I worked in a now-closed pit in the Lancashire coalfield, and lived and worked among miners and their families until I was injured in an accident underground and subsequently discharged on medical grounds. That experience of being in a mining community,

and working (however inefficiently and ineptly) among coal miners, was one which radically changed my outlook, my political attitude, and my awareness – or, rather, my previous lack of it – of the class-based nature of our society, and particularly of how the materially poor and educationally underprivileged are always at the mercy of the wealthy, the comfortable, and the frequently uncaring. I also became gradually aware of the deep-running and deeply-imbued mystique of coal mining to those involved in it, of the strength of the bonds between miners and mining families, and of how being able to say 'I'm a coal miner', 'I'm the wife of a coal miner', or 'my father was a coal miner' carries a cachet of specialness and pride . . .

(Parker, 1986: 194)

An account of Thurcroft in South Yorkshire provides an extension to the image of a pit village:

Compared with other local centres, Thurcroft was not considered a particularly glamorous place to live. It nonetheless had a closeness and solidarity which for its inhabitants more than outweighed its lack of large shops or other amenities. 'You know that when you die, there's going to be someone there to hold your hand.' Changes there had been, but it was unusual to face troubles alone and most inhabitants still felt their trust in others to be well-founded.

(Gibbon and Steyne, 1986: 38–9)

For close observers, as well as members of mining households, the experience of living and working in mining villages can take the form of a 'manifest community', creating identities and consciousness, which can be markedly different from those in other parts of the same society. The class character of such localities, the local social institutions and their separateness from other not dissimilar places, tend to lead to frequently repeated claims of a dual experience, hardness, ugliness and danger on one side, and friendliness, closeness and solidarity on the other. Death and other 'troubles' are not subject to quite the same taboos as elsewhere. Further while there is a clearly felt stigma in and about pit villages, there is also a sense of a shared glory and pride.

If we were looking for social psychological explanations, together these manifestations might perhaps be seen to make the cutting edge of the dominant political economy, in the lives of individuals and groups, a little easier to bear. They provide reasons for collective resistance in hard times and collective well-being on better days. Our task as sociologists is to explain the meaning of structures and processes within the localities and their relation to continuity and change at a much wider level. We have indicated in the previous chapter that we approach this task with reference to the conflict of interests and the processes of social closure.

Plate 2.1 Pit head gear (photo by Griff Griffiths)

THE CLASSIC STUDY OF ASHTON, IN *COAL IS OUR LIFE*

It was the great merit of *Coal is Our Life* that its authors chose to confront previous community studies by referring to 'extra-community factors' and their influence on the local organisation of work, leisure and family life. In this they stressed the conflict of interests that 'were the outgrowth of the actual economic relations and working conditions under the given form of nationalization' of the coal industry (Dennis et al., 1969: 8). In doing this, they showed that the miners, their households and the social networks of which they were part, were subject to the interplay of political and economic interests at a national and international level. Fundamentally, they wanted to suggest that the combinations and division of interests which lead to conflict at the level of social classes, and the working through of such conflict in the institutions and processes of mining communities, were still the main means of explaining social experience in such communities. Though they do not use the language of social closure theory, it is clear that they would have agreed with Murphy that any form of closure around locality was secondary to that based in the form of capitalism, whether it was organised by and on behalf of private coal-owners or subject to state management, under nationalisation.

Centripetal and centrifugal forces

Their sense of 'community' is one which, based in the conflict approach, admits of variability. In their discussion of 'Place and People' (Chap. 1), the authors say:

> Ashton is predominantly a working-class town owing its development to the growth of its collieries. The latter have drawn people and houses around them, the main pit is almost in the centre of the town. But the collieries have exercised a centripetal influence in other ways. Most of the men in Ashton are miners. The cohesive results of this fact are well-known . . . Common memories of past struggle have undoubtedly helped to bind a community such as Ashton.
>
> While the nature of the work and the history of the industry in Ashton have thrown the men together in this way, they have exerted an opposite or centrifugal influence on the women. The coal industry provides no paid work for them . . . [At the nearest estimate] there were only 6 insured women to every 100 insured men . . . [An unknown number of others] were working outside their own . . . area.
>
> [On the basis of a comparison between Ashton, which] has never been physically isolated . . . [and] Fullwood [to the south, which] is 10 miles from Barnsley, the nearest town to exceed it in size . . . Ashton has a looser hold upon the leisure-time activities of one section of the men [in terms of club membership which was lower than in Fullwood]. Another set of figures seems to show that the Ashton housewife in going about the business of shopping goes farther afield than does the Fullwood housewife . . . Both towns are dependent on mining to a similar extent, [and] although it cannot be said with confidence that the observed differences in social behaviour result from location, [the relative closeness of Ashton to other places] might therefore be deemed to exercise a strong centrifugal influence on social life in Ashton.

These two tendencies, the centripetal and the centrifugal, help to determine the 'community' for the citizen of Ashton. Clearly what is the 'community' for one person may be much less than the community for another.

(Extracts from Dennis et al., 1969: 14–17)

These concepts, 'centripetal' and 'centrifugal', are introduced without any definition, but seem to emphasise the dynamic processes of community formation, which may lead to a sense of integration or, alternatively, segregation. They can be seen to underline the thrust of the explanation and discussion of Ashton and its household and community relations. This consists of three propositions. First, these relations are similar to those of wage-workers everywhere in Britain; they are based in class divisions. Second, 'this similarity is modified by the particular conditions and history of the coal industry as such; at this level Ashton has social relations in common with other mining communities' (ibid: 26). Third, there are 'local' factors, linked to the economy and culture, which 'give an individual, unique bias to the life of Ashton' (ibid: 27). Such 'local' factors are the character of the local labour market, the particular physical conditions of coal-getting and the market for coal. Thus any experience of 'community' may at least be be marked with contradictions and tensions. People are driven outwards (centrifugal influence) or pulled inwards (centripetal tendency).

The language of the explanation at this point is one which suggests that Ashton's way of life was created, is maintained and will be changed by forces beyond the control of individual members and households. Between them and the externally driven forces, the authors suggest that there is a 'certain autonomous community life' (ibid: 27). The extent of this autonomy, however, is not delineated.

The working class and the miners of Ashton

In a chapter on 'The Miner at Work' (Chap. 2), the authors provide an analysis of the miner as a wage-worker in Marxist terms, stressing the alienation of the wage-earner in conditions which are dictated to him by capitalist owners and managers. This is shown to contradict a need for reciprocity in the social relations of production. Though there is some evidence of the development of class consciousness, workers on the whole have not seen this in a 'political sense' and

[t]hey see it as natural that the employer wishes to make profit out of their work; . . . But their aim also is to make money, and for this reason their relationship with the employer is one of struggle for the division of the spoils . . . [They think] not in the abstract terms of social and economic relations.

(ibid: 32–3)

Miners are, however, somewhat distinct from other wage-workers. The book gives a very full account of the detailed division of labour in and the means of coal production. This stresses the difference between fully experienced underground workers on contracts giving the possibility of relatively high earnings, and younger, older and disabled workers on day wages. There are also divisions within the contract workers and the day-wage men, but the division between them is a very significant basis of stratification in Ashton and elsewhere. With regard to the means and technology of production, the key fact which is given prominence is the shift from hand-got methods of mining towards a full implementation of mechanised longwall faces with power-loading of coal on conveyor belts which was occurring in the newly nationalised industry. This was likely to bring more changes to the social relations of production. The authors then point to

> the complex pattern of social relations in at least one pit in the nationalized coal industry of 1953. In any of the day-to-day lives of Ashton . . . one could discern the interplay of [several] factors. Many years of hard toil and social conflict had given rise to a social structure and an ideology in mining which were fraught with dissensions, contradictions and suspicions. The ideology of the days of private ownership, the days of depression, unemployment and bitter social strife, certainly is operative in everyday social relations in mining.
>
> (ibid: 76)

Nationalisation had, however, changed little in this sense. In this most dangerous of industries, the wage-workers at least kept alive the sense of struggle, and there were some who saw beyond the more concrete fight for security of employment and a good wage.

The uniqueness of Ashton was shown to rest in the fact of common residence, and a common set of persisting social relations. 'Solidarity, despite the division into interest groups among the miners in a given pit, is a very strongly developed characteristic of social relations in mining' (ibid: 79). It also comes from the singular way in which the miners and their households shared the common miseries of unemployment, the hardships of a strike, the closure of a colliery and, in Ashton's case, one of the bloodiest incidents in British strike history in 1893 (see Chapter Three).

It was the authors' impression that any uniqueness in Ashton's way of life added

> no new quality to the characteristics of the miner already described. But the participation in and sharing of a common set of community relations and experiences through time gives confirmation to those characteristics, considerably strengthening them.
>
> (ibid: 83)

This then confirms the approach of Dennis, Henriques and Slaughter to community study. 'Community' is very much a dependent variable. For them the miners of Ashton were active within the class struggle sited in the coal industry. They gave little weight, therefore, to that 'certain autonomous community life' as a force in the struggle for social change.

The miners, their union and growing corporatism

In their chapter on 'Trade Unionism in Ashton' (Chap. 3), the argument seems to be that, with nationalisation, even the sense of struggle in which miners as wage-workers have engaged locally, as well as regionally and nationally, has been muted. The local branch of the National Union of Mineworkers (NUM) in Ashton had, like most other branches in the days of privately owned coal mines, been a centre of resistance to, and conflictual negotiation with, owners and managers. It had been based particularly in the need for the representation of the interests of face-workers and other contract workers in the pit, whose disputes with management always tended to be fiercest. Indeed, it is shown that the branch and the branch committee had been and still were dominated by contract workers and their disputes, while the interests and disputes of day-wage workers were not necessarily well represented. The latter tended to be around the varying load of work related to an unvarying day-wage rate, whereas the former were over a much contested price-list concerned with the changing quality of coal in the seams, the relative amount of stone in the coal and the problems of day-by-day access to and the safety of working the coal. Mechanisation was adding further issues for debate and conflict. All of them, as anyone who knows the physical conditions of mining would agree, are essentially local problems, because even though they occur in coal-mining generally, the conditions are different in every pit. Nationalisation has not changed this situation.

Before nationalisation, however, the union branch could uncompromisingly act as advocate for the men in dispute, claim the authors. The interests of mineworkers were distinct from those of management. After the nationalisation of the coal industry in 1947, the union and union officials were required to some extent to cooperate with management in the organisation of work. The union had official representation at all levels of decision-making and branch officials tended to be given facilities for carrying out their union duties during working hours. So

> the predicament in which the miners' union in Ashton finds itself today is not only that it has abandoned a policy of single-minded opposition for the more complicated one of co-operation, but that it is trying even more to pursue both policies together.
>
> (ibid: 104)

Nationalisation was requiring a tendency on the part of the NUM to become both more bureaucratised, to match the National Coal Board, and similarly more professionalised, as the educational credentials of officials came to be as important as experience in the industry, and careers within the union offered chances of social mobility, not available to men on the coal face. The Ashton branch committee of the NUM, like others, stood at the pivot between the conflictual relations at the grassroots and the newly required cooperative relations in the industry. Hence, for Dennis, Henriques and Slaughter, change taking place outside Ashton was reducing the relative autonomy of the workers in the community. Their union was being compromised by what we now term 'corporatism', and was being incorporated into the management of capitalism. This seems to overlook the effect of the growing gap between the union and its members, which was leading to many 'unofficial' disputes, and over time could lead to grassroots movements in mining communities based in 'pit politics' against the incorporation of 'mineworkers' politics' at a national level. (See, on the distinction between 'pit politics' and 'mineworkers' politics', Gibbon, 1988.)

The alienation of leisure

The remaining chapters of the book discuss 'Leisure' (Chap. 4) and 'The Family' (Chap. 5). In the former, two categories of social influence are discussed. These are (a) the mining industry, which through the pit itself and the Miners' Welfare Commission (later to be called the Coal Industry Social Welfare Organisation) sponsored a number of organisations, including a brass band, a division of the St John's Ambulance Brigade and the Welfare Institute, with a number of functions; and (b) the development of a local culture in the context of a dangerous industry, where the probabilities of being killed or injured were high, where financial insecurity as a consequence of injury or unemployment was always probable and where the pattern of life-time's earnings tended to be one of decline after a mid-period of relatively high wages. Of the first category, the authors speak, somewhat scathingly, of 'artificially fostered institutions' (ibid: 128) which did not attract much participation, except for the dances. In the case of the second category, the authors stress how relatively autonomous institutions have been moulded by a predominantly 'frivolous' orientation of miners to their dangerous and insecure work. This contrasts with a more 'serious' attitude, which a minority express:

> [I]t should be explained that the word frivolous is used in the sense of 'giving no thought for the morrow'. It is used in this way as a contrast to those forms of recreation which pursue a definite aim such as intellectual improvement by means of study in adult classes or discussion groups, or spiritual improvement through membership of a church.
>
> (ibid: 130)

Both attitudes exist side by side, almost as false consciousness resides along with true class consciousness, we can assume. The book provides no explanation for this bifurcation, except that the culture of poverty based in capitalist exploitation contains these two possibilities. The majority of men are said to seek immediate gratification in drinking, gambling and sport, in the clubs, pubs and betting offices. Rugby League is the key sporting activity. The men participate largely to the exclusion of women, whose 'frivolous' leisure tends to be 'callin', or meeting and talking with other women, usually kin and neighbours. Television watching had hardly impinged on Ashton, but probably would have been judged, as going to the cinema was, to be both frivolous and 'atomistic'. Gala days and other activities were also put in the frivolous category. Allotment gardening to some extent provided an escape for the men, while the public library seemed to do no more or no less for the women, who tended to choose light romantic fiction. 'Frivolity' or immediate gratification was seen to be characteristic of the majority in all the status divisions of mine-working, though variations in leisure form are shown to exist between contract workers and day-wage men. The gender division of leisure activities permeates the whole, and there are fewer 'serious' women than men, according to the authors.

The book seems, thus, to indicate a failure in the local culture. It was not the cutting edge into the deprivations and inequalities of a class divided society. The serious institutions, like the Labour Party, Adult Education and the churches, were judged either to be largely ineffective in promoting serious causes, or to have declined in membership and lost the impact they might have had in the past. All the authors have to say by way of attempted explanation is a rather cryptic comment: 'The *mechanism* by which change is minimized is that of avoidance' (ibid: 170, original emphasis.) Presumably, the serious-minded and their voluntary associations failed to face up to the work of consciousness-raising because they are caught in a system ('mechanism') which diverts them from the real issues. The word 'avoidance', however, does have more of a connotation of deliberate action on the part of the 'serious'. This should, perhaps, have been considered more carefully by the authors, who seem at key points to use mechanistic concepts, like 'centripetal' and 'centrifugal' in the first chapter, or 'mechanism' here, in an attempt to reinforce their overall theoretical approach, but then give intimations of another, with their reference to 'autonomous community' or 'avoidance'. There were grounds for a theoretical reappraisal, stressing the possibilities of both external structural forces at work in Ashton, and the power of human agency within and beyond the locality.

The conflictual production of social personalities

In the final chapter, on 'The Family', all the social forces which have been introduced in the study of Ashton are brought together in the analysis of this institution:

An attempt is made to show that the basic features of family structure and family life derive their character from the large-scale framework of Ashton's social relations.

(ibid.: 171)

Despite admittedly significant differences between younger and older, smaller and larger households, tenants of council houses and those of private landlords or the Coal Board, between those of higher relative incomes (contract workers) and those with lower (day-wage workers), the authors claim that they 'exist within a basic framework of similarity' (ibid.: 171). This is because the vast majority of households were either directly or indirectly dependent on the pit for occupation and income, and linked together in networks of face-to-face relations, based in kinship and propinquity, in what was still a relatively small settlement (c. 14,000 persons in c. 4000 houses in 1951).

More than four-fifths of the families at present living in Ashton originated in that period of 1895–1908 when the community truly developed from a village to an industrial town based on the collieries at Ashton and Vale. These families have given individuality and continuity to a community, Ashton, to which their attachment is maintained through the continued existence of the primary cause of coming together, employment (with little immediate alternative) at the local collieries.

(ibid: 172)

Such a claim of continuity is not backed with clear evidence from a survey or historical records, and may be an exaggeration (see p. 59), but the existence of social networks embedded in a local culture, 'common living standards limited by the weekly wage . . . and the growth of an institutional life and an ideology which accentuate the confinement of the mother to the home' (ibid.: 174) seems a valid description.

At the time *Coal is Our Life* was written, there was a shortage of workers in the coal industry. It was partly being assuaged by recruitment from elsewhere, but partly by the tendency of mining households to socialise their young men into the local culture and to provide opportunities for their daughters to marry miners. Admittedly, seventy percent of parents in mining households claimed in interviews that they 'would not encourage their sons to be miners' (ibid.: 176), but they neverthless did tend to become miners.

Clearly the function of the family is as a mechanism for perpetuating the social structure, not only in terms of biological reproduction, but in terms of the production of the social personalities required by such a community as Ashton.

(ibid.: 245)

The family was helped in this function by the state, through the schools and the health and social services, but these are not examined in the book. The emphasis is on the family being an agent ('mechanism' again) in reproducing the system. It did this despite the strict gender division which was culturally demanded, basically because of the wage which the man earned. In most households the women were expected to create a homely atmosphere by means of an allowance, which the main earner presented to them each week. This expectation was occasionally reinforced by symbolic gestures, like throwing a meal 'straight to t'back o't' fire' (ibid.: 182) if the husband was displeased.

For the authors, male dominance and the segregation of the men's world from that of the women were merely a consequence of the particular circumstances of the mining industry, in communities where there was little paid work for women. There was some assessment of the quality of family life and the personal relations between spouses and their interaction with children. This was based in interviews (number not specified) and the authors claim that apart from a few households where the men are 'irresponsible' (ibid.: 193), marriage relationships had a high degree of stability. Even under pressure, as in strikes, despite the women seeing that the men were driven by

> quite other considerations than those of their families' welfare . . . if it comes to the question of solidarity the wives usually defend their menfolk strongly . . . against the enemy . . . [Nevertheless] the development of deep and intense personal relationships of an all-round character is highly improbable . . . Marriages in Ashton are a matter of 'carrying-on' pure and simple . . . husband and wife live separate, and in a sense, secret lives.
>
> (ibid.: 227–8)

The fact that at least a considerable minority of girls were pregnant at marriage was claimed by the authors (ibid.: 206) to be a strong factor in pressing women and the men they had to marry into these restrictive relationships. There was some indication that this might change under the influence of the mass media among the younger generation, but since the same economic system was likely to continue for some time, the authors did not consider the change would be very significant. Children were not given great personal attention by parents, but presentable children were a sign of women's adequacy as mothers. Educational success was approved, but parents had little real knowledge of how to help their children and often home conditions, both material and emotional, were thought not to contribute to such achievement. The book indicates that miners tended to be cynical about 'book learning', sceptical about 'theory' and saw only technical education as of much value, except in terms of escape or 'getting on' (ibid.: 236).

In sum, the social and economic conditions of Ashton disadvantaged the adults and children. Their culture, their lives and their community were closely bound by a very inequitable and conflict-ridden economic system, over which they had little control. Despite the struggle of the labour movement, now much compromised by increasing incorporation, the people of Ashton lived relatively bleak and insecure lives, which were made easier only by seeking frivolous pleasure.

With some prescience, Henriques, writing an introduction to the second edition of the book in 1969, added:

> The mining industry, or certainly a large part of it, has been condemned to death . . . For miners today, the death of their industry means that the heart is torn from their communities. There is no overall planning of new industries or of training or of education for leisure; there is no more than marginal provision for economic security . . . this community without the mine and mineworkers is in danger of becoming merely an aggregate of socially isolated and culturally condemned human beings . . . The very fact that miners do *not* live only in communities, but as part of their class . . . means that the alternatives transcend what can be observed or deduced from the life of the community . . . [T]he miner has still not said his final word.
>
> (ibid.: 9–10)

This points very clearly to the underlying motive for studying and writing *Coal is Our Life*. In adopting a Marxian framework of analysis the authors were examining the potential for the awakening of an emancipatory interest among what they took as proletarian workers. In exploring the social divisions of Ashton, between management and mineworkers, between contract workers and day-wage workers, between the frivolous and the serious, and between the men's world and the women's world, they were posing questions about the conditions for and limitations on the emergence of a revolutionary consciousness. Despite the evidence to the contrary, they still hung onto the view that a little optimism ('The miner has still not said his final word') was possible. Class was still the most important basis for social closure and cohesive social action. Communities were, if not derivative from class, no more than contingent forms of closure which might or might not contribute to successful emancipatory or usurpatory movements. They were sites for the conflictual 'production of social personalities' required by a hard economic system.

ARCHETYPAL PROLETARIANS, ISOLATED MASSES AND OCCUPATIONAL COMMUNITIES

We have commented lengthily on *Coal is Our Life* because it is the classic social scientific account of a coal-mining community. It has become a basis around which other studies have been undertaken. Bulmer (1975a) gives it a central status in his account of sociological models of the mining community, which draws material from world-wide studies. It can be seen to have provided some evidence either in justification for, or to be criticised in, the formulation of hypotheses about mining communities and the working class more generally. Lockwood (1966) in a very influential paper on changes taking place in the working class uses 'Ashton' as evidence of survival of traditional working-class consciousness, which he labelled 'proletarian' and which could be found in single-industry communities. It was distinct from another traditional form, 'deferential' class consciousness, found in other more mixed or rural working localities, and contrasted again with what he argued was a new form of working-class consciousness, that of the 'privatised, instrumental collectivist' worker to be found in contemporary mass production industries.

Bulmer (1975a) looking at studies of mining communities, and taking clues from Lockwood, suggests that they have thrown up four main systematic attempts to provide generalising hypotheses. The first is that which argues that mining communities, as a consequence of the whole ensemble of capitalist exploitation of mineworkers, provide a solidary base for the emergence of the 'archetypal proletarian'. This is based in the account to be found in *Coal is Our Life*. A second, known as the Kerr–Siegel 'isolated mass' hypothesis, based in its American authors' international comparison of the strike propensity of industries like seafaring, dock working, lumbering and cloth working, as well as coal mining, suggests in criticism of the first, with its emphasis entirely on the class factor, that isolated but homogeneous industrial communities, like those in mining, have a culture which promotes strike action by workers and conflict with owners and managers (Kerr and Siegel, 1954: 189–212). A third, promoted by a German sociologist, Rimlinger, criticises both the previous hypotheses, on the basis of a comparison of strikes in the mining industries of America, Britain, France and Germany. He suggests that there is a variable tendency to strike-proneness in mining communities, dependent on the existence of a 'separatist group' tendency, which might or might not, depending on the historical, economic and political circumstances, and the interaction between them and the miners and their community, come into conflict with the management of the mines (Rimlinger, 1959: 389–405). A fourth hypothesis departs from the others in the sense of focussing not on 'structural' variables, but on 'meanings'. Drawing on the work of American sociologists, Blumer (1964: 132) and Blauner (1960: 337–60), among others, mining communities are defined as 'occupational communities', where interaction in work spills over into non-work time, and where workers and their families are relatively self-enclosed, so forming the main reference group for those who belong. On this an occupational culture may develop, which becomes the basis for solidary action, in the defence and promotion of worker interests.

Bulmer prefers the fourth characterisation, and on it builds his 'ideal –
typical' mining community. His preference is stated in terms of 'voluntaristic'
rather than 'structural' (more deterministic) approaches.

> 'Occupational community', then, is an attempt to characterise sociologi-
> cally the mining settlement in a way which permits consideration of
> the orientations and social meanings held by social actors in particular
> situations . . . It can be used, moreover, as a means of characterising and
> even explaining the industrial and political orientations and world-views
> of members of the occupational community. Lockwood's discussion of
> variation in working-class images of society, for example, constructs an
> ideal-type of the 'traditional proletarian' . . . as a starting point . . .
> suggest[ing] a possible way of connecting up the study of a worker's
> structural situation with his consciousness of that situation and of the
> world at large.
>
> (Bulmer, 1975a: 82)

It is crucial for Bulmer that sociological analysis must contain reference to
both structure and human agency and express it as an essential duality of
social condition and consciousness. He clearly intends this as a criticism of
the classic study by Dennis, Henriques and Slaughter.

> Although the origin and basis of the existence of an occupational com-
> munity of miners may lie in technological and economic organisation, its
> maintenance and persistence may be due to other sociological factors, such
> as constituting a separatist group, the development of an occupational
> identity by miners, and its reinforcement by a multiplex pattern of
> social relationships in which work and non-work spheres overlap. The
> *gemeinschaftlich* ties of kinship, residence and friendship help to bond
> an ongoing local pattern of social interaction which may in time even
> become relatively autonomous in relation to the dominant local economic
> activity.
>
> (ibid: 84)

It is therefore all the more surprising that, when he puts forward the
elements of his ideal type of the traditional mining community, it consists
virtually of a restatement in stereotypical form of the major aspects of
Ashton portrayed *Coal is Our Life*, but without the reference to its
location in corporatist Britain, so that it can be used in the comparison
of such settlements based on minerals in any part of the world. It follows
the Weberian definition of an ideal type.

> It is a one-sided *accentuation of reality* which emphasises the dominant
> characteristics of the phenomenon under study and orders these charac-
> teristics in a logical manner in relation to each other.
>
> (ibid: 84)

Bulmer's ideal type of traditional mining community

It consists of the following characteristics:

1 Physical and geographical isolation – little contact with the outside world.
2 Economic predominance of mining – the paid work available in the mining organisation forms almost the whole of the local labour market. The town or village is a virtually a 'company town'.
3 The nature of work – dangerous, unhealthy, but a source of pride and cohesion among workers, despite the status difference among the miners.
4 Social consequences of occupational homogeneity and isolation – virtually a one-class community with little social or geographical mobility.
5 Leisure activities – 'gregarious patterns of communal sociability' outside the home, usually with workmates.
6 The family – sharp division between men's world and women's world. Home is the woman's domain. Each household is involved in a supportive kinship network, and there is much continuity between generations.
7 Economic and political conflict – interests of owners and miners are fundamentally opposed over the division of the 'spoils', and the politics of distribution and control. Each side forms associations/unions to pursue its ends, but power tends to be in the hands of the owners, especially in a 'company town'.
8 The whole – close-knit and interlocking collectivities based in a shared history, and meaningful social interaction confined largely to the locality.

Bulmer states of the ideal type that it

> is a theoretical construction intended to aid empirical analysis of social change in mining communities currently being undertaken. It is a tool of investigation, and the elements included cannot of themselves *explain* how or why observed changes take place . . . It states in extreme and deliberately accentuated form the hypothetical dependence of all community relationships upon the dominant technological and economic conditions of action in the community, within a capitalist economic system . . . [It does so] in order to find out to what extent this provides an adequate explanation of mining settlement structure and to what extent it does not . . . The overall strategy is one of attempting *disconfirmation* of the social structural characteristics delineated in the ideal type.
>
> (ibid: 88–9, original emphasis)

Bulmer refers to the intention to make comparisons across three societies, but the project unfortunately does not seem to have been completed. In the Acknowledgements in Bulmer (1978), it is said that research at

Durham University, funded by the Joseph Rowntree Memorial Trust (as well as by the Social Science Research Council), was affected by changes of direction and leadership, and that it was difficult to maintain the sense of cumulative research and continuity. Nevertheless, a number of publications, including two influential monographs (Moore, 1974; Williamson, 1982), articles (Moore, 1975; Taylor, 1979) and the compilation *Mining and Social Change* (Bulmer, 1978), show that much work was completed in the study of mining localities in the North East of England by erstwhile members of the research group. The work, too, was linked with a more general interest in 'occupational communities', including a study of shipbuilding workers (Cousins and Brown, 1975). This connected them into the contemporary debates about working-class consciousness and culture, and was the basis of a conference in Durham in 1972, on 'The occupational community and the traditional worker' (Bulmer, 1975b). In the late 1960s, much empirical research was devoted to the changes taking place in working-class life, as a consequence of old industries declining, occupational communities disappearing, new technologies being introduced and new settlement patterns emerging. Further, of course, many pits were being closed in the 1960s, and the salience of mining localities in the industrial economy and as objects of research into working-class life and culture was reduced.

CRITICISMS OF *COAL IS OUR LIFE*

There never has been a systematic attempt therefore to revise the ideal type of mining community, traditional or otherwise of *Coal is Our Life*. Nevertheless, a number of criticisms of its assumptions and of the empirical research on which it has emerged have been made (see Frankenberg, 1976; Brook and Finn, 1977). In the mining localities which we have studied, initially we asked a number of residents whether they had heard of or read *Coal is Our Life*. There were varied responses. The existence of the book was fairly widely known or remembered. Some told us that they would not want to alter one word of the account that it gave about mining. The conflict relations which it portrayed still, in their view, existed. Informants also agreed with the contention that Ashton was male dominated, had seen men throw meals 'on t'back o't'fire' when angry and reckoned that girls and women had limited ambitions. The view that men and women tended to lead very separate lives as a consequence of pit work was confirmed, even if qualified, by the elderly man who claimed that he had always helped with the housework and shopping. He could bake and cook meals, he could do the washing and ironing, adding that 'married men who talk about "men's work" and "women's work" ought to face up to reality and accept that times have changed'.

On the other hand, other informants remembered that the researchers were around in the town in the year that the local Rugby League team first played (and lost) in a Wembley cup final. 'They spent a lot of time in the pubs and clubs' was a repeated comment. Another interviewee said that much of the information had been obtained from talking to old miners, some retired or on the point of retiring, one of whom, he recalled, was 'able to keep up an endless stream of anecdotes and information, so long as the beer flowed'.

The most dismissive comments on it have come from former union officials or local councillors. One remembered that there had been much adverse discussion about it when it was first published. The *Yorkshire Post* daily and evening newspapers carried prominent features and pictures of the town with the name 'Ashton' concealed and told their readers that there had been an emphasis on the seamy side of life (*Yorkshire Post*, 10 February 1956). A second 'official' view poured scorn on the book, and claimed that it painted a distorted picture of the town and its people. A third, someone who was both a trade unionist and a local Labour councillor, took time to reflect when one of our interviewers asked him to give his opinion of the book. Our field notes report the later reply:

R. also thought it bad, because it gave a thoroughly distorted picture of the town. Some aspects of life were over-emphasised, even caricatured, some hardly alluded to or even ignored completely. He considered it a bad piece of research. The researchers, in his view, had come with firmly fixed stereotypes in their heads and with preconceived ideas. They had looked only for evidence which would support these stereotypes and preconceived ideas, and of course had not failed to find them. R. and many other people, he claimed, had been outraged and deeply hurt when the book was published. They had believed the researchers were devoted supporters of the Labour Party. Every possible facility had been granted to them, their paths were smoothed as far as possible, everybody did everything they could to help them. They had been made honorary members of Green Lane Club in which they spent a great deal of time. When they read the book, they realised they had been conned, they had been used. The researchers had been sniggering at them behind their backs all the time. They had seriously betrayed the trust that had been placed in them, abused the great hospitality that had been showed to them, bitten the hands that had fed them with information. The place was represented as a cultural desert, full of drunken, wife-beating miners who only thought of beer, baccy and betting, Rugby League football and girls of low morals. Of course, there were people like that, but they were not at all typical. R. was not denying there was sexual promiscuity but it was certainly not greater here than anywhere else. His wife, he said, was outraged by the bit about pregnant brides.

Very little attention was paid in the book to the role of the churches and chapels in the community or to cultural activities, especially music and musical shows. It was the 'popular' type of culture that was emphasised:

Rugby League, drinking in working men's clubs, etc. R. was particularly unhappy at the way women were portrayed in the book. He thought that the researchers had made little attempt to understand local life and local people.

(field notes, 1981)

There seems to be much of substance in this criticism, even though it takes a position different from some of our other informants. It comes from someone Dennis, Henriques and Slaughter might have called 'serious'. It is relatively balanced and based in a deep understanding of 'Ashton', which has come from many years of residence and representative activity. It cannot be dismissed merely as moralistic and lacking in objectivity. Other informants have also stressed the point of view that outsiders continually get the place and its people all wrong. The criticism that the authors had used a powerful local political network to achieve entry, and that they had had other privileges offered to them, implying that they should have got their account right, must stand as a significant warning to anyone who tries to comment without first reaching some agreement with the subjects of the research as to the appropriate framework of analysis. The question of how to reach such a negotiated product is difficult to answer, especially if it is taken that there is a local status system in which some people are more powerful than others. Do the powerful locals have a clearer understanding of the locality and its culture than either the less powerful or professionally trained sociologists? Can a community study ever be a negotiated product in which sociologists are not the only definers of the situation?

We shall comment on the first of those questions in Chapter Four when we draw from the biographical material which we collected in an attempt to examine the content and meaning of the local culture. The second question is more rhetorical, and is meant to form a basis for the critical reader to offer alternative views and to consider the usefulness and appropriateness of sociological work. It is quite clear that Bulmer in hypothesising the ideal type of traditional mining community was hoping to form a basis for a theoretically aware empirical sociology, which would add to our scientific understanding of occupational communities. Considering that, it is very surprising that the ideal–typical construct focussed rather more on the social entity than on the social forces which were creating it. As we have said there was no reference to the predominant corporatism of decision-making in Britain, or in many other industrial societies. There was no reference to the dependency status of many primary producing economies in the Third World, and the effect of that on mining communities. There is little place for the consideration of the wider social processes which we can now see to be operating in many nation states and economies, causing polarisation between industrially advanced and developing societies and within such societies, such as urban versus rural regions, and economically restructured and advancing versus deindustrialised and declining regions and localities.

CONCLUSION

In this chapter we have looked at the basis of studies of coal-mining communities and in particular have presented a summary of the classic study, *Coal is Our Life*. We have seen that Dennis, Henriques and Slaughter emphasised the external forces operating to cause segregation within Ashton, creating oppositions between workers and management, between 'serious' and 'frivolous' elements of the culture and between the men's and the women's worlds. At the same time there were forces, or 'mechanisms', at work which could create class solidarity, and derived forms of community solidarity. There were hints at 'autonomous community life' but these were largely unexplored. The local culture, if anything was shown to have failed. It failed to be the cutting edge against the dominant culture of capitalism. Social institutions like the household and other social networks tended to be agencies for the reproduction of this failed culture. There was a small sense of optimism that mineworkers as a class might still have more to say about the capitalist social order, particularly as pit closures threatened the existence of their own social institutions and communities.

We have seen that this study became the basis for the formulation of the hypothesis in Lockwood's work (1966) that such isolated occupational communities were the context for the emergence of the 'archetypal proletarian' worker. Indeed the relative isolation of such communities is taken up as a key element in the ideal–typical formulation of the traditional mining community. This, we have indicated, is a probable weakness in the ideal type, for it encourages an overemphasis on seeing it as an entity not primarily created by the interests of capitalists, industrialists and entrepreneurs. As we have come to recognise, industrial development, whether in terms of innovation, restructuring or disinvestment, can have many effects on industrial localities, in terms of opportunities in the labour market, in the structure of the labour force itself and in the spatial distribution of economic activity and life chances. Forms of social closure which produce industrial localities and occupation communities may be countered by others which produce social polarisation, variation in life chances and the destruction of local cultures.

In the chapters which follow we shall focus on the question of the adequacy of Bulmer's ideal type of mining community, and in them we shall be taking note of what seem to have been major weaknesses both of the classic study on which it was based and of the ideal type itself. Briefly, these are questions of the historical development of the mining industry and the pit villages, the dominant and oppositional forms of local culture, and the labour market and the gender division of labour in those localities. We shall also focus on the forces at work creating the contemporary social divisions within the mining localities, and make some reference to education. Finally we will address the question of the miners' strike of 1984/5 in Britain, for it seems to have arisen as a consequence of both contemporary social trends and polarisation, and historical memory embedded in local culture and mineworkers' politics.

Chapter 3

The historical background of West Yorkshire mining communities

INTRODUCTION

Bulmer's ideal-typical mining community fell back on the stereotype which emerged from *Coal is Our Life*, despite, as we have shown in our presentation of the classic study, the ambiguities of theoretical and empirical presentation. These had questioned the concept of the organic or systemic view of community drawn from functionalist anthropology, had made the question of isolation an empirical question and gave many hints, through emphasising dichotomous attributes, of the duality of experience. True, the study of 'Ashton' had presented somewhat unquestioningly the notion of continuity of kinship networks and family residence, the segregation of men's world and women's world and the sharing of values about the locality, its history and the world in which it was placed.

HOW STABLE WERE THE MINING COMMUNITIES AND THEIR CULTURES?

One of Bulmer's colleagues seems to have accepted some of the stereotypical views of the history of mining communities in his study of migration to and from pit villages in County Durham (Taylor, 1979). In this work, Taylor criticises those who concentrate on continuity rather than change, but does not himself examine the rather 'organic' view of community, with its assumptions of continuity, which is adopted in his own work. His aim is to examine, in the context of cross-cultural studies, the 'migration system encompassing both sending and receiving communities . . . linked by the migrants themselves' (ibid.: 476). The focus is on the migrants and their reasons for migration from or return to the mining villages after a period away from them, and not on the communities. 'The five study villages were sufficiently alike to obviate the necessity of individual description' (ibid.: 477). The chief reason for migration was the closure or reorganisation of the local pit. The communities seemed to have a life of their own, independent of the people who formed them, passing through three stages. These are:

Youth, characterised by immigration and population increase; Maturity, characterised by a falling off in immigration but continuing population increase; and Old Age, characterized by declining population and emigration.

(ibid.: 482–3)

The villages reached old age simply when the coal gave out. Then the miners were offered the possibility of jobs in pits eleswhere, and in this case in the Midlands. Those who chose to migrate were generally from households who were not as closely linked into the community's social networks as those who chose to stay. Those who eventually came back (just less than one in five of the households studied) tended to be ones who sought the closeness of the mining village they had known, rather than stay in a place where they were only newcomers. Thus the closure of the pits and the migration system that was necessitated did not immediately destroy the Durham communities, though clearly it threatened them.

Interestingly, this last fact did not encourage Taylor to question his three-stage hypothesis about the residual mining communities in Durham. The difficulties which some Midland pits had in recruiting miners highlights a point which has been made in other studies. Gerard Engrand (1975) in his study of mining in North Eastern France notes that the 'organic' or 'culturalist' approach, as he calls it,

seeks above all to confirm the idea of a well-defined social milieu, of a vertically differentiated community nevertheless exhibiting a profound unity, because it is entirely caught up in the mine and its fate.

(Engrand, 1975: 67, author's translation)

and then questions its legitimacy. Has it not been true, he argues, that the problem of mining has been the problem of recruiting miners?

Private or nationalized, the mine does not retain its men. The social group always has to be remade. Even after a century, it is still a question of forming and reforming the teams in the mines.

(ibid.: 69)

Controlling the continual turnover is a major problem. In France, Engrand indicates that in order to get one extra man in the workforce it has always been necessary to set on more than one, and in many years in the late nineteenth century or early twentieth, when the army, the railways or new industries were recruiting, it was very difficult indeed. He calculates that over short periods some sixty to seventy percent of workers left the mines. In particular, this was often the young and most productive miners, in their twenties or thirties, who deserted the mines. Danger, early and sudden death, respiratory diseases, and foul working conditions always provided very real reasons for miners to look elsewhere for work.

The degree of labour mobility in British mining districts has varied both within and between them. In Harrison (1978), the mobility of miners is but one factor used in support of the attempt by this labour historian and his colleagues in *The Independent Collier*, to 'recover a "lost" historical character', as the dust jacket announced. Only as the enumerators' books have become available for successive decennial censuses in the nineteenth century – there is a hundred-year ban on examining them – has it been possible to begin to measure with accuracy the levels of labour mobility in the industrial districts, and to tie them down to particular occupations. Campbell, in Harrison's book, presents some calculations of 'persistence' rates for the Lanarkshire coalfield between 1841 and 1871, which reveal that only from about a tenth to one half of the miners in some settlements stayed for as long as a decade. Sometimes this was mobility between pits and sometimes occupational mobility. James Brown, for instance,

> claimed in 1877 to have worked in more than two hundred pits in fourteen different Scots mining districts ... [but] superimposed on this geographical mobility was occupational mobility in and out of the mining industry, for example in 1866 during a depression in the shipbuilding industry (on the Clyde) large numbers of shipyard workers sought temporary jobs in the mines.
>
> (Campbell, 1978: 95)

Campbell also shows, in trying to account for varying rates of trade union militancy, that mining localities vary considerably on a wide range of variables from the geological through the technological, economic, geographical, demographical, political and social to the cultural. They can also vary through time. In the Coatbridge and Larkhall districts, he shows that, based on the decennial census reports from 1841 to 1871, 'persistence' rates for miners changed. Thus for Coatbridge the percentage of miners present through each decade was 14.2 from 1841–51, 16.7 from 1851–61 and 23.3 from 1861–71, while in Larkhall, among a smaller mining population, the comparable figures were 42.5 percent, 46.8 percent and 32.0 percent. Using the marriage registers for 1855–75, he showed that 46.3 percent of miners who married in Coatbridge had fathers who were miners. The corresponding figure for Larkhall was 59.5 percent. This suggests both some continuity and some change. Larkhall seemed to have in those decades a greater, though possibly declining, level of continuity than Coatbridge. The level of militancy, judged from historical records of disputes, seemed to be higher in Larkhall than in Coatbridge, but many other variables might have accounted for this and, in particular, much depended upon the determination of employers to repress employee resistance. In other studies, for instance Spaven (1978) on South Yorkshire, it has been shown that miners were more prone to militancy in more mobile mining settlements with harsh employment practices, and that moderate trade unionism was linked to communities with lasting social networks, which tended to be associated with employer paternalism.

To come back to Taylor (1979), it seems to be inadequate to conceive simply of unvarying, stable mining communities, with migration forced on the colliers only as the coal seams have been declared spent or 'uneconomic'. Migration and mobility have to be seen as part of the texture of mining localities, and as variables which relate to the history of community processes and institutions. They have to be set against the possibility of the formation of stable social networks and the sharing of historical memory. Further, such variable attributes of pit villages are likely to be associated with employment practices, be they paternalistic or harshly entrepreneurial.

This has been clearly spelled out in Moore's study of Methodism and mining (1974). Moore does not find evidence from his study to dissociate himself entirely from the ideal–typical view of the traditional mining community, but he indicates clearly that religious affiliation may vary and that this will account for differences in consciousness and trade union practices. In another study from the 'Durham' school, Williamson (1982) also shows that such variability has to be recognised. He combined biography with historical and sociological analysis in a study of his own predecessors, particularly his grandparents, who lived in Throckley, Northumberland.

The lives of Williamson's grandparents within the context of their family, work and community, were taken as 'illustrative of some of the major complex moments of social change over the last one hundred years' (1982: 2). At a wider level the context was one of class relationships, and the community in which they lived was constructed out of the impulses of landowners and colliery entrepreneurs as well as out of the responses of the miners and their families within that context.

> The coal company appears . . . as the representative of industrial capital, of ownership and of the political dominance of a bourgeois class. The Throckley miners' lodges, the Labour Party, the cooperative store symbolise organised labour. The relationship between these two forces defines the character of Throckley as a community.
>
> (ibid.: 7)

The whole study attempts then to point up the changes and crises in the configurations of production, power and class, which mark a transition from 'paternalistic' to 'corporate' capitalism. In many ways then it repeats the analysis which we saw in *Coal is Our Life*, except that Williamson includes much more data on the social history of Throckley, its miners and the labour movement generally. It is based, too, on a much more sensitive understanding of the people, who are not treated as members of dichotomous categories. The study suggests that the notion of the miner as the archetypal proletarian, which had arisen from the account of 'Ashton' miners and their relations with the managers, does need modification. In stressing the transition from 'paternalistic' to 'corporate' capitalism, however, Williamson may also be suggesting a generalisation about mining industry relations, which overlooks considerable variations in the nineteenth-century experience of British miners. Not all owners were in any sense 'paternalistic', but some were, not only in Throckley, but also in South Yorkshire, and this made a difference to pit-working and the villages.

Thus it is necessary in a reassessment of the ideal – typical model of a traditional mining community to examine evidence about the continuity of residence and community relations, and second, evidence concerning the relation between mine-owners and managers, and the labour force. To what extent is stability a more significant characteristic of mining communities than mobility of population? How far should the sense of conflict relations between workers and bosses be the one that forms the typical view?

These questions now are taken as the central themes of the historical description of our research area.

THE CREATION OF WEST YORKSHIRE MINING COMMUNITIES

The research area where we have collected information for the past decade as we indicated in the Preface, is situated in the same area where Dennis, Henriques and Slaughter carried out their study. Geographically it is situated to the east of the Pennine valleys of the Aire and Calder, where the woollen textile industry grew and where coal seams outcropped. The rich agricultural lands of the Vale of York begin here and stretch to the east. Politically and administratively, it is located in the present Hemsworth constituency of West Yorkshire, which includes the towns of Featherstone, South Elmsall and Hemsworth and a number of other smaller settlements. It covers an area of some sixty square miles, and its total population in 1981 was some sixty thousand.

In the mid-nineteenth century the area was predominantly one of small villages with Hemsworth somewhat larger than the rest, having a workhouse, an endowed hospital and a grammar school in a state of decline. Even a trade directory for the area in 1889 describes it in somewhat bucolic terms:

> The soil is clayey, marly and sandy; subsoil, clay and limestone. The chief crops are wheat, oats, barley, potatoes and pasture ... Here are several stone quarries of good quality for building, brick-yards and a steam corn-mill.
>
> (Kelly's Directory, 1889: 462)

The population of the research area in 1881 numbered seventeen thousand, and the industrial revolution was still having relatively minor effects on the social structure and economic activities. The emphasis in the same Kelly's

Directory is on informing potential traders of the chief landowners, the location and character of their stone-built mansions, and the architecture of the churches, the educational background of their incumbents and the names of the patrons. The landowners included descendants of families of the nobility and gentry of a pre-industrial age, but there were also some whose wealth had been made in banking, commerce or industry in the early nineteenth century. The Directory thus notes that railways were being built and from about 1870 deep coal mines were being sunk.

When George Bradley, one of the area's coal entrepreneurs, decided to sell the Ackton and Featherstone estate in 1890 in a period of relative decline in coal prices, and possibly because of bankruptcy, the bill of sale described it as an 'Agricultural and Mineral Estate'. It consisted of over a thousand acres of arable, pasture and woodland, including seven farm houses, one public house and two 'capital' houses, 'Featherstone Old Hall' and 'Ackton Hall', as well as two working collieries, which had been opened in the previous twenty-five years. 'Ackton Hall' was described as 'situate amidst pretty scenery on the higher portion of the Estate, whence extensive views are to be obtained of the surrounding country'. The rural imagery was evidently still important to the sale of property, even though the major marketable aspect of the sale was probably the coal resources.

The estate was bought by Lord Masham, using Lister family capital or credit built up through land-ownership and textile manufacturing in the West Riding of Yorkshire. The reasons for this purchase are not known, but probably relate to a need for new sources of coal in the textile enterprises of Bradford, Halifax and Addingham as seams nearer at hand were worked out. The purchase indicates also the growing tendency in the late nineteenth century for the vertical amalgamation of capitalist enterprises (that is, primary and secondary sector activities linked together in a large organisation) in the face of growing overseas competition, the increasing strength of trade unions, and changes in the structure of financial markets (Mathias, 1969).

The development of textiles and engineering industries in West Yorkshire especially after 1850, the growth of the cotton industry in Lancashire, the extension of the railway network, the expansion of the shipping industry, and the relatively small size of the Lancashire coalfield generally, explain the increasing exploitation of coal resources in Yorkshire. The richest coal seams, outcropping on the edges of the Pennines in West Yorkshire, dipped quite steeply under the surface to the east, and it required new technology related to the sinking of shafts, ventilation of coal workings and the pumping of water, as well as increasing demand for coal to encourage the eastward extension of coal mining. The profitability of deep mining was probably thought by some entrepreneurs to be not worth the risk of capital involved. One of the largest coal companies in West and South Yorkshire, the Charlesworth concern, never invested significantly here, though their mine holdings extended almost to the boundaries of the research area (Goodchild, 1978: Chap. 8). If we add the probability of some difficulty in assembling a large enough workforce and keeping it there in largely rural surroundings to the risks of investment, we can understand the relative reluctance of individuals and companies to begin the exploitation of the area's coal.

Deep mining began with the opening of the Featherstone Main Colliery on George Bradley's estate in 1865. Other pits were sunk in this northern part of the research area in the next ten years, but to the south nearer Hemsworth and South Elmsall, the development came only in the last decade of the nineteenth or in the early twentieth century. The family business enterprise like that of the Charlesworths gave way to amalgamated concerns like that of Lord Masham, or to companies created out of family businesses, like the South Kirkby, Featherstone and Hemsworth Collieries Limited, which owned several collieries. Managers or Company Agents tended to replace owners as the immediate authority over mine-working in the locality, as was the case when George Bradley, who lived in Ackton Hall, Featherstone, sold out to Lord Masham. Alfred Holiday was appointed as Masham's Agent and he came to live in Featherstone Old Hall, from where he would be able to look over the colliery workings. Industrial relations in the pits of the research area rarely began with a relationship between the mineworkers and an owner who had roots and a home in the locality where the pit was situated.

All the pits that were sunk in this part of West Yorkshire were situated in or near to small towns or villages, where the number of resident potential mineworkers was too small. The opening of mines had to be accompanied by the recruitment of workers and this was usually preceded by the construction of some houses for them to occupy. At no point according to our evidence was there any attempt to set up mining compounds, but the assumptions of the house builders, who were either the mining companies or local speculators making a cheap investment in housing, were that migrant workers would not need over much comfort. The Medical Officer of Health for Featherstone Urban District Council noted in his report for 1901 that in a survey undertaken of the housing in the area in 1886, the surveyor had noted that many houses were '"jerry built", damp, dilapidated, ill-ventilated and dirty' and that there was some overcrowding. This latter note is probably an understatement, since the MOH did not think that overcrowding was a problem in 1901, even though sixty percent of the four-roomed houses in the town (the modal type) had more than four persons living in them and twenty two percent of all dwellings had two or more persons per room. Sewers had been built along principal streets by 1886, but they were subject to rupture through mining subsidence and often overflowed.

One part of the town occupied mainly by mineworkers even in 1901 is described as

> a colony living in brick houses erected in parallel streets, . . . near by the Don Pedro Colliery. Altogether there are 152 houses. Some of the dwellings are arranged in sandwich fashion, the front and the back being alternate in each pair. There are no back or front yards, and on washing days the tenants dry the clothes on ropes stretched across the road from house to house . . . There is a most objectionable open privy midden at the bottom of Albany Street which . . . is a very great danger to health near these dwellings.
>
> (Featherstone Urban District Council, 1901)

The tendency of the inhabitants of the whole town to keep fowls, ducks, pigeons and pigs was also deplored, mainly because they were assumed to add to the insanitary conditions.

In each of the small towns and villages which became home to mineworkers and their households, there was a 'population explosion' of sorts. We have examined the reports of the Census Enumerators in the parishes of Featherstone and Hemsworth for the Censuses of 1871 and 1881, that is the documents on which the official Reports of each Census are based. They include details of every household member, principally their age, sex, marital status, occupation and birth place. Since there is a rule banning researchers from examining them until one hundred years after they were completed, this is as far as we can go (until 1992) in gaining any reliable evidence about continuity of residence, extent of migration and the composition of households in the new mining localities.

In our examination of Featherstone and Hemsworth, in the period of early development of the deep mining industry, the effect of the time differential in the starting of pits between the south and east of the research area and the north and west is clear. Featherstone parish in the north was already much more densely populated and miners were a much greater element in the population structure than was the case in Hemsworth in 1871. By 1881 this was still the case, though changes had taken place in both. In Featherstone parish, too, the concentration of housing near to the pits had produced several distinct parts which were developing in different ways. This can be exemplified by noting the contrasts between the former separate hamlet of Purston Jaglin and the rest of Featherstone. In Hemsworth parish there was little development of parts of the parish away from the old centre of the town until after 1881. Thus in presenting our findings from the Census Enumerators' Reports we make distinctions between Featherstone and Purston Jaglin, but give information for Hemsworth parish as a whole.

In the whole of Featherstone parish in 1861 there were 833 persons, of whom just over half were women. Hemsworth, with 993 persons in 1871, also had a rough balance in the sex distribution. In both cases

Table 3.1 Age structure, Featherstone, Purston Jaglin and Hemsworth

1871 and 1881
Males and females

| | 1871 | | | | | |
| | Featherstone | | Purston Jaglin | | Hemsworth | |
Age groups	*Males*	*Females*	*Males*	*Females*	*Males*	*Females*
0– 9 yrs	197	216	92	97	117	133
10–19 yrs	123	83	51	45	120	100
20–29 yrs	136	94	57	50	78	82
30–39 yrs	91	82	57	45	72	70
40–49 yrs	54	48	25	18	64	58
50–59 yrs	31	18	11	19	40	31
60–69 yrs	10	12	13	9	39	42
70–79 yrs	3	6	6	5	27	23
80–89 yrs	2	1	3	2	9	4
90 yrs +	0	0	0	0	1	1
Total	647	560	315	290	567	544

| | 1881 | | | | | |
| | Featherstone | | Purston Jaglin | | Hemsworth | |
Age groups	*Males*	*Females*	*Males*	*Females*	*Males*	*Females*
0– 9 yrs	524	554	110	108	213	202
10–19 yrs	383	243	70	53	153	131
20–29 yrs	322	211	61	50	175	122
30–39 yrs	272	205	52	45	135	112
40–49 yrs	179	127	34	32	98	80
50–59 yrs	90	65	21	18	55	42
60–69 yrs	26	31	13	16	45	38
70–79 yrs	8	11	5	5	22	30
80–89 yrs	2	2	3	2	9	5
90 yrs +	0	1	0	0	0	0
Total	1806	1450	369	329	905	762

Source: Reports of Census Enumerators, Featherstone and Hemsworth Parishes, 1871 and 1881

this was a situation immediately prior to the major development of coal mining. (In both parishes there are records of the extraction of coal from surface workings going back into the middle ages.) The apparently obvious effect of the new pits, which can be gathered from the sex distribution in Featherstone in 1871 and 1881 and Hemsworth in 1881, was the immigration of male workers, many of whom came without partners. This is shown in Table 3.1, and illustrated in Figures 3.1 to 3.6. In the youngest age group, the under ten-year-olds, there are more girls than boys in Featherstone, Purston Jaglin and Hemsworth. In Featherstone in 1871, where large pits were already established, among teenagers and those in their twenties, there were over thirty percent more males than females. In contrast, in Purston

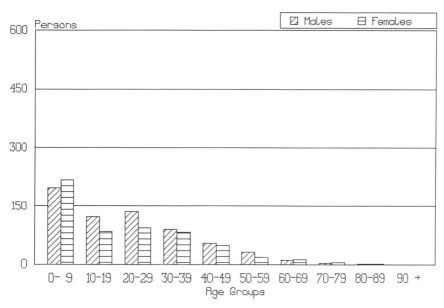

Figure 3.1 Age structure, Featherstone, 1871

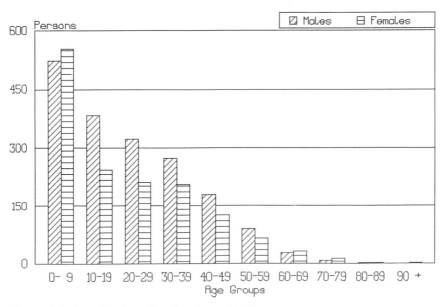

Figure 3.2 Age structure, Featherstone, 1881

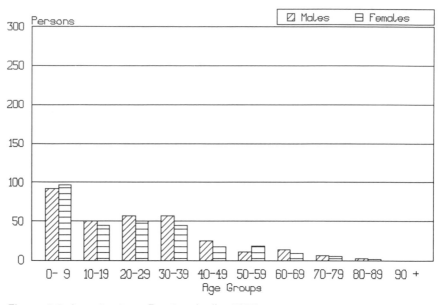

Figure 3.3 Age structure, Purston Jaglin, 1871

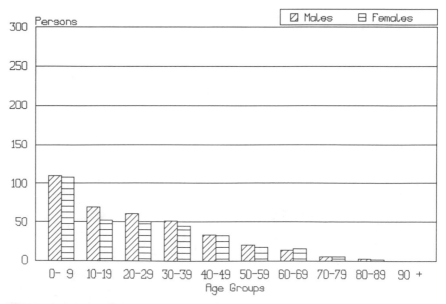

Figure 3.4 Age structure, Purston Jaglin, 1881

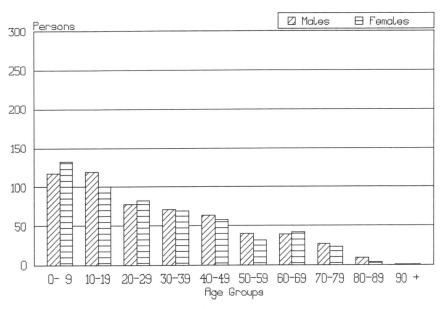

Figure 3.5 Age structure, Hemsworth, 1871

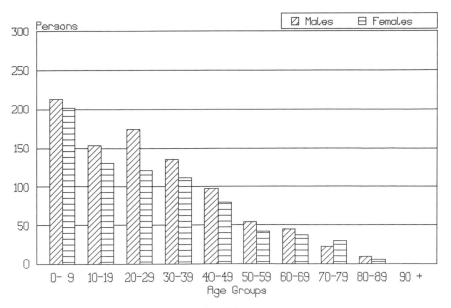

Figure 3.6 Age structure, Hemsworth, 1881

Table 3.2 Birthplaces of heads of households, Featherstone and Purston Jaglin, 1871

| | Featherstone | | Purston Jaglin | |
	Number	Percent	Number	Percent
Born within same parish – 'locals'	26	13.1	27	19.1
Yorkshire born (a) within 10 miles	33	16.6	47	33.4
(b) more than 10 miles away	51	25.6	24	17.0
North and North West England	27	13.6	5	3.5
Derby, Notts. & Lincs.	17	8.5	16	11.3
Other Midlands	35	17.6	18	12.8
Eastern, Southern and South Western counties	6	3.0	3	2.1
Rest of British Isles	3	1.5	1	0.7
Overseas	1	0.5	0	0.0
Total	199	100.0	141	99.9

Source: Reports of Census Enumerators, Featherstone Parish, 1871

and Hemsworth, the distribution of the sexes in those age groups is more balanced, and not consistently in favour of men. By 1881, in all three places, there is a similar majority of males over females in these teenager and young adult age groups. The older age groups, up to and including people in their fifties, show a clear and similar tendency between 1871 and 1881 to have more males. Demographically, the coming of the pits created settlements with a predominance of men, a fact which persisted into the mid-twentieth century.

The pattern of this inward migration is shown to some extent in our analysis of the birth places of the heads of households, given in Tables 3.2 and 3.3. Featherstone already had a large pit by 1871 and among heads of households only thirteen percent had been born within the parish. More than seventy percent had migrated from more than ten miles away in Yorkshire or from other counties. Among those coming from within Yorkshire, the majority were from the west. Likewise, where they came from other counties, they tended to come from the north, the west or the Midlands, where industries had been established. Many were probably from other coal-mining localities, where pits had closed or where disputes had led to outward movement, just as was indicated in Harrison's account of the 'independent collier' (1978). The Census Enumerators' Reports do not indicate previous occupations, though sometimes where a man had migrated

Table 3.3 Birthplaces of heads of households, Hemsworth, 1871 and 1881

| | Hemsworth 1871 | | Hemsworth 1881 | |
	Number	*Percent*	*Number*	*Percent*
Born within same parish – 'locals'	72	30.9	86	24.1
Yorkshire born (a) within 10 miles	91	38.2	76	23.9
(b) more than 10 miles away	51	21.9	42	13.2
North and North West England	3	1.3	16	5.0
Derby, Notts. & Lincs.	6	2.6	24	7.5
Other Midlands	3	1.3	42	13.2
Eastern, Southern and South Western counties	8	3.4	19	5.9
Rest of British Isles	1	0.4	12	3.8
Overseas	0	0.0	1	0.3
Total	233	100.0	318	99.9

Source: Reports of Census Enumerators, Hemsworth Parish, 1871 and 1881

with his family, it is possible to envisage the path of migration by noting where the successive children had been born. Henry Lawley, a miner aged forty-two, for instance, had been born in Shropshire, later moving to St Helens in Lancashire, where his wife, aged forty, and their first three children, aged eighteen, thirteen and ten, had been born, then to Normanton, less than three miles from Featherstone, where the fourth child, aged seven, was born. They had a baby aged twelve months born in Featherstone. All the localities with which Henry Lawley was associated were in mining areas. Not surprisingly the eldest child, a male, was a miner.

Purston Jaglin had more locals and was not quite so dominated by coal mining. Both places had more immigration by 1881, roughly following the same pattern of movement from other industrial parts of Britain. This was also a period of decline in the numbers employed in farming, however, and some moved here from the agricultural districts to the east and south east. Edward Lomas aged fifty-six, who had found work as a farm labourer in Featherstone, had been born in Norfolk. His wife, aged thirty-six and two eldest children, both boys and working as coal miners, were born in Norfolk too. Two daughters, aged ten and eight, had been born in agricultural villages in eastern Yorkshire, and three other younger children, aged six, four and two had been born in nearby Ackworth. This household seems to exemplify what had, earlier in the nineteenth century, been the typical mode of transformation of a farming into a mining or industrial household.

The father, possibly driven by poverty in farm labouring, migrated to other farming areas in search of a similar outlet for his skills, and his sons later found work in newly developing mines, mills or factories. The father may have combined seasonal or part-time farm labouring with some other work in the same locality.

In Table 3.3, the change taking place in the local economy and labour market around Hemsworth from 1871 to 1881, from farming and local trades to one where coal mining was increasingly important, is illustrated by the increase in migration from outside. Taking those born within the parish or ten miles of it as the 'locals', they formed nearly seventy percent of heads of households in 1871, and less than sixty percent in 1881. Over a quarter of them came from the mainly industrial counties bordering on Yorkshire in the later year, compared with only five percent in 1871. As in the case of Featherstone, though, this migration was not necessarily directly into Hemsworth. Isaac Whitehead, a colliery engine driver aged twenty-nine in 1881, had been born in Derbyshire. He migrated to West Ardsley in the South Yorkshire coalfield, where he married Louisa aged twenty-eight. Their two eldest children aged seven and five were born there. They probably moved to Hemsworth some three or four years before 1881, as their two youngest children, aged three years and five months respectively, were born in Hemsworth.

There was a particularly large migration from the Midlands, and this consisted very largely of the new employees of Hemsworth Colliery. Many of these were housed in a new row of terraced houses to the north of the town, called Fitzwilliam Terrace after the landowners. The Census Enumerators' Reports for 1881 show that there were thirty-four houses in the row, one of which remained unoccupied. Almost two-thirds of the heads of households were from the Midlands, with a large number from south Staffordshire. Altogether thirty of the heads of household were miners, two others were railway workers, possibly connected with the pit, and the last one was the local shopkeeper (also from the Midlands). In twenty-four houses there were sixty lodgers, who in the main were single miners, two or three per house. The households averaged 6.5 persons and altogether there were 136 males and 95 females, again showing the over-representation of men typical of mining localities. Even from this objective information it would not be difficult to recognise that Fitzwilliam Terrace could be thought an 'alien colony'.

The terrace was situated about a mile north of the centre of Hemsworth, and occupied by people whose earnings were gained in dirty, underground workings, evidence for which resided in growing mounds of 'slag' and cinders, and noisy, ungainly pit head gear, disfiguring the rural landscape. Undoubtedly, too, the miners and their households spoke with very different dialects, which added to their separateness. Even the manager, who lived near the pit, too, had come from Lancashire and his chief engineer, also nearby, was from Durham. This new settlement might have seemed to the 'locals' of Hemsworth an entirely unwelcome intrusion, against which it would be easy for the influential among them to cast many aspersions, which would be likely to stigmatise the mining households. It would take some years before Hemsworth would accept that it was becoming a very different social whole. Less than a third of the miners living in Hemsworth in 1881 would be likely to speak with a Yorkshire accent.

In both Featherstone and Hemsworth, it is possible to give some shape to the changing social whole in terms of the varying occupational status of inhabitants revealed by the Enumerators' Reports. It is always difficult to make a retrospective 'class' analysis, because the evaluation of occupational status has both temporal and spatial attributes. We have to 'think' ourselves into the nineteenth-century social values attached to landowners, mine managers, small and large farmers, clergy and other professionals, as distinct, perhaps, from people who were shopkeepers and those who practised craft skills, and who saw themselves as different from or better than labourers, domestic servants and others likely to have low incomes, not to mention the coal miners. What had been a fairly clear-cut rural social structure was changing to accommodate new industrial workers and their managers and supervisors. It is in some trepidation, therefore, that we offer a 'class' analysis using terms such as 'higher social class', 'intermediate' and 'working' classes for 1871 and 1881. The entries are somewhat uncertain, in that we have only the Census Enumerators' word for the accuracy of their designation of individuals' occupations. The descriptions are often no more than one word, either, and so without much wider discussion and comparison of such a classification, our analysis cannot serve to link with a more general picture of the British class structure at this period in any valid sense. It does, however, provide some internal comparison.

A comparison of the 'class structures' for 1871 and 1881 of Featherstone, Purston Jaglin and Hemsworth, makes clear that while there is little general change in numbers of heads of households in the old rural occupations and statuses, farmers and farm workers, it is the incursion of mineworkers which alters the percentage relationships of each group. The coming of these workers, along with other industrial labourers, has also provided a reason for the expansion of trades and shops, and there is some growth in the 'intermediate' class. What appears as a big growth in the numbers of landowners and persons of independent means in Hemsworth, between 1871 and 1881, is likely to be explained by such people not being at home at the time of the earlier census. (In much work on Census Enumerators' Reports, we have found that people known to live in large houses are often missing on the night of the census, possibly because they owned more than one and were away from the one in question.) The point is that at this stage of the assembly of what were to become mining localities (at least for a century or so) the social structure was not in any sense homogeneous.

Table 3.4 Heads of household by social class, Featherstone, Purston Jaglin and Hemsworth, 1871

	Featherstone		Purston Jaglin		Hemsworth	
	Number	%	Number	%	Number	%
Higher social class						
Landowners and those of independent means	1	0.5	3	2.8	5	2.1
Farmers	16	7.2	13	11.9	35	14.8
Mine-owners/ managers	1	0.5	1	0.9	0	0.0
Manufacturers	2	0.9	0	0.0	0	0.0
Professionals	3	1.4	8	7.3	14	5.9
Intermediate class						
Craftsmen and women	20	9.0	9	8.2	32	13.5
Traders/shopkeepers	15	6.7	8	7.3	27	11.4
Working class						
Colliery workers	126	56.7	45	41.3	4	1.7
Transport workers	2	0.9	0	0.0	8	3.4
Industrial labourers	11	5.0	8	7.3	14	5.9
Farm labourers	21	9.5	5	4.6	47	19.8
Domestic servants	0	0.0	3	2.8	11	4.6
Others*	4	1.8	6	5.5	40	16.9
Total	222	100.1	109	99.9	237	100.0

Source: Reports of Census Enumerators, 1871
*Note:** 'Others' includes 'retired', 'paupers', 'widows' and some where no, or too little, information is given

The divisions which created the heterogeneity were already based in those of earlier rural social structures, and the immigration of large numbers of mineworkers began to create the basis of others.

Demographically the new miners created an impact on the localities because generally they were of a much narrower age spread than the rest of the population (see Table 3.6 and Figures 3.7 to 3.12).

They also seem to have begun quickly to establish, perhaps on the basis of their common immigrant status, some traditional social networks. By an examination of the marriage registers for All Saints Parish Church in Featherstone for the years 1870 to 1880, we can see that there was a clear tendency for mining families to intermarry, and for fewer cross-status or cross-class weddings to take place (Table 3.7). Using the same classification of occupations and statuses as in Tables 3.4 and 3.5, we conducted a cross-classification of wife's fathers with husband's fathers in 166 marriages registered in Featherstone. Among seventy-eight miners' sons, forty-eight

Table 3.5 Heads of household by social class, Featherstone, Purston Jaglin and Hemsworth, 1881

	Featherstone		Purston Jaglin		Hemsworth	
	Number	%	Number	%	Number	%
Higher social class						
Landowners and those of independent means	1	0.2	1	0.6	17	5.0
Farmers	18	3.0	12	7.7	27	8.0
Mine-owners/ managers	2	0.3	2	1.3	3	0.9
Manufacturers	1	0.2	1	0.6	0	0.0
Professionals	8	1.3	6	3.8	10	3.0
Intermediate Class						
Craftsmen and women	32	5.3	11	7.0	50	14.8
Traders/shopkeepers	26	4.3	10	6.4	27	8.0
Working class						
Colliery workers	429	71.5	77	49.3	75	22.2
Transport workers	22	3.7	0	0.0	21	6.2
Industrial labourers	17	2.8	5	3.2	29	8.6
Farm labourers	12	2.0	15	1.0	31	9.2
Domestic servants	2	0.3	5	3.2	14	4.1
Others*	30	5.0	11	7.0	34	10.1
Total	600	99.9	156	100.1	338	100.1

Source: Reports of Census Enumerators, 1881
Note: *'Others' includes 'retired', 'paupers', 'widows' and some where no, or too little, information is given

(or sixty-two percent) were married to miners' daughters. Another sixteen (or twenty-one percent) were married to daughters from working-class homes. About a fifth married into a higher social class. The position is reversed for those belonging to the highest status groups. Twelve of the twenty sons of upper and middle class fathers, or sixty percent, married daughters of similar class fathers. Only in the intermediate class of shopkeepers and craftsmen was there a high degree of cross-class marriage. The tendency here was for both sons and daughters of intermediate class fathers to marry into the working class, rather than into the intermediate or a higher class. Although these findings relate to a much smaller sample and have not been subject to the same methodological rigour, they are similar to those of Penn and Dawkins (1983). Over a longer time span in another northern industrial area, Rochdale, they found a tendency among their upper and lower class groups to class inter-marriage, but they also found a much wider grouping in the intermediate stratum where there

Table 3.6 Mineworkers and the age structure, 1871 and 1881

Age groups	1871 Featherstone		Purston Jaglin		Hemsworth	
	Non-miners	Miners	Non-miners	Miners	Non-miners	Miners
0– 9yrs	197	0	92	0	117	0
10–19 yrs	75	48	37	14	120	0
20–29 yrs	39	97	20	37	77	1
30–39 yrs	29	62	21	36	70	2
40–49 yrs	17	37	12	13	63	1
50–59 yrs	19	12	7	4	40	0
60–69 yrs	7	3	11	2	39	0
70–79 yrs	3	0	6	0	27	0
80–89 yrs	2	0	3	0	9	0
90 yrs +	0	0	0	0	1	0
Total	388	259	209	106	563	4

Age groups	1881 Featherstone		Purston Jaglin		Hemsworth	
	Non-miners	Miners	Non-miners	Miners	Non-miners	Miners
0– 9 yrs	524	0	110	0	213	0
10–19 yrs	217	166	46	24	137	16
20–29 yrs	58	264	29	32	105	70
30–39 yrs	61	211	14	38	87	48
40–49 yrs	48	131	16	18	67	31
50–59 yrs	32	58	8	13	42	13
60–69 yrs	12	14	12	1	40	5
70–79 yrs	5	3	5	0	21	1
80–89 yrs	2	0	3	0	9	0
90 yrs +	0	0	0	0	0	0
Total	959	847	243	126	721	184

Source: Reports of Census Enumerators, 1871 and 1881, Featherstone and Hemsworth Parishes

was much inter-marriage. Penn and Dawkins were not willing to conclude that there was clear class polarisation from their study, and we could only cautiously suggest that in Featherstone between 1870 and 1880, there were the beginnings of social closure around working and upper/middle-class positions.

As well as class endogamous marriage, as a factor in a process of social closure, it was also the case that miners were recruited, if not from migrant workers, from among the sons of local miners. Using the Census Enumerators' Reports for 1881, it is possible to see how many sons of working age living at home were employed in mining. In Featherstone, in the district nearest to the two largest pits, among sons living in a mining household (that is, where the head was a coal miner or worked in the colliery) seventy-nine percent were also working at a colliery. (In 1881, the

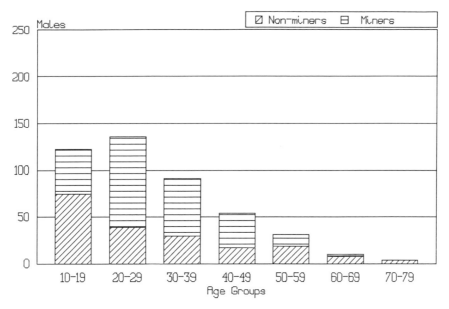

Figure 3.7 Mineworkers and the age structure, Featherstone, 1871

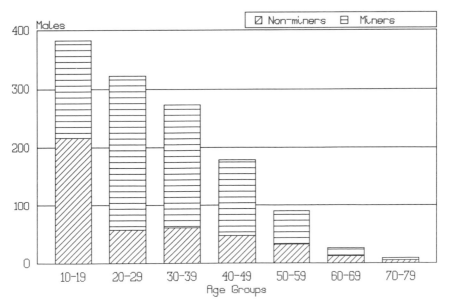

Figure 3.8 Mineworkers and the age structure, Featherstone, 1881

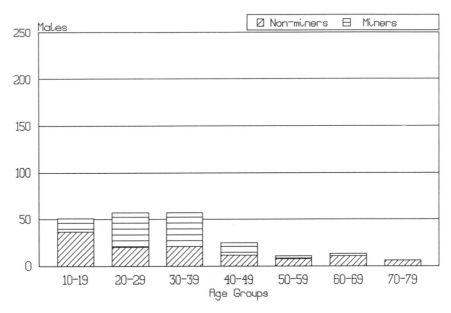

Figure 3.9 Mineworkers and the age structure, Purston Jaglin, 1871

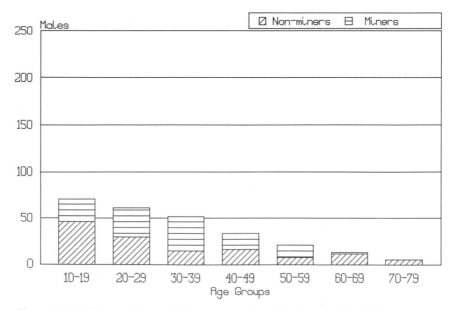

Figure 3.10 Mineworkers and the age structure, Purston Jaglin, 1881

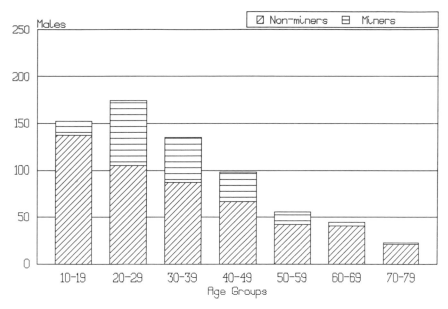

Figure 3.11 Mineworkers and the age structure, Hemsworth, 1881

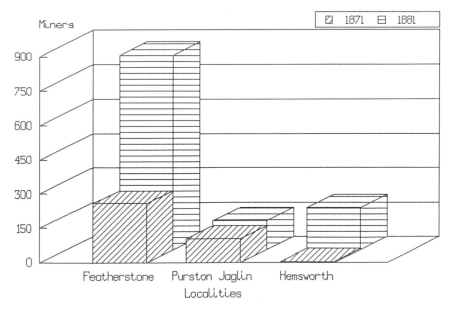

Figure 3.12 Increase in the number of mineworkers 1871–81

Table 3.7 The class pattern of marriages in Featherstone, 1871 to 1880

	Social class of brides' fathers				
Social class of grooms' fathers	Upper & middle classes	Inter- mediate class	Colliery workers	Other working class	Total
Upper & middle	12	2	2	4	20
Intermediate	3	6	14	8	31
Colliery workers	2	12	48	16	78
Other working class	6	6	10	15	37
Total	23	26	74	43	166

Source: The marriage registers, All Saints Parish Church, Featherstone (kept in West Yorkshire County Archives, Wakefield)

youngest coal workers were thirteen years old.) In non-mining households, where the head of household was not working at the pit, fifty-seven percent were colliery workers. Among the households of Purston Jaglin, which we have already noted as being a little more distant from the pit, and a little less dominated by colliery workers than the rest of Featherstone, eighty-six percent of sons aged thirteen or over living in mining households were already mineworkers. Only twenty-eight percent of those in non-mining households were mineworkers. In a local labour market that was already very skewed towards coal mining, it is clear that kinship was an important determinant of entry into the market. Perhaps it is also interesting to note that in the households of a colliery manager and a mining engineer, teenage sons were not mineworkers and had entered non-manual occupations. This seems to indicate a class and aspiration gap between mineworkers and their managers and controllers.

This survey of the beginnings of Featherstone and Hemsworth as mining localities has emphasised the heterogeneity of the structures and processes involved in their assembly. It suggests lines of cleavage and boundaries of social closure that would mark these places during the twentieth century, and were reflected in the analysis of 'Ashton' by Dennis, Henriques and Slaughter. It also suggests that if there is any validity in the ideal–typical view of the traditional mining community, with its emphasis on solidarity and continuity, then these are characteristics which have had to be socially constructed onto social collectivities which were marked by heterogeneity. There was certainly no evidence that mineworkers necessarily came to Featherstone and Hemsworth with clear intentions to stay. Many were migrant and probably 'independent' colliers. It is not possible yet to check whether there was an increased tendency to stay put, as a consequence of the development of kinship networks, and of kinship being a basis for recruitment into the mines, after 1881. In Featherstone

Table 3.8 Employment in coal mining, Featherstone and Hemsworth, 1881 to 1951

Year	Featherstone		Hemsworth		
	Number	Percent	Number	Percent	
1881	1541	63.1	184	26.6	(% males age 10 & over)
1921	3790	75.0	2476	67.1	(% males age 12 & over)
1951	2153	47.0	2291	53.0	(% males age 15 & over)

Source: For 1881, Census Enumerators' Reports, and for 1921 and 1951, occupational tables in the Reports of the Registrar General on the Censuses of those years
Note: The age when most boys left school in 1881 was approximately twelve years, in 1921, thirteen years, and in 1951, fourteen years. We have not found records of boys being employed under thirteen years in the pits in 1881, nor under fourteen years in 1921

and Purston, the staying-on rates of mining households between 1871 and 1881, were twenty-nine percent and fifty-three percent respectively. That for Featherstone was similar to those reported earlier for Larkhall and Coatbridge in the period 1861 to 1871 (see p. 38). Purston mining households were more persistent, however, and their staying on rate was higher than that for other types of household in the village. Later information will also indicate that kinship networks did become very significant in the area, but it is impossible to check the validity of the claim made in *Coal is Our Life*, that four-fifths of the households in 'Ashton' had roots going back to the end of the nineteenth century. Certainly in the 1980s a number of household names in Featherstone can be traced back to the 1881 Census Enumerators' reports: Bullock, Cording, Cranswick, Dyas, Hale, Heptinstall, Herrington, Hufton, Jepson, Jukes and Luckman are examples.

LATE NINETEENTH-CENTURY CAPITALISM AND INDUSTRIAL CONFLICT IN THE MINING DISTRICTS

However we look at the processes and institutions such as households, kinship, marriage and social classes, it is very clear that the transformation of the local economies into ones in which coal production predominated is what gave these localities their distinctive structures and cultures. The growth of mining as a male occupation here (see Table 3.8) corresponded with a period of somewhat uncertain development in what was a very large industry. There were over half a million coal miners in the 1880s in Britain. The development was marked by consolidation and concentration of mining companies in an attempt to cope with a relatively poor market situation for coal between the mid-1870s and the mid-1890s, the period that marks the beginning of Great Britain's economic decline relative to Germany and the United States (Mann, 1988). Industries were stagnating rather than growing, so that prices, profits and rates of interest tended to decline or to remain relatively low. Prices of coal fell from over eight shillings per ton at the pit head in 1890 to below seven shillings in early 1893. Mine-owners and managers attempted to constrain their costs by keeping the price-lists for production in and development of their mines as low as possible. Conflicts over methods and conditions of coal cutting, transporting and weighing, and over the quality and quantity of production as well as safety and access in the mines, were always occurring at every point of production, and they escalated during this time.

Unions of mineworkers and associations of mine-owners formed and reformed in the nineteenth century to cope with the conflictual character of the industry. Allen (1981) looking back over this time, when discussing the background to the amalgamation of separate county unions of mineworkers into the National Union of Mineworkers in 1944 points out that

> [a]lthough the coalfields were physically isolated and the workers in them tended to be insular and chauvinistic, it was not inevitable that trade unionism in mining should have been organised on a county basis. The unions were formed after the establishment of the railway system and after the coal markets had become national in scope. The coalfields possessed many divisive factors, including competitiveness, but the unifying ones were strong.
>
> (V. Allen, 1981: 23)

He goes on to claim that it was groups of owners who preferred the miners to be divided and who sought to break down any militant national unionism. A loose alliance of county unions, called the Miners' National Union had formed in 1863, but this tended to be led by men who favoured compromise with the owners rather than conflict. It eventually came to be known as the Miners' Federation of Great Britain in 1889.

The late nineteeth century was also a time of political change. Up to the 1890s labour leaders tended to seek political representation through the Liberal party, but it was in conflicts emerging in the coal industry, as well as elsewhere, that the idea of labour representation separate from the Liberals began to gain ground. A dispute which had a relationship to this national issue, but also had very significant implications for industrial and community relations in our research area, occurred in 1893. There was a Liberal government in office – Gladstone was serving his last term as Prime Minister and Asquith was his Home Secretary – and there was widespread industrial unrest. The labour movement was responding to the depressed state of the economy and the tendency of employers to cut back wages. The Independent Labour Party had been formed in 1893, with socialist leaders like Keir Hardie and Cunninghame Graham. New trade unions were recruiting rapidly among transport workers, dockers, and railway men. There were still many divisions among the working class, however, and though the opposition to the new unionism which came from employers was a potentially unifying force, many labour leaders were still members of the Liberal Party (Bedarida, 1979).

As 1893 unfolded Gladstone's government clearly supported the employers. The Home Secretary gave permission for police and troops to be moved at the request of employers to break strikes and guard their property. There was, understandably, much hesitancy among trade unionists, especially their Liberal leaders, such as Ben Pickard and Edward Cowey of the Yorkshire Miners' Association, over decisions to withdraw labour. Hostility to the constabulary and military were on the one hand easy to justify, when they seemed prepared to back up employers' wishes somewhat ruthlessly, as they had done when drafted into Hull at the time of a dock strike in April and May. On the other, they were there as the forces of a Liberal government, and hostility to them should not be encouraged. Such conflicts and contradictions formed the background to the events of the spring, summer and autumn of 1893 in the coalfields, which included a 'riot' in Featherstone when two miners were killed and others wounded by soldiers.[1]

The Featherstone massacre

At a conference of the Miners' Federation held in London at the beginning of May, 1893, a majority decision was taken to resist any further attempt by mine-owners to reduce wages. The owners for their part, however, responding to what they saw as a crisis in the coal trade, had in late June proposed a cut in wages, which the unions said amounted to a twenty-five percent reduction in increases agreed in the two years up to 1890. In any case, it is very probable that many miners were on short time during 1893 and were not able to take home anything like a full week's pay. While various county miners' unions balloted their members on the proposed cut, owners in some areas gave their employees a fortnight's notice of intended reductions on 8 July. The Miners' Federation held a delegate conference in Birmingham on 19 July, and, although not all county unions and their members were represented, a unanimous decision to refuse the wage reduction was taken and all miners were advised not to allow coal to be moved from the pits. The owners were notified of this at a joint negotiating conference held in London two days later. Negotiations were curtailed, and while coal prices in London markets rose by two shillings and sixpence per ton, the owners notified their miners that they would be refused work from 28 July, unless they withdrew their objections to the cut in pay. This 'lockout' started in every coal-field except in the North East of England. The Durham miners refused to be bound by the July Miners' Federation delegate conference.

Elsewhere, and particularly in Yorkshire, the 'lockout' produced much conflict. Some miners did not accept the union decision to refuse the cut and worked on, and pickets often clashed with such 'blacklegs'. In Featherstone, a new shaft was being sunk, and surface workers involved in this did not join in the dispute. Some coal extracted in this process, known as 'smudge', continued to be loaded into wagons and sent to Lord Masham's mills in Bradford. This was the cause of much concern to pickets, and eventually in September led to a clash. Before this, however, coal stocks quickly disappeared throughout the country, and railway companies laid off many drivers and firemen. Negotiations between coal-owners and the Miners' Federation continued, and with some irony the latter offered not to seek pay rises again until market prices for coal reached the level they had in 1890, just before the big downturn. In fact the shortages had brought prices back up to the old levels, and a *Punch* cartoon in August showed a fat 'mining capitalist' enjoying champagne and cigars. The Coalowners' Association offered to submit the dispute to arbitration at the end of August. The conflicts continued, however, and there were disturbances at collieries all over Yorkshire and adjacent counties leading to the movement of troops into the area.

On Thursday, 7 September 1893, disturbances broke out at Ackton Hall colliery, Featherstone, as local miners and pickets at last disputed with the management about the removal of 'smudge' from the pit yard. That morning wagons were turned over and windows broken. Troops were requested to protect the colliery, the police being fully stretched because it was the time of the St Leger race meeting at Doncaster. The arrival of twenty-eight armed troops by train at Featherstone in the afternoon seems to have inflamed the local miners, and it seems possible that they invited assistance from miners in other villages and towns. In the early evening groups of pickets, possibly numbering two or three hundred, arrived in Featherstone, reportedly carrying sticks and cudgels. A confused situation followed in which two local police officers, the manager of the pit and the squad of infantrymen with officers were besieged in the colliery engine house.

Following some negotiation, the pickets allowed the group in the engine house to leave, on the understanding that the soldiers would go back to the station. Soon after this some timber in the pit yard was set alight, and this attracted more people to come out to see what was happening. The crowd, according to witnesses who were questioned by the Bowen Commission, contained both men and women. The arrival by train of a magistrate, called by the manager in the hope of quelling the unrest, signalled the return of the troops to the colliery about eight o'clock in the evening, and they proceeded, with bayonets fixed, to clear the pit yard of pickets. Despite resistance, in which stones were allegedly thrown, they were pushed back to the main entrance. There the magistrate is said to have read out the Riot Act about 8.40 p.m., after a number of unsuccessful appeals to the crowd to disperse. Witnesses called by the Bowen Commission disagreed about the ferocity of the resistance put up by the pickets, but it was that which at 9.15 pm led the magistrate, according to his own testimony, to give the order to the troops to fire on the crowd, even though according to the provisions of the Act, an hour should have been given after the reading of the Act for the crowd to disperse. He asked for blanks to be used, but the soldiers only had live ammunition, and in firing two rounds they wounded a number of bystanders, two of whom, James Gibbs and James Duggan, later died. The Bowen Report claims that between eleven and fourteen people were shot, some of whom were nowhere near the pit, but happened to be in the line of fire.

Fierce disagreements about the meaning of the incident followed, in which accusations of massacre and the re-establishment of military repression by a Liberal government were made. At the two inquests, one returned a verdict of 'justifiable homicide', while the other on James Gibbs, 'a Sunday School teacher', refused such a justification of the shooting and merely noted that he was 'shot by the military after the Riot Act had been read'. This made it necessary for the government to set up the Bowen Commission to enquire into the events, and into the conduct of the magistrate and the troops. Not surprisingly Lord Bowen, advised by military and legal experts, was able to dismiss any charge of unjustifiable homicide, despite evidence from witnesses that neither of the dead men were ringleaders or among those who used sticks, stones or other weapons. Few violent incidents were seen by witnesses drawn from the local working class, and it was mainly the evidence of police officers, the commander of the troops and the management which suggested that a riot was taking place. Nevertheless outrages were committed, claims the Report, so that the magistrate was therefore right to call upon the soldiers to shoot.

> [A]s things stood at the supreme moment when the soldiers fired, their action was necessary. We feel it right to express our sense of the steadiness and discipline of the soldiers in the circumstances. We can find no ground for any suggestion that the firing, if it was in fact necessary, was conducted with other than reasonable skill and care.
>
> (Bowen Report: 11)

The 'if it was in fact necessary' was perhaps a concession to the critics of the action, but there is no concession to those who were 'imprudent' enough to be standing watching the events, or to those who were locked out of work and sensing considerable grievances in their situation.

The 'massacre' produced enormous storms of protest throughout the country, and particularly from the growing labour movement. The funerals of the two who died were attended by large crowds of mourners, estimated in the thousands. At one of them ILP leaders were present and the occasion was turned into a protest meeting on behalf of the locked out miners. Keir Hardie came to the area about ten days later and in a speech in nearby Normanton urged the miners to carry on the struggle, although by this time local Yorkshire Miners' Association leaders were recognising that their

Plate 3.1 The gravestones of James Gibbs and James Arthur Duggan, shot and mortally wounded on the streets of Featherstone, 7 September 1893 (Photo by Zygmunt Bauman)

hardship funds were running very low, because of the increasing claims as the dispute lengthened. Edward Cowey, the Liberal Yorkshire Miners' President, attacked both the socialists and the police and military for increasing the temperature of the conflict.

Through the rest of September and the whole of October, distress among mining households grew, and the local papers printed stories of hardship and near-starvation. Negotiations repeatedly broke down over the issue of the cut in wages which the owners continued to demand. It was not until the government openly intervened in the situation in mid-November and a Home Office Minister, Lord Rosebery, was called upon to arbitrate that the dispute was settled. The mines were reopened on 20 November with the old wage rates intact.

Future wage disputes were to be the subject of proceedings at an official Board of Conciliation, on which government, the owners and the Union would be represented. This can be seen to be a precursor of twentieth-century 'corporatist' solutions to industrial and class conflicts, to which Williamson (1982) also draws attention in his account of a north-eastern mining community.

More immediately, the settlement represented respite in a bitter conflict, the first of a series of major disputes in the four decades from the 1890s which indelibly marked the working class in mining localities. The return to work did not end the sense of opposition or resistance to the owners or the government, for in the months that followed miners who had been arrested in neighbouring villages and towns during so-called riots were put on trial. Though the majority were acquitted, some were sent to prison for periods up to fifteen months. Further, coal prices dropped once production levels rose, and the Conciliation Board insisted on a ten percent reduction in wages in 1894. This was just a part of the experience which eventually led to and confirmed the shift in the political allegiance of the miners' union from the Liberal Party to Labour and gave impetus to the labour movement. Ben Pickard, the Liberal MP for Normanton, by the end of the 1890s is recorded as attempting to persuade the Miners' Federation to set up a political fund in support of the election of MPs who were clear supporters of the labour movement, though he still held to his Lib–Lab affiliation and was an outspoken critic of Keir Hardie and the ILP. The Yorkshire Miners' Association saw its role as promoting 'not industrial passivity . . . but collectivism and industrial solidarity' in association with political liberalism (Howell, 1983: 18).

Another even longer dispute in our research localities, though it was much more local, and one of many that were instrumental in bringing about that political realignment, occurred in Hemsworth over several years from 1904 and particularly affected the mining households in the north of the parish, in Kinsley and Fitzwilliam.[2]

The Hemsworth lock-out

Hemsworth colliery was opened by 1880, and by the mid-1890s three seams were worked, the Shafton, Barnsley and Haigh Moor seams. About 1600 men were employed by the Hemsworth Colliery Company, some of them living in houses built by the company, near to the colliery. Coal prices had risen during the time of the Boer War, in 1900 and 1901, and the Miners' Association had through arbitration negotiated a wage increase, which was agreed until 1903. The price of coal fell after the war, and the Hemsworth Colliery Company indicated that they could not continue paying at the agreed prices. Unsuccessful arbitration followed in September 1903, and the dispute simmered until July 1904, when the company gave notice to lock out the miners in the Barnsley seam, where some of the highest wages were earned. Work continued in the other seams, while negotiations proceeded, but in April 1905 the Shafton seam was also closed. The YMA had supported the Barnsley seam miners with hardship funds, during the negotiations, but the second lock-out spurred a more militant reaction within the Hemsworth Union Branch, and a ballot was held to determine whether to give notice of strike action in support of a claim that the company should pay the prices in force in 1903. By a large majority they agreed to give that notice, but the company, despite pressure from the Yorkshire Coalowners Association to honour what had been a legally arbitrated price-list, refused to pay. Thus what had been a lock-out now became a strike, from August 1905.

The bitterness of relations between the company and the miners led to the company evicting miners from the houses which they owned and virtually bribing other local landlords to do the same, which some did. (Such 'landlordism' had already occurred only three years previously in Denaby and Cadeby, mining villages in South Yorkshire.) Further the Board of Guardians in Hemsworth, the body responsible for granting poor relief, seemed to take the side of the owners, when they refused to provide free school meals and support for local children, whose parents' income was hit by the lock-out during 1905. The Guardians refused the repeated appeals of miners' branch leaders, John Potts and William Bull, that children were undernourished and that the miners had not chosen to be locked out of work. They let the appeals run on until the strike began, and then accepted the view of the company that there was work for all the men to do and the seams were now open, if they wished to return to the colliery. Support for the miners and their families from local church leaders was also disregarded.

The eviction of many miners from their company and privately rented houses in August 1905, and the publicity around this in the local press led to demands for more militant action by the Miners' Association leadership. The creation of a tented compound for evicted miners and their families, in a field behind a nearby hotel (with the support of the landlord, who seems to have gone against brewery instructions) was the focus of widespread attention within the labour movement. Socialist groups and newspapers, such as the *Clarion, Labour Record* and the *Labour Leader* (see Howell, 1983), gave support by encouraging donations and collections among their members and readers. Local newspapers, including the *Yorkshire Post*, also reported the events to the region, and this encouraged wider charitable support.

The camp lasted for two months, until a large donation, by the Miners' Federation of Great Britain in the middle of October, 1905, enabled the YMA to lease a large number of the empty houses. These were let back to the miners at small rents, and most of the evicted could now be accommodated for the winter under solid roofs. The dispute continued, however, for neither side would alter their positions and the Colliery Company went into liquidation, claiming bankruptcy. Part of the problem was its inability to pay the rates to the Overseers of the Poor, who funded the Board of Guardians!

Indeed the dispute continued into 1907 without a complete settlement, for a new owner bought up the mine to create the South Kirkby, Featherstone and Hemsworth Colliery Company in the summer of 1906, but refused to pay the rates awarded up to 1903. There were several attempts at negotiation,

Plate 3.2 The Kinsley camp (Photo courtesy of Hemsworth WEA)

but none produced any agreement acceptable to all the local miners. Some men were engaged however at the end of 1906 to begin to make the mine safe once more for working, after a closure of over twelve months. Many found work in other pits and by March 1907 there were just under 400 men who remained on strike, mounting pickets to try to prevent the repair men continuing with their work, until the dispute was settled. The sense of solidarity was obviously much strained by this time, and there were reports of protests, street fights with police and the breaking of windows of houses tenanted by 'blacklegs'. Outside labour was recruited, and only about two hundred remained on strike in November 1907, after rates on offer were raised slightly (possibly as a pre-Christmas incentive). Potts and Bull led this small group of strikers until January 1909, when the Yorkshire Miners Association exerted pressure on them to come to a final settlement. In the end nothing appreciable was gained, and over half of them were refused work at Hemsworth. Some of these remained officially in dispute, in fact, until June 1910, when the YMA ceased to pay hardship funds to them.

Such a long-term dispute had many implications for those involved throughout, but chief was its politicising tendency. John Potts, for instance, became an active local politician, along with several other leaders of the miners. He later became the first Labour Member of Parliament for

Plate 3.3 Camp life: evicted miners (Photo courtesy of Hemsworth WEA)

Barnsley, from 1922 to 1938. For others who went back to work, it is difficult to know how the conflict between loyalty to the cause and the need for a living wage was felt. There must have been many internal arguments. It was during this dispute that those who supported the break of the Yorkshire Miners' Association from the Lib–Lab alliance won a majority. The Hemsworth miners, under Potts and Bull, continued their militancy, partly because of support given by the Independent Labour Party and a stream of notable visitors, including Philip Snowden and Keir Hardie, especially during the 1906 General Election, when an ILP candidate fought the nearby seat of Wakefield. Though the Liberals won a landslide election victory nationally, in Wakefield they were pushed into third position by the Labour candidate. The Tories, however, held on to the seat, and of course there was much recrimination between Lib–Lab supporters and the more socialist ILP members. Potts and Bull used the result to suggest that the Lib–Lab alliance should end, that miners should all vote for clear Labour candidates and that the YMA should alter its affiliation. The leftward political shift which we noted at the end of the 1893 dispute was now very much more obvious in miners' politics, and this was a consequence of experiences of disputes like these, affecting many of Britain's industrial localities.

Plate 3.4 Evicted household (Photo courtesy of Hemsworth WEA)

CONCLUSION

In this historical account, we have concentrated upon the formation and early development of settlements based in the exploitation of coal measures in the latter part of the nineteenth century and in the first decade of the twentieth. We have drawn the material together in the light of Bulmer's ideal–typical model of traditional mining communities, and of comments on that drawn from the work of the members of the Durham research school with which Bulmer was associated.

The early structuring of mining localities in our research area began in the 1860s, and the extension of deep coal mining continued into the twentieth century. From the examination of records we have shown that ownership was changing from the family dynasty type of mine owning to the company and vertically integrated concerns, and that there was little or no evidence of paternalistic ownership. The labour force which was assembled was drawn from a wide range of localities, and the sense of mobility which marked this assembly was sufficient to raise some doubts about how far this could or would become the basis of relatively homogeneous and solidary 'working class communities'. Many internal conflicts based in rivalry between 'locals' and 'incomers', between more militant and more

Plate 3.5 Evicted children (Photo courtesy of Hemsworth WEA)

deferential mineworkers, and between more and less religiously oriented men and women, undoubtedly existed, and the characterisation of 'Ashton' as experiencing both segregated and solidary relationships seems accurate. Events like the Featherstone 'massacre' and the Hemsworth lock-out and evictions, backed by experiences of stiff-necked attitudes deriving from magistrates and Boards of Guardians, were capable of creating working-class solidarity strong enough to bring about local political change and contribute to the growth of the labour movement generally. At the same time we can see in the Hemsworth dispute a tendency for division between local pit politics and more general mineworker politics at the level of the County and Federation. This, too, has become part of the consciousness and culture of mining communities. Its influence can be seen in the 1984/5 miners' strike, a point which is made by Gibbon (1988) in his analysis of that strike and to which we will refer later in Chapter Seven.

It was not merely hostility between mineworkers and mine-owners and managers, then, which created the consciousness of mining communities, but a whole complex of social relations which existed in industrialising societies at the same time. In the next chapter we start by examining biographical data drawn from the twentieth century in the West Yorkshire mining localities, the variations we have found there in our research project,

Plate 3.6 Kinsley evictions, 3 October 1905 (Photo courtesy of Hemsworth
       WEA)

and in particular how the local culture of one of them developed, its key
aspects, its reproducers and definers. The variations which we observed
will emphasise not merely the significance of community structures and
cultures, but also the wider social trends, new forms of social closure and
polarisation.

Chapter 4

Research in four mining communities in the 1980s

INTRODUCTION

In one sense the very reason for interest in the ideal–typical model of the traditional mining community in sociological research has not been because of the links between the isolated occupational community and the development of working-class consciousness, but because of the atypical character of such localities in the twentieth century. Many mining localities, not only in Britain but also elsewhere in the world, have remained outside the urban sprawl, and this has made them quite different from urban neighbourhoods, in terms of labour market opportunities, access to urban services and ethnic heterogeneity. Nevertheless they have been caught up in modernising tendencies, in conflicts over the organisation of capitalism and of state economies, and in debates about changing forms of energy production.

At the same time as they have become untypical, they have continued to make a mark on modern societies, because within them has developed a culture which has enabled them to act with some autonomy in times of stress and change. Our research localities provide us with indications of that culture, which has been a product of a whole century of development.

In this chapter we wish to indicate the main lines of our research in the 1980s, both to indicate the local culture and to show the social organisation of such communities in all their complexity.

HOW WE SEE OUR RESEARCH LOCALITIES

Mining communities are composed not only of miners, but of households in which there are men, women and children, and it is in them as well as in trade union branches, pits, clubs, churches and schools, as well as many other institutions, that the development has occurred. Thus we will focus not only on men, but also on women. Both history and sociology have often been blind to the lives, consciousness and action of women. Bulmer's (1975a) model of the mining community notes in accordance with the stereotypical view that the home is the women's domain, that there is a men's world and a women's world. The men's world is the world of economic and political activity, where the working-class consciousness is made and remade. Women are the domestic managers, and their lives are at the centre of a web of kinship and other traditional social networks which make up the close-knit and interlocking collectivity, the community with its shared history and culture.

How far this ever was entirely the truth is a good question, and how far this has been a product of men's own definition of the situation is another. It is only as a consequence of feminist critiques, arising in the women's movement, that we have come to look again at questions of roles, of consciousness and of interpretations of the world, which in the past have taken men's definitions as adequate. Now women have challenged that male supremacy, not only in their lives but in the culture around them. This is another aspect of twentieth-century change, of course, and one that must be embodied in a discussion of mining localities. One of the problems of *Coal is Our Life* was that it was written in the middle of the twentieth century when feminist critiques were hardly ever heard and therefore not taken account of in social science. When its authors wrote about 'Ashton', they certainly were concerned with the possibility of the development of revolutionary consciousness, but it was furthest from their thoughts that this might have anything like the meaning that contemporary feminists have when they talk of cultural revolution (see Frankenberg, 1976).

We as male authors cannot seriously claim to be able to do much better of course, but our whole approach has been to work with women researchers, and to give priority to women as respondents in the localities. Women researchers interviewed and participated in the lives of women in the mining localities. Their reports form the basis of our writing. Inevitably our own interpretations may be seen by feminists as inadequate, but we ask them to look upon it as a contribution to the on-going work of listening, recording and interpreting.

In the early 1980s, we collected the biographies of local inhabitants mainly in Ashby but also in other parts of the research area. We used a schedule which sought to gain both biographical details, and impressions of change in the locality. The respondents were selected by reputation as being persons with a 'good local knowledge', whom we heard about in earlier conversations. Twenty-nine of them were over sixty-five years of age, and there was no doubting that Ashby was regarded by all of them as a mining community, where a majority of men had found employment in the mines, or in work which depended on mining, such as on the railways. Households varied but, increasingly as the twentieth century passed, fewer of them were distinctively mining households. The memory of the first three decades, when mining employed almost three-quarters of the local men, has left an indelible mark on Ashby. Unfortunately for reasons of space we are only able to refer to small extracts from the biographies and our main task here is to draw out the major facets of the local culture which they revealed.

THE LOCAL CULTURAL CAPITAL: BIOGRAPHICAL DATA

Among the women of pensionable age, we noted some differences of outlook according to whether they were born and brought up in the locality or were 'incomers', and on grounds of having or not having had some further education and training. There were also differences according to their self-defined class or status position within the locality. All of them, whether they were partners of miners or not, tended to remember that the early decades of the twentieth century were hard times, not made easier by the exigencies of the wars, when there were great shortages of food, and queuing for what there was could take hours. Some could remember the long strikes in 1912, in 1921 and in 1926. Coping with hardships by one means or another was what many women recalled. Different attitudes were expressed about this which seemed to be based in varied backgrounds.

The majority clearly coped through the use of social networks and their own efforts to make ends meet. Local women born and brought up in Ashby and married to miners told us, like Mrs V.R., that improvements, among which she listed the birth control pill, better housing and a higher standard of living, have been bought at the cost of 'charity and companionship . . . In the old days everyone helped each other, even if they were poor. Today people seem to be only looking after themselves, never thinking of others.' Mr E.G., daughter of a miner, had been employed at a liquorice sweets factory in Pontefract on leaving school at age thirteen. She had had to give that up when her mother asked her to help her nurse her brother, dying of cancer. She returned to her paid job briefly, before marriage to a miner in her early twenties, and then had six children. She had gone to the Methodist chapel when young, and generally remembers those years as ones of friendliness, as 'people helped each other'. 'There is more money in the world today . . . but the young ones are very cheeky and . . . there is no control over them.'

Early attendance at Chapel or Church is mentioned by many of the women and this seems to have given some a moral basis for the effort of coping, which sometimes went beyond household and kin into community action. Mrs D.S., eighty years old when interviewed, married a miner when she was eighteen. Her husband contracted arthritis in the 1930s and was unemployed for seven years until the Second World War. Her part-time and casual employment as a cleaner and domestic assistant helped to make up the household income and to provide for her three sons and two daughters. She also found time to help organise a centre for the unemployed in Ashby during the 1930s. D.S. said that she now got very annoyed when people grumbled. 'They should be thankful for what they have.' On the other hand, she knows that we still live in a divided society; 'there is one law for the rich and one for the poor'. Another, Mrs M.P., a woman who married into Ashby, said it was 'still a close-knit community on the whole . . . a working-class town, but in a society that has a class system'.

Most recognised that kinship was very important but the 'incomers' seemed to be the ones who mentioned it most. Mrs G.T., who had married a miner in the 1930s, found Ashby a friendly place, but for her the problem was that 'a lot of them are related, so you have to be careful what you say about anybody when you're passing remarks'. Her contacts were built up through her husband's kin in Ashby, and through using the tailoring skills she had learned in her 'teens to assist the local rugby club. (She repaired the team's 'strip'.)

It is these subtle differences between the 'locals' and the 'incomers', and between class and status levels, that make boundaries between those who feel part of the local culture and those who are not sure and are in some sense strangers in an ambivalent position. Somewhat different perspectives marking another boundary are expressed by those who had had further education and training. We talked to women who had been clerical workers and shopkeepers, to another who had been a midwife and to several who had been school teachers. Almost all felt a little social distance between themselves and those who had had no educational or training qualifications. They tended to turn this distance into something of a class barrier and felt opposed to what they took to be the predominant local class outlook, even though in many cases they knew of and had participated in the common heritage of hardship.

A.C.'s father had gone down the pit at the age of eleven, and remembered the strike and the events of 1893 which he used to recall to the family. As a former clerical worker she had come to believe that the experience of hardship was related to personal morality and effort. Mrs F.S., a former teacher, was just over seventy when we interviewed her. She wanted to believe that hardship was always relative, and like A.C. that living carefully as a conscious member of a moral community, particularly as a Christian, was the best way to overcome difficulties. She was and continued to be a regular church attender. For her, organised public bodies like local Councils were best defined as avenues for local charity.

Mrs F.R., also a former teacher, told us that teachers were a class apart, and so were the deputies in the pits. It was they who raised the level of the town, being its cultural leaders, and encouraging the widening of educational opportunities. Shopkeepers and other self-employed people formed another class. Other parents locally, she declared, 'can be divided into two classes: those who are interested in and concerned about their children's education and those who are not'. The determinants of social class, she thought, were 'your standards and beliefs and your whole way of life, not how much money you've got. It's futile to expect everybody to be the same.' She also told us that she was a Conservative voter, who believed in giving people equal opportunities; 'but it is difficult', she said, 'because there is such a lot of favouritism and pulling strings'. F.R. was not happy with Labour leaders locally, who had encouraged a dilution of educational standards in introducing comprehensive secondary education. 'If they put up a donkey in a red rosette, they'd vote the donkey in round here.'

Not all the educationally qualified women were so opposed to the dominant values, however, and one, M.S., a former teacher told us that in her view Methodism and the Labour Party were a way of life. She recognised that miners and their families have been stigmatised 'as donkeys, blundering and uncouth', whereas 'they are honest and hard-working people – their wives included'. The militancy of miners had always been justified, she thought.

The women on the whole were much more ready to talk about change in terms of the domestic sphere and the locality rather than the wider society, unless they had had long-term paid employment outside the household. The men, probably because of their greater participation in paid employment and the patriarchal nature of British culture, were perhaps more confident in their views of the world as well as the locality. Among them the clearest expression of what was a dominant outlook came from a former miner and Labour Councillor.

T.M. was in his eighties, when interviewed, and living in sheltered Council accommodation. T.M's parents had had nine children (he was their third) and his father became unemployed because of contracting nystagmus in the pit about 1905. He recalled the degrading appearance of the family before the Board of Guardians in order to claim ten shillings a week for subsistence. Then there were strikes, in 1912, in 1919, 1921 and 1926 which T.M. thought possibly created more hardship than they relieved. The victories which were achieved were often meagre, he thought. There were some 'good' memories, like the day in 1912 when blacklegs at a local pit were given a 'real pasting' by the pickets as they came off their shift. No doubt, however, this 'pleasure' would have been bought at a high price in further hardship.

T.M. was a moderate, but forthright man who remembered the continuing struggle for better conditions in the pits and the locality with stories not only of individual, but also of collective action. His approach to his household was to be as careful with money as possible. He grew vegetables in his garden, and though he liked a drink of beer, he restricted himself. He and his wife were Methodist chapel-goers and saw that as an essential activity, 'to be on the right side'. He did not feel that there was any necessary connection between Chapel attendance and leadership in Ashby, though he confirmed the point made by M.S. that Labour politics and Methodism tended to have strong elective affinities.

For T.M. it was clear that being a Union man and being a Councillor were aspects of his sense of being responsible and trying to promote better conditions for the community. This was never easy because you could not trust everybody to see their responsibilities in the same way. Some were too prone to waste their money on pleasure, particularly beer drinking. Some were always ready to be aggressive but unable to resolve their conflicts afterwards. Some would resort to deviance, like poaching or vandalism. In general he thought it was possible to overlook all these things, provided there was some 'progress'. In his view there had been some progress, and the working-class households like his were subject to less hardship. 'Yes, honestly, . . . I think we're better off. Aye! There seems to be a bit more money floating about – I know it varies a bit – but people are on the whole well-dressed, different from what we used to be in our station of life.'

What we term the dominant view is based, as T.M. indicated, in a moderate sense of 'progress' and 'responsible' action, requiring both local and national political action. B.P., a man both in age and other ways similar to T.M., was suffering from arthritis when we interviewed him, but when younger had been very athletic, involved in playing rugby, cycling and swimming, for which he had been awarded numerous trophies and certificates. These now were displayed prominently in his terraced house. He was also very keen on music and as a tenor had sung in male voice choirs and in concerts and shows organised by the local amateur music and drama society, of which he was a founder member. He had been an 'ambulance man' in the pit, and for twenty-one years was in the local Auxiliary Fire Service. He told us that he had always been careful with money and with his savings he and his wife had been able to buy their house. Like many other working-class men, he had been a keen gardener, had grown many of his own vegetables and had always been willing to sell off the surplus to neighbours. Now, with his wife an invalid, he did all the cooking, cleaning and laundry in the house, though they had a visit from a home-help once per week.

T.M. and B.P. had not lost the sense of class which derived from their background and work experience. Ashby, B.P. said, was 'a real working-class town, always has been, always will be and will never be anything else'. Changes in house tenure would not make a difference, either, he claimed. They had an image of a working-class community, based on the morality of self-help and solidarity, in which everybody knew and tried to care for each other. This was based in knowledge of large kinship networks, clubs and association membership. It was a community which recognised the importance of class politics and T.M. and B.P. seemed to characterise most typically the 'active' working-class man in Ashby, at least of that generation which had seen the hardship of the early twentieth century. They remained quiet socialists, committed to the idea of strong trade unions, convinced of the decency of working-class people, though worried that there had been a decline of caring for others and some loss of solidarity.

There were variants from this dominant type. For some, sociability was more important than 'responsible' action. E.W., for instance, claimed to know a large number of 'locals' because he was a member of all but two of the social clubs, so that he saw (and drank with) many of them, including men and women. He was also a gregarious and a talkative man, even with 'a bit of a reputation locally for being outspoken' on political issues. Social groups still exist around the membership of the clubs and men like E.W. tend to belong to several. This ensures a place to drink the relatively cheaper pints which are on offer, and a chance to take part in weekly cash prize draws which clubs promote as a means of maintaining membership and funds. The pubs attract their clientele differently by the particular beers which they sell and their sponsorship of junior Rugby League clubs. Social drinking is a major cultural feature among the men, and women are now much more part of the same scene than they were thirty years ago. Not all men are involved, but it is very difficult to avoid being so, because of the strength of the cultural expectations and the sociability which it ensures. Some of the heterogeneity of Ashby, however, still derives from attachment to club rather than pub.

E.K. was not so convinced of the general goodness and decency of his neighbours. Also a former miner, E.K. had a more oppositional approach to community and politics than T.M. and B.P. He recalled intense rivalry between locals, played out not only in family conflict but also in rugby matches between neighbourhood and local club teams. He described these in language which emphasised their roughness and aggression, but maintained the code of silence which accompanied knowledge of legal transgressions. 'Poaching is still rife around here!' For E.K. community was a matter of tensions between solidarity, conflict and silence. There had to be class solidarity, but there also had to be watchfulness, and so neighbours were criticised if they became 'too nosey'. The traditional neighbourly ritual of 'calling' (pronounced with 'a' as in 'cat') had a dangerous edge to it. It was almost the case that E.K's house celebrated the famous wartime slogan, 'careless talk costs lives'. Our interviewer found them both suspicious of 'outsiders' and 'troublemakers', but very friendly and hospitable, willing to get out the family photograph album and talk about their kin and friends.

These four men showed an overt political consciousness, but not all our respondents did. This was largely a product of the sampling method which took us to meet men and women who were 'known' and respected for their local knowledge, and who thereby were expected to be, and had responded by being, more active in the locality. Our observations in Ashby led us to believe, however, that there was a 'silent majority' of long-standing and long-suffering members of the local community who rarely gave vent publicly to the values which T.M. and the others expressed.

There were, however, those like V.W. a former blacksmith in the local collieries, who pursued a more serious view of the world which he found reflected in the pages of *The Times* and the *Observer*, the newspapers which he regularly read. He felt as a blacksmith he had a different status from the face-worker and his team. Others interviewed had employment outside the industrial sector altogether. There are still a number of farms and a small number of farm workers. P.S. had not, in his own terms, done well at school, and he seemed destined to follow his father into the mines. He liked the open fields which he explored with his school-mates, however, and decided to try farmwork. He found the work like 'slavery', and tried unsuccessfully to form a branch of the Farmworkers' Union. Farmwork could be a very isolated experience, and it is interesting to note that P.S. particularly stressed the sense in which Ashby tends to be a locality which is cut off from other places. ('It was a great event to go to Wakefield or Leeds.') Mineworkers lived in a separate mining village or town, with its own local culture, but unlike P.S., many also had a sense of being part of a class or a nation.

Promotion within the mining industry also caused internal differentiation of the workers. J.B. was born and brought up in Ashby in a mining household. He was very bright at school. His parents, however, 'could not afford to let him go to Grammar School'. At the age of seventeen he turned towards mine work because it seemed to offer more security and higher wages. His latent ability led him into night school and at the age of twenty-eight years he passed his Deputy's Certificate. Thus he became an 'official' and responsible for work teams underground. He remained a Deputy until early retirement in the 1970s. He was sixty-eight when we interviewed him. He felt himself to be part of the community, but he was also different because of his status. Other deputies have also told us of this sense of social distance, which is emphasised by the existence of the National Association of Colliery Overmen and Deputies, a separate trade union from the NUM.

Another variant is the person who follows the common working-class destiny for a time, but then branches off either as a result of educational success, or a move into another occupational track. H.L., first a miner then a local preacher and lecturer, said 'if I could be born again, I would like to come back to the same place and the same people'. J.W. was one of six Ashby children in his school year to pass the local grammar school entrance scholarship at the age of eleven and this led to opportunities not available to most of his associates. Five of these scholarship holders had in fact migrated away from Ashby. He was the only one to have remained all his life, apart from the years when he trained as a physiotherapist. Though economically H.L. and J.W. could have changed their class position, culturally they remained part of the same mining community. This fact adds some support to the hypothesis about local cultural capital, and its significance in the reproduction of communities. The place had been a kind of cultural 'magnet' to them (a metaphor that other 'displaced' persons have used of their 'home-town' or village that for one reason or another has been adopted as 'home'). Ashby, Oakton, Willowby and Beechthorpe have all been felt to be 'magnets' to some of our erstwhile 'displaced' respondents, whether 'displaced' by migration or by educational qualifications. (See also the reference to Taylor, 1979, in Chapter Two.) It is often they who expressed the strongest resentment at 'outsiders' making what they call derogatory remarks about their home-town. F.G.S. was no exception, vigorously condemning those who call Ashby a 'dirty hole' and miners, 'earthworms, who ought to stay underground'. He countered the Tory jibe quite nicely when he said of Labour Party candidates in elections: 'If they put up a donkey with a red rosette, I'd vote for the donkey, because I'd know when it nodded, it nodded for me.' He had been a member of the local Urban District Council and its committees, of school governing bodies, of hospital management committees and of various voluntary groups, such as the Miners' Welfare and, in keeping with his interests in sport, on the local Rugby League club committee. As we have said, sports participation and watching is a key constituent of the local culture.

A former physiotherapist, J.W. was a perceptive observer of the changing life of Ashby. His comments ranged widely, covering changes both in the locality and external forces, for instance the erosion of local power through reorganisation of local government. A keen naturalist, he was also concerned about the introduction of more intensive and subsidised farming, which has transformed the landscape around Ashby. He told us about the decline of the churches as meeting places, and the closure of many small shops, particularly the old corner shops, which played a very important role in times of hardship in offering short-term credit. The pubs and the clubs had been refurbished and women were now involved in what had tended in the past to be a purely masculine culture. To some extent he put this down to a change to a more mobile clientele, as motor vehicles enabled people to come from other localities to drink in Ashby. Local institutions were much less local these days. Nevertheless the Working Men's Clubs retained the local male predominance through their committee structures, which still gave a few men a chance of a slightly elevated status, and possibly a few free drinks.

We also interviewed a middle-class man who had lived and worked for over forty years in Ashby, though now living in Oakton. J.D., the son of a Leeds shopkeeper, was born in 1900. Educated in Leeds at school and university, he had qualified as a medical practitioner in 1925, and had virtually come straight to Ashby after qualifying. Before the National Health Service existed each pit had a medical committee which ran the communal medical fund or club for the miners and their families. Miners had a small payment (five pence, if married, and two pence, if single) deducted from their wages and this entitled them to be on one of the local doctors' 'panels'. Another of our respondents claimed that 'doctors came to Ashby in droves' at the time when this fund was set up, because they could be certain of their fees. It was clear that doctors gained their income by grants from the fund in proportion to the number of patients who were on their 'panels', but whether they came in 'droves' is questionable.

The former doctor confirmed all that others have told us about Ashby in the inter-war period and added detail from his own perspective and approach. He thought that the bosses of the local pits tended to be 'tyrannical', but that there were some very militant miners, and in consequence much conflict. The poverty which he saw was a consequence of low wages and intermittent unemployment rather than laziness and free-spending. Generally people coped, but the conditions in some houses neglected by their landlords were no better than they had been described at the beginning of the twentieth century (see Chapter Three). The level of public health was very low indeed, with a prevalence of heart and chest diseases among men and women. Polluted air consequent on mine working, burning pit stacks and coke-ovens, not to speak of the terrible working conditions in the mines themselves, created an injurious environment for all.

Poverty meant relatively poor diets, and women and children were particularly affected by malnutrition. Babies were born and people died without the kind of attention from medical and paramedical staff that is now normal. Instead of health visitors and midwives, there were 'handy ladies', local women whose skills had been learnt from other local women. There were numerous outbreaks of virulent infectious diseases, against which isolation, either in hospitals or in virtually sealed off households, which had warning placards posted on doors, was the only defence. Miners' nystagmus, a neurological condition, was very prevalent, and meant that men had to be taken off underground work. Malnutrition and stress were the main contributory factors in the incidence of nystagmus, though J.D. thought that better lighting in the pits would have helped. Conditions had improved since the Second World War, but as Table 4.2 below indicates, our research survey in 1987 showed that health conditions are still poor in the area, compared with the rest of West Yorkshire (see Littlejohn et al., 1990).

There has been some continuity in the social conditions which J.D. remembered in the later part of his life in Ashby. He noted the significance of kinship and the considerable interrelation between families, and said that 'you had to be terribly careful what you said about anybody, because they seemed to be related somehow'. He also remembered the story which is often told to indicate the complexity of local kinship. 'A little lad once came into the pharmacy for some ointment for a baby. I asked if he was the baby's brother. He grinned and replied that he was his uncle.'

J.D. also commented on the significance of certain 'dominant families' who seemed to run things. For his part, he felt that 'they exerted undue influence, often by something approaching strong-arm methods . . . they'd get relatives elected to the Council . . . or as Union Officials . . . or get them promoted at work . . . They'd organise and settle strikes.' On the other hand, the middle class was relatively small, and in J.D's mind probably did not have the influence which they should have had. There were a few school teachers, ministers of religion and white-collar workers, like bank clerks and colliery officials. Apart from his medical colleagues there was hardly anyone 'with whom to play bridge or tennis'. Thus at the time of his retirement he decided to move a respectable distance down the road to Oakton, where he would find a few more people in his class. Again there is some ambivalence, however, for there was no outright class enmity in his approach. There was indeed much respect for the way households coped, and he obviously shared something of the displeasure with which respondents like F.G.S. viewed the derogatory comments made and the prejudices held about miners and mining communities by outsiders.

At the same time as these interviews with older people, that is in the early 1980s, we also interviewed members of younger generations in Ashby. Among these the differentiation between 'locals' and 'incomers' was possibly more pronounced. The longer you live in a locality, the more likely it is that you become integrated, but you can still carry the stigma of being a 'foreigner'.

There are still jokes in Ashby about 'Staffies', that is migrants from Staffordshire, who had come here when miners were being recruited in the late nineteenth century. They were roughly equivalent to 'Irish' jokes, and were meant to raise a laugh about outsiders who were rather slow in 'learning the ropes' or were deviant in some way.

> One was about a lad called Staffy Jones who had bought a clock from a travelling salesman and had not kept up with his weekly payments. He avoided the salesman every time he called for his money, but one day Staffy was standing on the street without his cap as a funeral went by when he saw the salesman approaching. Quickly he put on his cap and pulled it down over his eyes. The salesman stopped by him, but not being sure that it was Staffy, to open the conversation, said 'Whose funeral is it?' Staffy quick as a flash replied, 'Staffy Jones, mister! Isn't it sad!' The salesman looked crestfallen and said, 'Oh God! I have lost my money then.'[1]

Others refer to the context of work, and carry interesting ambiguities such as this one. They tend to reproduce a sense of local chauvinism and so to mark off the boundaries between 'insiders', 'outsiders' and 'strangers' (see Clayton et al., 1990).

The distinction between those with some further or higher education and training and those without, which we noticed particularly among the older women, still seemed to create contrasting outlooks on the locality and its people. Experience of church membership had further declined. Among our younger interviewees under forty, only three out of fifteen, all women, said that they were or had been church or sect members. Among the middle aged, four out of ten, three women and one man, talked of religious affiliations. The elderly were or had been far more religiously active, five out of the fifteen men and twelve out of the fourteen women were still or had been active attenders of churches or their organisations. The local Methodist minister, who had been in Ashby for over twelve years in the early 1980s when we talked to him, noted that there were two Anglican churches within the locality, but whereas there had been five Methodist churches, there was now only one, operating in a relatively new building and the result of amalgamation in the late 1960s, because of declining membership. There is one Roman Catholic church in Ashby, which is quite well attended, and a Mission Hall which is organised by an evangelical sect. The Salvation Army also has a band of adherents in the locality. All of these still created around them little 'sub-communities', adding to the cultural heterogeneity.

The decreasing proportion of men working in the coal industry means that the salience of the NUM is less now than it was in the first half of the twentieth century. Among the older men we noticed in general an attachment to a less militant form of trade unionism, which often came over in interviews as 'support for Joe Gormley's approach rather than Arthur Scargill's'. Among the middle-aged men we interviewed were the Branch President (D.G.) and the Branch Secretary (T.B.), the two key functionaries of the local branch. They were interviewed in 1981 and at that time both of them declared themselves to be for the Gormley approach, that is they said they believed in tough negotiations rather than striking. Cooperation between the NCB and the NUM and corporate management of the coal industry was what they saw as beneficial to the locality, even if it meant some 'rationalisation'. They were both Labour Party members and had been elected members of the local Urban District Council or its successor the Town Council (after 1974). They represented very much in their general outlook what we have termed the dominant local culture, and could be seen as significant reproducers of the knowledge, skills and values which that entailed. They had grown used to being respected, and did not talk of the conflict which more elderly men like T.M. and B.P had experienced. They spoke of the improvements brought about through the institutionalised actions of the labour movement, of better education, more affluence and good local social services. They were not class warriors, though they recognised the importance of vigilance with regard to inequalities in society. Class still existed and they saw themselves as part of a working-class community.

The three miners we interviewed at this time, who were in the under forty age group, were split two to one in favour of a more militant approach to trade unionism. T.P. and M.S. did not recognise all the improvements to which D.G. and T.B. referred, and agreed with Arthur Scargill that they had to fight for retaining their jobs in an increasingly hostile world. The defence and improvement of Ashby depended on the maintenance of strong mining unionism and militant politics. The third, J.R.S., was more in tune with the approach of the Branch officials, though not entirely sure that his future in mining was secure. Among the women in the younger age group, there was a greater tendency to support the less militant approach, though they all saw the significance of the decline of the mining industry.

There were now more employed men in Ashby not working in the mining industry and among the young and middle-aged interviewees there was a recognition of the changes this entailed. For women, the changes in the culture were seen as important for they thought they detected changes in the status of women. Where mining was not quite so dominant in the labour market, there could be more equal status for both genders, brought about by a more open competition for jobs. On the other hand they did not want to live in Ashby bereft of job opportunities. The younger men who lived in Ashby but worked outside mining tended still to be very much influenced by the local culture. It was a kind of benchmark against which they judged their life and opportunities.

THE MAJOR ASPECTS OF THE LOCAL CULTURE

From this biographical data, we can possibly draw four major conclusions. First, there is heterogeneity within localities; second, there is a local culture and it is held as a kind of capital; third, there are key figures who operate to maintain, reproduce and change the local culture; and fourth, there is a boundedness to this local culture which is formed as a consequence of social closure. These points suggest some modifications in the ideal-typical model of traditional mining community. Nevertheless, these mining localities in the late twentieth century are social entities unlike the urban neighbourhoods which form the majority of community spaces in the contemporary world. Further, they are caught up in processes which, despite protest and resistance, are modifying them inexorably.

The heterogeneity within Ashby reflects the composition of the population in terms of class, generation and community identity. Further variations are based in membership of different social associations, in a changing gender balance, in the particular collection of social institutions and in the changing labour market.

The local culture is the outcome of the sharing of knowledge about the place, its history as a mining locality and the social networks and institutions which have developed. Further it is the sharing of skills, particularly those of communication which help to maintain, confer and renew identities and membership among them. Finally, it is the set of dominant values which characterise relationships and activities in the locality. These are based in a history of hardship and conflict, and the slow improvement which has come from trade union and labour movement organisation, negotiation and success in modifying and creating a legal framework and political institutions in the interests of coal miners and the working class more generally. The dominant values are nevertheless contested, on the one hand by those who hold a more deferential view of capitalist market morality combined with a more individualistic view of human capabilities and power. On the other hand they are contested by views which emphasise the essential opposition of class interests and the need for continuing vigilance and struggle.

From the biographies, it is possible to sense that the dominant local culture is held as a kind of capital which is transmitted and sometimes modified from generation to generation. It then forms benchmarks around which individuals and households can trace their identity and interests. As we saw it can bind and draw people into a locality despite alternative or 'centrifugal' forces.

It would seem possible too that in each generation there are key people who become significant reproducers of this local cultural capital, who define its limits and to some extent create modifications. Such people as T.M., and B.P. seem to have had such a function. Centrality to such a local culture may, however, be a transient phenomenon, say for a generation or less, or as long as such individuals have the knowledge, skills and values, and the credibility to remain authoritative. This seems to be confirmed not only in the assessment of the meaning of what those key informants told us, but also by J.D., the local doctor, and his reference to influential families, whom he defined in somewhat negative terms. In other words the position of key reproducers of the local cultural capital, just like its central values, are contested and subject to opposition. Several of our respondents like F.S., and F.R. may well be characterised within that framework.

This would seem to add to the dichotomous characterisation of the mining community being formed by men with either a 'frivolous' or 'serious' orientation to its processes and institutions, as Dennis, Henriques and Slaughter (1956) did (see above, Chapter Two). Robert Moore (1975) pointed out that the miner should not be seen as the unexplained, serious or frivolous, traditional proletarian, culturally deprived and socially isolated, but as the product of a society and culture, and his own response to them, in the mining locality of which he is part. Edward Thompson (1976) reviewing Moore's study of mining and Methodism in Durham suggests that the situation is more complex still. Any study of the culture of mining communities requires, he argued, attention to the variants within and between them, and in particular an analysis of the cultural transformations that are taking place there. The transformations which have already taken place have left, he argued, three components of miners' culture. They are indicated by

> One, the officious, self-respecting, class collaborationist methodist lay preacher; two, the irreverent blasphemer with his constituency not in the chapel, but in the pub; and, three, the observant, class conscious, self-disciplined secularist (sometimes a Marxist) suppressing his own distaste for religion in the interests of a larger solidarity.
>
> (E.P. Thompson, 1976)

Even Thompson's categories, however, do not seem to exhaust the possibilities, by overlooking differences between church and chapel, between club and pub, and in particular by not referring to women at all, nor to non-miners.

Our respondents frequently repeated that they saw Ashby as different, as an entity which, despite the internal heterogeneity, was special for them. It had an identity which they shared. It housed the social networks and institutions, the kinship, friendship and neighbourhood links, the clubs, the pubs and the many associations with which they were familiar. Further, it was identified by outsiders, usually negatively ('that dirty hole'), as different. Its coal mines, its mean rows of houses and its 'rough' miners were thought to distance it topographically, economically and socially from their towns. Also, as we will show in later chapters, with reference to all four localities which we studied, other mining localities within our research area were defined as different, and in some ways objectively displayed that difference. In those senses, Ashby, as a community of persons living in a distinct location, has been created and changed through the processes of social closure (see Chapter One). These processes, too, were not only internally generated. As our respondents at times indicated, they were involved with outside forces, the forces behind industrial and economic development generally, and the bureaucracies, national and local, which often mediate these other forces.

Thus we must widen our analysis and turn to the evidence which we have collected comparatively across the four localities which illustrate both the developments of the late twentieth century and the responses and adjustments which people in the localities are making to them.

FOUR MINING LOCALITIES

At this point, we are going to describe the localities where we gathered our information in the 1980s, and because of the need in some cases to protect the identity of those whose lives were observed, whose opinions were collected and whose actions were discussed with us, we have given them fictitious names. The localities are, however, in the area of Featherstone and Hemsworth, where the historical data used in Chapter Three was collected.

We had contacted people in the research area, outlined in the previous chapter, from 1978 onwards. During 1981 and in 1984 we conducted over seventy biographical interviews mainly in Ashby on which the discussion of the local culture has been based. Also in 1984 we interviewed eighty men and women about the miners' strike then in progress. Then in the four localities we carried out two-hour long interviews in randomly selected households in the summers of 1986 and 1987. We also carried out a small follow-up survey in 1989 in some of the households contacted in 1987.

Table 4.1 Number of households surveyed in 1986 and 1987

	Oakton	Willowby	Ashby	Beechthorpe	All
1986 survey	30	32	31	31	124
1987 survey	50	50	50	50	200

1986 SURVEY

Households were chosen randomly from the 1986 electoral register and our interviewers contacted women householders, but in a quarter of the households we also interviewed a male, normally the partner of the woman. In one case we interviewed a single male, and there were thirteen women who had no partner. In the course of the interviews, averaging two and a half hours, we collected data on one hundred and twenty-three women and thirty-one men. We asked about their work situation, work histories, education and leisure interests, family background and links in the locality, domestic arrangements in the household, their attitudes to and experience of the miners' strike of 1984/5, and the future prospects of their localities. During 1986, Val Carroll, our full-time research assistant, also contacted and interviewed former members of women's support groups about their experience during and after the strike.

1987 SURVEY

Fifty households were chosen in each locality, some of which had been interviewed in 1986 (forty-six households overall), and the rest randomly chosen from the 1986 electoral register. The interviewers were asked to interview the 'householder' and his/her partner, provided they were of 'working age', that is 64 years or under. In the two-hundred household interviews, lasting on average just over two hours, we collected responses from 176 men and 187 women. The interviews covered household structure and living arrangements, work histories, records of children's employment, household decision-making and division of labour, use of and attitude to state services, voting intentions, income, details of general health and indicators of respiratory disorders and related factors.

Table 4.2 is a summary of indicators of the socio-economic conditions of the four localities from the surveys. We shall return frequently to these indicators, which reveal some of the variations which we have found in the four research localities. Essentially they show significant differences between Oakton and the other three in the economic position of men, in the distribution of household income, in educational experience and

Table 4.2 Socio-economic conditions in four mining localities, 1986/7

Indicator	Percentages			
	Oakton	Willowby	Ashby	Beechthorpe
1987				
Tenure				
Owner-occupiers	83	58	67	75
Council tenants	17	42	33	25
Age				
Women aged 41–64 years	44	60	36	56
Men aged 41–64 years	45	45	43	62
Paid work				
Women in paid employment	64	44	60	66
Of women in paid work: % P/T	30	57	61	48
Unemployed women	2	8	0	0
F/t housework and non-employed	33	48	38	34
Men in paid employment	96	63	71	73
Men ever worked in coal mining	22	60	36	43
Unemployed men				
In mining households	10	23	27	21
In non-mining households	3	41	15	16
Household monthly net income				
Less than £850	44	78	65	73
More than £850	56	22	35	27
Report severe coughing (women)	12	11	10	3
Report severe coughing (men)	6	31	14	15
1986				
Mean household size (persons)	(3.3)	(3.5)	(3.5)	(3.2)
Single households	13	13	6	13
Education				
Left school by 15 yrs (women)	43	69	84	70
Left school by 15 yrs (men)	50	86	88	75
Educ. quals: o level+ (women)	37	6	6	17
Educ. quals: o level+ (men)	33	0	0	0
Attended school locally (w)	48	78	57	23
Attended school locally (m)	50	67	50	63
Attended FE since school (w)	57	31	46	45
Attended FE since school (m)	100	17	86	67

Note: Figures in brackets are not percentages

qualifications and in health, as indicated by self-reported severe coughing. Further differences are seen in the proportions of owner-occupiers and tenants, in the age distribution of the population in the localities, and in the extent to which respondents were 'insiders' or 'locals', as suggested by the proportions attending local schools. Myths about women in mining households being tied to the kitchen sink are dispelled by the data on women's paid employment. Whether this makes much difference to the domestic division of labour between men and women will be the subject of comment later.

A BRIEF DESCRIPTION OF THE FOUR LOCALITIES

Oakton is a spread out settlement based on an old village, which grew in the nineteenth century as a result of nearby mining and quarrying. At the 1981 Census it had a population of 5836, and twenty-three percent of its male labour force in mining. The nearest pit closed in 1985. Twenty-eight percent of heads of households were in the Registrar General's Social Classes I and II. Oakton straddles an important cross-roads in the area, and has been a preferred 'dormitory suburb' for white collar workers in Wakefield and other West Yorkshire urban centres.

Willowby grew up in the late nineteenth and early twentieth century around a colliery. This closed in the 1960s but a new drift mine was opened with the prospect of twenty-five years mining in 1979. It was closed in 1986. In 1981 it had a population of 4931, fifty-six percent of the male labour force in mining, and only five percent of the heads of household were in Social Classes I and II. In the last two years, new residential development has been taking place and a nearby 'leisure park' has been opened. It remains primarily a working-class locality, with many streets and terraces of Council or Coal Board built houses. Many of these have been bought by the tenants.

Ashby is a small mining town, but as a consequence of pit closures and new land use, including open cast coal working, parts are now physically separate from the main urban area, which in 1981 had a population of 10,726. There were two large collieries nearby, and forty-one percent of its male labour force was in mining. Only one of the collieries was still working in 1989. Ten percent of heads of household were in Social Classes I and II. They occupied small detached houses and bungalows along the only main road, while most residents lived in old brick-built terraces or in 1920s and 1930s Council built houses, which have recently been renovated. About half of the former Council houses have been sold to tenants.

Beechthorpe consists of mainly twentieth-century housing which grew around a pit opened in the 1920s between two small villages. The pit closed in the 1960s but a large proportion of its male labour force continued to travel to other pits. In 1981 its population was 5284, fifty-nine percent of male workers were coal miners and eight percent of heads of household were in Social Classes I and II. A high proportion of the houses were Council built and owned but a large proportion have been bought by tenants. By 1989 only one pit within easy reach of the locality remained in production.

All of these localities are within one parliamentary constituency and fall in an area of some sixty square miles of small towns and villages. Oakton and Ashby are in the north of the area, Willowby and Beechthorpe to the south. They had had historically different experiences of the coal mining industry, but in the 1980s they have all been affected by pit closures which have reduced the number of jobs in mining in the area from about seven thousand ten years ago to less than two thousand in 1990. Prospects for the end of coal mining in the area are very strong. In Table 4.2 the distribution of household income shows that the three localities with the highest proportion of households where someone has recently been employed in mining were the poorest localities. Oakton had a distribution of household income which roughly matched the national average as indicated by the 1987 *General Household Survey* carried out by the Office of Population Census and Surveys. The heritage of hardship and deprivation which nineteenth-century capitalism imposed on these localities is a historical memory which is still to some extent reinforced by contemporary conditions.

The historical link of these localities with coal mining still, however, gives them a strong sense of being different from communities which have other salient local economic activities. Not far away are towns and villages once dominated by the woollen industry of the West Riding. Nevertheless, even within our four localities, as we have said, there are obvious differences between them. Oakton has the lowest proportion of households where men have ever been employed in mining, but in the other three the proportion rises from over a third to over a half. It is difficult to speculate what the 'critical mass' is, in terms of the proportion of mining households to all households, which gives a locality its distinctiveness as a 'mining community'. Some authorities have suggested that it might be about twenty-five percent (Winterton and Winterton, 1985), but this is probably a question that cannot be resolved, except through a much wider study. Oakton, however, clearly falls into the margins of what might be defined as a mining locality or community. We have included it in order to show that a coalfield area can be socially and spatially differentiated.

In the next chapter we present evidence about the changing labour market, the households and the division of labour both in the wider market and in the domestic units themselves. This will add further comment on Bulmer's model and widen our understanding of the social divisions which characterise contemporary society.

Chapter 5

Paid employment, traditional social networks and the gender division of labour

INTRODUCTION

In this chapter we will focus on four coal-mining localities, and the social divisions existing among and within them, which we researched in the 1980s. Such localities can be a site of social closure and integration around a common identity and a common culture. By that is meant a shared sense of belonging to a collectivity which has a location (in our case) in a market economy. It is experienced not only as solidarity around dominant values but also as segregation, both from the outside world and to some extent within the community. Such segregation may be brought about by the tactics and strategies of external groups and associations, which may have opposed interests in terms of relations of production and power, or it may be a product of locals or insiders simply holding a different subjectively held identity. We would suggest that the common identity has elements of a class identity. Indeed many, though not all, of the respondents in our biographical interviews did agree that the common identity held by people in Ashby was a working-class identity.

In mining and other 'occupational communities' sociologists have examined various tendencies, including, as in the case of *Coal is Our Life*, the formation and expression of class consciousness. The influence of other forms of social closure, such as around kinship and gender, have also been noted but not extensively researched. The integration of a focus on kinship and gender into the study of change in industrial societies is based in the view that the social reproduction of the labour force is of major importance. By social reproduction, we refer to the whole set of processes which lead to the formation, renewal and socialisation of a potential workforce, imbued with the knowledge, skills and values which enable it to be employable. Hence it is important to include an examination of the whole household, not merely the men, for it is in the household that significant orientation to society and culture begins. In our localities, too, we have stressed the importance of an identity based in a local culture, the learning of which commences in the household.

Furthermore, women as well as men are key definers of that local culture, despite the effects that patriarchy can have. In our interviews they sometimes posed alternatives and oppositional views to the dominant local culture. This is particularly the case where women have taken up full-time or part-time, permanent or temporary, paid employment. The teachers and the nurses were particularly prominent. The ideal–typical model of the traditional mining community, however, took little note of women's significance. It merely posed the division between the men's world and the women's world. It is clear that the local culture is based in an economy in which coal mining was predominant, and coal mining largely excluded women from its labour force. The local labour market therefore did not offer many opportunities for women to find paid employment. This is no reason for overlooking women in the way that some studies have done. There have always been some women in the labour market and we need to explore how that has been reflected in the division of labour. Changes which have taken place in our localities, particularly in the closure of pits and the restructuring of the local economy, have also had their effect on the gender division of labour. This of course is reflected to some extent, and we need to ask to what extent, in the domestic division of labour within the household.

Households are part of social networks. Our respondents recorded how important networks of kin, friends and neighbours were in creating and maintaining the sense of membership of the local community. They have also recorded how much reciprocity there is within and between such networks. We refer to these as traditional social networks. Recent research has pointed to the continuing importance of such networks, as we indicated in Chapter One (see p. 6).

In this chapter therefore we will start with a description of the local labour markets, in terms of men's and women's work. We shall then focus on the social conditions of households whose main characteristics are related to the present or former occupational status of their adult members. Following that we will examine a number of hypotheses about the gender division of labour, which will draw in information about households and the social networks of which they are part.

MEN'S EMPLOYMENT

The coal-mining industry

We have already noted that the predominance of coal mining and work in the mines has been much attenuated. In the mid-twentieth century, there were some twenty pits and over fifteen thousand miners. In 1990 there are just two with just under two thousand men employed in them. The current percentage of men who in our sample of households in 1987 were

Table 5.1 Percentage of employed men in four localities working in coal mining

Year	Oakton	Locality Willowby	Ashby	Beechthorpe
1981	23	56	41	59
1987	21	65	27	25

Note: The percentages for 1981 are of all economically active men aged sixteen to sixty-four, but those for 1987 are drawn from the sample survey of fifty households in each locality and refer to male heads of household or male partners of female heads of household who worked in mining at the time of our survey

employed in mining, varies from the percentages which the West Yorkshire Metropolitan County Council Planning Department supplied to us, using data derived from the Office of Population Censuses and Surveys.[1]

Table 5.1 suggests that there has been a drop in mineworkers as a percentage of economically active men in all but one of our localities. For Willowby, the Table is confusing, for there has certainly been a drop in employment in the mining industry, but there was also a dramatic decline in other employment. Over forty percent of men who had not been associated with the mining industry were unemployed at the time of our survey in 1987 in Willowby (see Table 4.2). It so happened that of those remaining employed, workers in the mining industry formed a higher percentage than they had done in the 1981 Census.

The coal industry was, from the nineteenth century, in Britain, and in our research area, the epitome of capitalist industrial relations with its owners and managers not only commanding the workforce and the technology but also the production of raw material itself. During the mid-twentieth century the organisation of the industry went through major developments, including nationalisation of management and control, and most pits in our area changed from being 'hand-got' to mechanised. The tradition of 'hand-got' coal working operated with small teams of colliers and mates hewing, filling and shifting coal competitively on contracts with managements.

H.L., interviewed in Ashby in 1984, remembers such working conditions:

There were three shifts, days, afternoons and nights. On days, the hours of work were from six in the morning to two in the afternoon. There was a system of buzzers at each pit. The first was blown at 5.30 am presumably to wake you up, although most people relied on 'Mam' or 'Our lass' [partner] or the 'knocker-up'. The next buzzer went at 5.45 am to remind you to set off, because if you were not at work by the time the six o'clock buzzer went, you were too late . . . I worked in a team of three, as haulage hand at first, coupling and pony-driving the tubs to and from the coal face. Later I filled tubs as my mate, the hewer in the team, brought down and broke up the coal from the seam. The team would be allocated a place or 'stall' for each day's work in a system of bargaining with the deputies and other teams.

When I first started I was in the 'market', and was sent to whichever team had a man short that day. If no team was short, I was sent home with no pay. Permanent teams to which you moved eventually, were made up of families or very close friends. Each team had their own number and this was stamped on metal oval-shaped 'motties', which were hooked on to the tubs before they were sent to the pit-bottom. When they reached the pit top, they were weighed by the 'Master's Weighman'. If they were too heavy, that is, contained too much stone in proportion to coal, they might either not be paid, or, if adjudged as having sent up too much stone or 'muck', be fined. The colliers elected a checkweighman as their arbiter in any dispute.

There were many disputes over the quality of the coal, the proportion of 'muck', the particular site for each team's work in relation to the quality and structure of the seam, over safety standards, over developing new seams, and timbering or propping up the worked seams. Each task would be priced and, as we saw in an earlier chapter, arguments over the price-list could be the cause of a major dispute. The teams could themselves be split by disputes, but generally the disputes and the method of working drew the team members together and this was an important basis for the development of solidarity.

The changeover to mechanised faces proceeded slowly in the coal field from the 1930s. Where it was possible coal seams were now worked on the 'longwall' method, that is, on horizontal faces about forty to sixty metres long, along which mechanical cutters could be driven. The coal would be 'filled' on to conveyor belts, rather than into tubs, with the intention of speeding up the process and cutting the costs of production. Instead of small teams, the new method required large teams, continuously supervised, and each member probably having a much more specialised task. Trist and Bamforth (1951) discussed the implications which this had in terms of a reduction of flexibility and of worker autonomy, an increase in differentiation among the workers at the same time as more coordinated effort was required, an increased dependence of the production process on an organised cycle of operations centrally controlled (more recently subject to computerisation) and probably an increase in dust generated diseases, consequent on the mechanical cutting. This required a big change in the culture of the pit, Trist and Bamforth argued, and it certainly meant a change in the wage structure, from individual and team contracts to various piece-work and day-rate systems with bonuses as incentives to increase pit production, sometimes accompanied by coal-field wide agreements. As we will see in the final chapter, this brought with it increased tensions between the national, area and local, or pit, levels of negotiations over pay and conditions of work.

T.B., local branch secretary of the NUM in 1981, commented on the newer methods when we interviewed him:

> Mechanisation has meant for the miners (apart from more dust, which is a common complaint) that many more skills are required for the job; training used to be more or less a matter of toning up to the actual physical work – now it is a matter of learning to use the machines which are more and more the tools of the miners' trade . . . Miners are more safety conscious and although there is some possibility that productivity schemes might endanger safety standards, the rewards aren't enough to drive the men to take unnecessary risks . . . Miners are a 'good set of lads' with a strong co-operative attitude; they help each other whenever they can.

In other words some of the old culture had not been eroded, but a new element had been added, that of 'training'. This has been a result of tendencies in most large organisations since the Second World War. It is related to concern for increasing productivity on the part of management, and for widening the application of the label 'skilled craft' to jobs and trades where specialisation and mechanisation were threatening old skills and earnings, on the part of trade unions and their members. The Coal Board, urged on by the NUM, introduced training at all levels in an attempt to enhance skills, management and safety.[2]

Further, as a part of the same modernising processes which affected the actual production technology, there has been an expansion of line management and the use of professionally qualified workers. In our 1987 survey, forty-two male respondents in the four localities were working in the mining industry. Their distribution among the various grades of staff is shown in Table 5.2.

There are women in the mining industry, particularly in secretarial work and catering, but only one of the women respondents in the 1987 survey was currently working in the industry as a canteen assistant. One woman who was not currently employed had worked as a wages clerk for the National Coal Board.

Other male employment

There is a considerable variety of other work in the research area, though the 1980s were a time of high unemployment in some sectors of the labour market, particularly as a result of the decline in the coal industry and the knock-on effect that had on other industries and services. A survey of employment in the Wakefield Metropolitan District, in which the research

Table 5.2 Grades of male staff in the coal-mining industry, 1987 survey of four mining localities

	Numbers	Percent
Administrative and managerial	2	4.8
Professionals (e.g. surveyors, engineers)	4	9.5
Supervisory (deputies, overmen)	8	19.0
Clerical (e.g. wages, sales)	1	2.4
Skilled manual (face-trained and craftsmen)	18	42.9
Semi-skilled (e.g. plant-drivers)	7	16.7
Unskilled (labourers)	2	4.8
Total	42	99.9

Source: Survey of two hundred households, 1987, in which 174 men were interviewed

area is situated, was carried out in the 1980s to illustrate changes which were occurring (O'Donnell, 1988). This apparently showed a relatively stable situation overall. On the one hand there was a heavy decline in the mining industry accompanied by an overall reduction in jobs in manufacturing and public administration. There was, however, some compensating growth of jobs in construction and professional and market services (see Table 5.3).

Table 5.3 Sectoral employment distribution and change in the Wakefield Metropolitan District, 1984

Occupational sectors	Numbers of employees 1984	Percentage of all 1984	Change 1981–4 in jobs as a percentage of 1981 sector total (+ increase) (− decrease)
Primary (mainly coal extraction	14,309	12.3	−23
Secondary (manufacturing industries, e.g. textiles)	29,421	25.3	−2
Construction	6,897	5.9	+25
Power and water supplies	2,978	2.6	−4
Professional and market services	35,210	30.3	+16
Public services	27,314	23.5	−1
Total	116,129	99.9	+ less than one percent

Source: K. O'Donnell (1988)
Note: This refers to all jobs whether filled by men or women

Table 5.4 Occupational status of men in mining and non-mining households, 1987

Occupational status	Mining households Number	Percent	Non-mining households Number	Percent
Employers and proprietors	0	0	4	3.8
Administrators/managers	2	2.9	13	12.5
Professionals	4	5.7	16	15.4
Supervisors/foremen	8	11.4	12	11.5
Clerical workers	1	1.4	3	2.9
Sales personnel/assistants	0	0	2	1.9
Skilled manual	21	30.0	13	12.5
Semi-skilled manual	7	10.0	16	15.4
Unskilled manual	2	2.9	8	7.7
Retired/non-employed	10	14.2	1	1.0
Unemployed	15	21.4	16	15.4
Total	70	99.9	104	100.0

Note: This is information drawn from the 1987 Survey in four mining localities in the Wakefield Metropolitan District. Two-hundred households were interviewed. In twenty-six of these there was only a single woman householder. The data is drawn from the other 174 households. A mining household is one where the male respondent worked or had worked in the mining industry until recently (in the last five years), or where he had had no other employment since leaving the industry. Other households are defined non-mining households if these criteria are not met. All respondents were aged between twenty and sixty-four inclusive

What was happening was what has happened elsewhere in Britain and in other Western type economies. This was a restructuring of occupations as a consequence of the decline of old established industries, and a change in the opportunities for employment as new qualifications and skills were sought by employers. To some extent this has been accompanied by spatial changes in the distribution of economic activity. In our research area, the unemployed men tend to be those made redundant by pit closures, and people without qualifications. Only three men in our 1987 survey, who had been made redundant by pit closures, had taken up other paid employment. One was a painter and decorator, another a plumber and the third had become a supermarket porter. O'Donnell (1988) notes that male unemployment rates were about twenty percent in the research area in 1987, but this may overlook the fact that a number of men were not seeking work, and saw themselves as 'retired', even though they had not reached statutory retirement age. Table 5.4 indicates the situation.

Table 5.4 suggests then that male unemployment was higher than twenty percent. If we include the non-employed as well as those who said they were unemployed, the rate rises to over thirty-five percent for men in mining households and to over sixteen percent for men in non-mining households. Overall, of all male respondents, twenty-four percent were either retired,

Table 5.5 Respondents employed by the Wakefield Metropolitan District Council, 1987

Occupational status	Men	Women
Administrators/managers	1	1
Professionals	5	14
Supervisors	0	7
Clerical workers	0	4
Skilled manual	1	1
Semi-skilled	1	0
Unskilled	3	4
Total	11	31

non-employed or unemployed. This indicates that the restructuring of the economy of the research area had in 1987 more of a 'shake-out' effect, than a replacement one, as far as men's work is concerned. It was clearly having more effect, too, on mining households than on the others, since the preponderance of work done is in the skilled and other manual categories. It is just these categories which are affected most by changes apparent in the Wakefield District.

As we have already indicated in Chapter Four there is no other employer who overall has created jobs in this area for as many male workers as the coal industry. Put together, however, the local public authorities are providing more work for both men and women. The Wakefield Metropolitan District employs over thirty-thousand men and women at various levels. Much of it, however, is at administrative, professional or clerical levels, and therefore does not, even if it were able in times of public sector cutbacks in funding, provide much alternative for less well qualified potential employees. Forty-two respondents in our 1987 survey were employed by Wakefield MDC (Table 5.5).

Working for the Council also sets people to some extent in an ambiguous position with regard to the culture of the localities. A number of the respondents to the biographical interviews expressed some concern about the relation between Wakefield MDC and Ashby. E.W., for instance, said that he was convinced that the former Urban District, which had existed before the 1974 reorganisation of local government, was 'being raped' by Wakefield. He thought that the Coal Board was 'hand-in-glove' with the MDC against 'great little working-class towns'. There was a strong view in Ashby that Wakefield MDC did not always operate in the interests of local people. It is vigorously contested by those who have represented the localities on the Council. We interviewed two such representatives and both argued that Ashby, for instance, has not been disadvantaged by Council policies. One claimed it was because of the tough representation which local Councillors made: 'We are real fighters and we have all stuck together through thick and thin to fight for what Ashby needed.' Another, a former leader of the Council, suggested that localities in the research area had benefitted from a kind of positive discrimination exercised by the Council. For instance, he said, 'Ashby has been the most improved area in the Wakefield Metropolitan District, in terms of housing, environment, schools and leisure centres . . . People who think that Wakefield doesn't care should stop first and look what's been done – they could never have done half so much with their own small resources' (as Urban District Council areas).

As far as those who are employed by the Council are concerned, there are tendencies either to accept the local view of neglect or disadvantage, or to reject the local culture. The former seem to support the local culture even more radically than some of its key reproducers do. K.G.S., a young graduate computer operator, was so inclined. He said he believed very strongly in the need for militancy in the labour movement and saw the local culture as somewhat conservative. Another was H.H., a gardener and grave-digger employed by the local Council, who, when interviewed in 1984, suggested that, during the so-called 'Dirty Jobs' strike by Council workers in the 'winter of discontent' at the end of 1978, local Councillors were more keen on remaining Councillors than supporting the solidarity of brothers in the labour movement. He saw collusion between Labour Councillors and trade union officials, sometimes in league with Council officers, as the problem for both local workers and local communities. He supported the motivation and action of the miners in their strike in 1984. Some local teachers are examples of the other tendency. C.G., a young woman teacher, said she was fully aware of the history of Ashby, and had been born and brought up in a mining household. For her the town was 'no longer a mining town', and she lived there not because of any cultural affiliation, but because of the relatively low prices in the housing market.

The paid employment, other than coal mining, in which men, and of course women, are involved is on the one hand not so significant to particular localities as the pits have been. On the other hand, its spatial distribution and the distance between employees' homes and their place of work are such that the organisational culture has little local counterpart. There could be some exceptions, as in the case of the branch of a large multinational organisation which has about five hundred employees in Ashby, where some comments were made by respondents that a new local sub-culture was being formed. There is not enough information to decide whether that is likely to replace or merely modify the local culture of the mining localities.

One factor that has to be taken into account is the location of work itself. Many men employed in the mining industry no longer work in the same locality as their household and this has become an increasing tendency both with the closure of pits and the diversification of male employment. In 1986, we asked all respondents the location of any paid employment both

Table 5.6 Women aged 12 and over, employment by sector, Featherstone and Hemsworth, 1921

| | Featherstone | | Hemsworth | |
	Number	Percent	Number	Percent
Professional occupations	80	1.7	223	1.9
Public administration	11	0.2	23	0.2
Clerical workers	19	0.4	34	0.3
Commercial & financial	116	2.4	223	1.9
Manufacturing industries	141	2.9	178	1.5
Mining and farming	3	0.1	45	0.4
Services including domestic work	282	5.9	843	7.1
Unoccupied and retired	4159	86.4	10,243	86.7
Total	4811	100.0	11,812	100.0

Source: Registrar General, *Census of Population, 1921, Yorkshire,* HMSO

their own and that of their partners, where appropriate. Only twenty-eight percent of males worked in the four research localities. Well over half the men's jobs were five miles or more from their homes. This contrasted with the situation of women in employment, where sixty-five percent had jobs which were within the research localities, though not necessarily in the immediate vicinity of their homes. Relatively few worked more than five miles from home. The increasing tendency of men to be employed outside mining and for them to become commuters is likely to have a weakening effect on the local culture. Women may in consequence be more significant reproducers of any local culture in future.

One of the very strong characteristics of the mining culture was the dominance of men, based in the almost total exclusion of women from paid employment in the mines. This had its counterpart in the opposition of some women to elements of the local culture, as we noted in Chapter Four. As we have also seen, in Table 4.2, many women now enter into paid employment either full-time or part-time and this is likely to have a further impact on the dominant local culture. It is appropriate to turn therefore to women's employment.

WOMEN'S EMPLOYMENT

When the localities were primarily coal-mining towns or villages, there were few employment opportunities for women. Some women, particularly after leaving school and before marriage found full-time work, and others like F.S. and F.R. continued in, or returned to, full-time or part-time employment. The Census for 1921 shows the employment situation of women in the areas of Featherstone and Hemsworth which are near to our localities. It

Table 5.7 Numbers of textile and garment women workers, Featherstone and Hemsworth, 1921 to 1951

	Featherstone	Hemsworth
1921	103	130
1951	356	332

Source: Registrar General, *Census of Population, 1921* and *1951, Yorkshire*
Note: Hemsworth changed its status from a Rural District Council in 1921 to an Urban District Council, and its boundaries changed. The UDC covered a smaller area and therefore the growth of employment of women in textiles in the Hemsworth area is possibly underestimated by the above statistics

is difficult to make detailed comparison between the 1980s and the 1920s. The Census data for 1921 is based on occupational categories used at that time, but they have been arranged in Table 5.6 so as to suggest some comparison between the occupational status categories we have used for our 1986 and 1987 surveys. There is no indication of how much of the women's employment was part-time in the 1921 Census data. What is very clear is that the proportion of women in paid employment was small. There is a very similar distribution of employment in both areas, with a predominance of domestic work. This possibly understates the proportion of women in the localities who went 'into service', as our elderly women respondents liked to call it. For working-class young women without qualifications, domestic service in other localities was one of the very few employment options, and they would have been recorded for Census purposes in the households where they were employed. Indeed going away to work could also be seen in other types of employment. From the time that motor transport became available, textile mills and other manufacturing firms in other West Yorkshire towns would recruit women from our localities and transport them each day by bus. In the First World War women from here were transported daily to work in a munitions factory near Leeds. Textiles, including the spinning of fibres, weaving of cloth and production of finished garments, employed small but growing numbers of women from the 1920s onwards (Table 5.7).

The restructuring and decline of the textile industry in West Yorkshire since the 1950s has reduced the number of women involved in textiles and garments. There has, however, been some attempt to bring garment making into the mining localities and a small number of women continues to be employed in sewing-up and pressing in relatively small firms. Some also do it as home-workers. In three separate surveys of women in our localities by Elaine Evans (1984), and by ourselves in 1986 and 1987, the proportion of women respondents who were textile and garment workers remained relatively constant at about six percent. Most of the jobs now fall into the semi-skilled category and involve the manipulation of small machines,

Table 5.8 Occupational status of men and women in four mining localities, 1987

| | Men | | Women | |
Occupational status	Number	Percent	Number	Percent
Employers and proprietors	4	2.3	1	0.5
Administrators/managers	15	8.6	8	4.3
Professionals	20	11.5	25	13.4
Supervisors	20	11.5	9	4.8
Clerical workers	4	2.3	11	5.9
Sales personnel/assistants	2	1.1	12	6.4
Skilled manual	34	19.5	7	3.7
Semi-skilled manual	23	13.2	13	6.9
Unskilled manual	10	5.7	23	12.3
Retired/non-employed	11	6.3	72	38.5
Unemployed	31	17.8	6	3.2
Total	174	99.8	187	99.9

Note: The men and women respondents in the 1987 survey were between 20 and 64 years of age inclusive

often in very cramped or trying conditions. One respondent spoke of the very steamy atmosphere of the pressing room of the factory in which she worked.

We have already seen that a number of women are employed by the Wakefield District Council (Table 5.5). Their jobs consist of teaching, library work, care supervising, catering and cleaning. Others are employed by public bodies such as the District Health Authorities, as nurses, nurse auxiliaries, catering staff and cleaners. Using the same categorisation of occupations as we have used for men in the 1987 survey of mining localities we can compare the occupations of men and women (Table 5.8).

There are some immediately obvious differences. Almost twice the proportion of women as men are not in paid employment, forty-two percent of women and twenty-four percent of men. Among the employed, men tend to have higher occupational status than women. There are more men employers, and a higher percentage of men in administrative or managerial grades. Among professionals there are more women than men, but a closer examination of the posts which the men hold, shows that they are among the higher paid professionals, accountants, civil engineers and surveyors, for instance, whereas women are among the lower paid, including teachers, librarians and nurses. In the intermediate categories, men are more numerous among supervisors, whereas women are more numerous among clerical and sales staff. In the manual grades, men are more often found among the skilled workers and women more likely to be found among the less skilled.

There is therefore no doubt of the tendency for male dominance to continue in the occupational sphere, despite the changes in the labour market which have taken place, and despite equal opportunities legislation which was passed in Britain in the 1970s. Women are much more obviously part of the labour market than they were in the 1920s, but the jobs which they do at all levels do not give them occupational equality with men. To some extent one can see the influence of a gender-segmented labour market, in that some jobs tend to be done only by women and some only by men. This too is reinforced by the fact that whilst all the employed men are full-time workers, women are not. Fifty-eight percent of women are in some form of paid employment, but of those almost a half are part-time.

Let us now move to look at how these changes in the labour market and the participation of both men and women in paid employment are reflected in the structure and conditions of such traditional social institutions as the household and kinship networks.

HOUSEHOLDS IN COAL-MINING LOCALITIES

The household was the subject of some interest in Dennis, Henriques and Slaughter, *Coal is Our Life*. Both it and the ideal–typical model of the traditional mining community, which we have shown to be based in that study, noted that in the separation of the men's world from that of the women, which was a consequence of the division of labour in such communities, the household itself was marked by a clear segregation of roles and the dominance of the male. Further, the study presented a view of the men's world which suggested that friendships developed in the pit were more significant than those of the household. There was no discussion of whether this also applied to the households where no-one was employed in mining. Nevertheless sociological research, particularly through the influence of David Lockwood (1966), has been dominated by the view that traditional working-class households had similar kinds of segregation and patriarchy. This notion has not been modified either by some other studies of coal-mining localities, such as Claire Williams's Australian study, *Open Cut* (1981). Her evidence supports the view that patriarchy and role segregation, with the wife virtually confined to household management and child care, are typical of households in mining settlements. Women are rarely able to enter the world of paid work. Bill Williamson's study of Throckley (1982) maintains the same image, though presenting a very sympathetic view of women's work and the relations between men and women there.

Recent research on the effects of unemployment and redundancy on working-class households has shown that they have reinforcing effects on the traditional pattern (McKee and Bell, 1986), whereas diversification of employment and residential patterns has been said to produce more egalitarian or 'symmetrical' households, a theory challenged by a number of feminist researchers (S. Allen, 1983; Leonard and Speakman, 1986). A number of questions therefore emerge about the assumptions of the ideal–typical model of mining communities with regard to the household, its division of labour, participation in the wider labour market and the social networks in which households are involved. These are put here in the form of five testable hypotheses.

1 Mining households are marked by a domestic division of labour in which there is a clear separation of tasks, with women taking sole responsibility for household management and child care.
2 Women are dominated by their male partners in mining households, and decisions are rarely taken by women.
3 Women of mining households rarely enter paid employment outside the household.
4 Women and their male partners rarely share the same outside interests, cultural pursuits or consciousness.
5 Men and women have different social networks, based in kinship, neighbouring and friendship.

The data which we will use to assess the validity of the hypotheses above is drawn from one hundred and twenty-four households interviewed in 1986, and two hundred households interviewed in 1987. We have defined mining households as those in which one or more male members have ever recently been employed in coal mining. This means that we have included in the mining household set some where there is no male currently employed in mining. This is because of the rapid closure of pits in the research area, which we have already noted. In 1986, there were forty-eight mining households and in 1987 seventy mining households so defined. For the purposes of comparability, we have in the following analysis concentrated on households which were male/female partnerships. In 1987, for instance, sixty-seven mining households out of the seventy had partnerships. Three had single males. Ninety-four out of one hundred and thirty non-mining households had male/female partnerships. Ten had single males and twenty-six had single females.

THE SOCIAL CONDITIONS OF HOUSEHOLDS IN THE RESEARCH AREA

Classifying the households as either mining or non-mining, it is possible to start by illustrating the social conditions of the sample, so as to indicate the context within which the hypotheses are tested. In terms of household size, that is the number of people living together in each, mining households tend to be slightly larger (Table 5.9).

When we turn to age structure we note that mining households tend to be older than non-mining households. Table 5.10 refers to the 1987 survey, but the same held in 1986.

As a consequence of the different age structures, there are fewer young

Table 5.9 Size of mining and non-mining households, 1986 and 1987

	1986 persons	1987 persons
Mining households	3.32	3.69
Non-mining households	3.27	3.09

Note: The greater discrepancy between the two types in 1987 seems to be a consequence of sampling and is not statistically significant

children of school age in mining households, but a slightly higher proportion of mining households have sixteen to nineteen-year-olds.

With regard to the marital status of all respondents, in our 1987 sample, seventy-seven percent were legally married to their partners. Eighty-one percent were living in partnership households, that is one hundred and sixty-one households out of the two hundred where we interviewed respondents. In our 1986 sample of households, eighty-eight percent were partnership households. Mining households tended to have a higher proportion of legally married couples than non-mining households.

The households had two main housing tenure situations, either being tenants, mainly in Council properties, or being owner-occupiers. The local authority and the Coal Board, the other main housing landlord up to 1987, both had policies of selling off their housing stock. A shift in tenure can thus be observed between the two surveys and the two sets of households by the time of our second survey shared roughly the same proportion of tenancies (Table 5.11).

We collected information about net household income only in 1987. This included all sources of income less tax and other statutory deductions. At a time when the national average net annual household income, according to

Table 5.10 Age structure of mining and non-mining households, 1987

Age groups	Households Mining %	Non-mining %
40 yrs and under	37.1	57.1
41 to 50 yrs	35.5	23.5
51 to 65 yrs	27.4	19.4
N =	67	94

Note: The age structure is based in the age given by the original male respondent in each type of household where there were men and women in partnership. In the 1986 survey we had a small number of respondents over sixty-five years of age. When they are excluded from the analysis, the age structures are virtually identical to those of 1987. There is little difference between men and women in the samples, though the women tend to be slightly younger than their partners

Table 5.11 House tenure, 1986 and 1987

	Owner-occupiers	Tenants	
1986			
Percentages of:			
Mining households	54	46	(N=48)
Non-mining households	67	33	(N=60)
1987:			
Percentages of:			
Mining households	70	30	(N=67)
Non-mining households	71	29	(N=94)

the Department of Employment's Family Expenditure Survey, was just over £10,000, the equivalent figures in our research area were £8774 in mining households and £8820 in non-mining households. The average for non-mining households, of course, is based in a somewhat wider range of net incomes as Table 5.12 shows. Mining households tend to cluster more in the the middle of the range. The non-mining households do not spread as much as those in the national sample, which, however, include single person households. Taking net earnings from employment alone, non-mining households tend to have higher earnings than mining households but again the range is greater among the former. In both types of household male earnings tend to be twice the level of women's earnings. This is accounted for largely by the factors we have already noted, that is, women tend to be in less well paid jobs and nearly half of the employed women (forty-nine percent in our sample) are working part-time.

The spread of household income is also reinforced by the fact that in partnership households there is a strong tendency for men and women to have similar occupational status. Partners tend to choose one another in terms of social background, educational qualifications and possibly work

Table 5.12 Net monthly income in mining and non-mining households, 1987, compared with that in a national sample of households, 1986

	Up to £400	£401– £850	£851– £1300	£1301 & over	N
Percentage of households:					
Mining	14.8	37.7	31.1	8.2	61
Non-mining	25.5	39.4	23.4	11.7	94
National sample (F.E.S.)	27.1	30.0	22.8	20.0	7,178

Note: The percentage distribution for the National Sample Households is drawn from the Family Expenditure Survey, 1986, (FES) published by the Department of Employment

Table 5.13 Partnerships in mining and non-mining households, showing partners' relative occupational status, 1987

| | Mining households | | | | | |
| Women's occupational status | Men's occupational status | | | | | |
	Salariat	Inter-mediate	Working class	Non-employed	Un-employed	Total
Salariat	3	0	3	0	2	8
Intermediate	1	3	4	1	1	10
Working class	1	3	13	1	3	21
Non-employed	1	2	8	7	8	26
Unemployed	0	0	2	0	0	2
Total	6	8	30	9	14	67

| | Non-mining households | | | | | |
| Women's Occupational Status | Men's occupational status | | | | | |
	Salariat	Inter-mediate	Working class	Non-employed	Un-employed	Total
Salariat	11	5	1	1	0	18
Intermediate	8	7	5	0	0	20
Working class	4	0	12	0	3	19
Non-employed	6	4	13	0	12	35
Unemployed	0	1	1	0	0	2
Total	29	17	32	1	15	94

Note: Occupational status is classified after Heath, Jowell and Curtice (1985) with the addition of two categories as follows:
   Salariat – employers, managers and professionals;
   Intermediate – supervisory, clerical and sales staff;
   Working class – all manual workers;
   Non-employed – retired and not seeking paid employment;
   Unemployed – having no paid employment but willing to work. This category includes
      some who are sick or disabled

experience. This to some extent replicates the situation we illustrated in the mining localities during the nineteenth century (see Chapter Three, p. 52). Table 5.13 shows the cross-tabulation of partnerships in mining and non-mining households according to occupational status, defined with reference to the categories used in Table 5.8 above.

The marginal totals and the numbers in the diagonal cells for each cross-tabulation of partners' occupational status show what we have just noted. In mining households most men are in manual jobs and most of the employed women are also in manual jobs. Where they are in what we can term high or intermediate status employment, their employed women partners tend to be of a similar status. Where men are either non-employed or unemployed their women partners tend to be non-employed. In non-mining households, men's employment tends to be more variably distributed across the categories and in more high status jobs, and their women partners are likewise more likely to be of higher status than in mining households. Their partners are even more likely to be non-employed where the men are unemployed, than in mining households. A link between the man's unemployment or non-employment and their women partners' non-employment has been recorded previously in studies of unemployment (McKee and Bell, 1986). It is interesting to note here that this can be seen to some extent as a part of the whole structure and culture of male/female partnerships, and of the more universal tendency to choose or be constrained to be like one's partner.

Many studies have shown that educational qualifications are related to occupational status and income, and the fact that non-mining households have higher incomes is related to their possession of more educational credentials. In 1986 we collected data on education, and among mining households, only 11.6 percent of respondents had any nationally accredited educational qualifications, while the figure was 25.9 percent among non-mining household respondents. These are both nevertheless below national averages which indicate that some forty percent of adults have a qualification of CSE level or equivalent and above. Most of our respondents in 1986 were, of course women, who tend to have fewer qualifications than men.

In sum, in terms of this data, we are dealing with households which do not display major differences when we categorise them according to their links to the staple (or former staple) industry of the locality. Mining households tend to be older, perhaps more stable in terms of marital status, slightly larger, somewhat poorer and with fewer educational qualifications, than non-mining households. In terms of house tenure, they are in 1987, similarly distributed with regard to owner-occupation and tendencies. There seem to be similar constraints operating on them with regard to choice of partners and employment as a base for income generation and style of life. Nor can we assume that all households in mining localities are working class. Our mining households include some that rank in terms of income and partners' occupational status as middle class.

There is however a strong difference when we take men's current employment status into account, for in 1987 among male respondents in those households which we categorised as 'mining' because of their former or present links with coal mining, only sixty-three percent were in paid work. All our respondents were of 'working age', that is between twenty and sixty-four years of age inclusive. In non-mining households, eighty-three percent of males were in paid employment. The unemployed made up twenty-one percent in mining, compared with sixteen percent in non-mining households. Another sixteen percent of the males in mining households were non-employed ('retired' or 'redundant'), compared with only one percent in non-mining households. The income of many mining households therefore depended very much on state benefits, in contrast with non-mining households.

It is with these conditions in mind that we examine the five hypotheses.

TESTING THE FIVE HYPOTHESES

The domestic division of labour

In order to examine whether the domestic division of labour in our households is gender segregated, we collected data about eight different aspects of domestic work in the 1986 survey. The responses from the males, who were interviewed separately from their partners, were almost identical with those of the women, and these indicated that while women were very largely responsible for several of the tasks, men did not play a negligible role. In terms of a rank order of responsibility Table 5.14 presents the findings.

Not all households do all of this work, but only in the last two task areas are men more likely than women to be performing seventy-five to one hundred percent of the work. It is obvious from this information that mining households do have a marked division of labour, but not significantly more than non-mining households. Women in most households do all or most of the laundry, tidying and cleaning, domestic production, child care and food preparation.

In the 1987 survey we also asked questions about the domestic division of labour. Very similar findings were achieved, though the categorisation of the tasks was different (determined by the requirements of a nationally coordinated research effort concerned with Social Change and Economic Life

Table 5.14 Domestic division of labour: rank order of women's work, 1986

	Mining households	Non-mining households
Percentage of households in which women do all or most of the given work:		
1. Laundry	93	83
2. Tidying and cleaning	67	71
3. Domestic production	54	54
4. Child care	52	34
5. Food preparation	50	71
6. Shopping	41	41
7. Home maintenance	36	20
8. Home improvement	5	0

Note: 'Domestic production' refers to work like gardening, making clothes, etc.; 'home maintenance' is decorating and minor repairs; 'home improvement' is major structural work, like new bathrooms, kitchens, etc. 'All or most' refers to a situation in which the person is said to do seventy-five to one hundred percent of that task

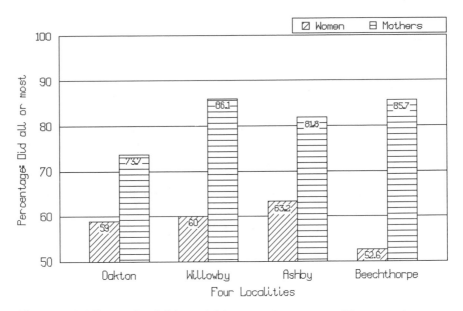

Figure 5.1.1 Domestic division of labour, 1987 survey: differences between generations – washing up

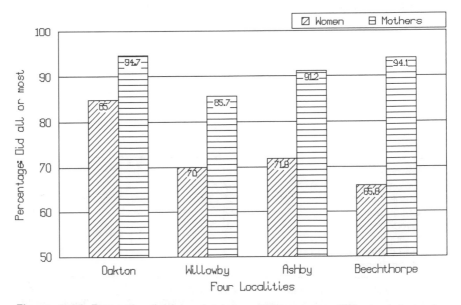

Figure 5.1.2 Domestic division of labour, 1987 survey: differences between generations – cleaning and hoovering

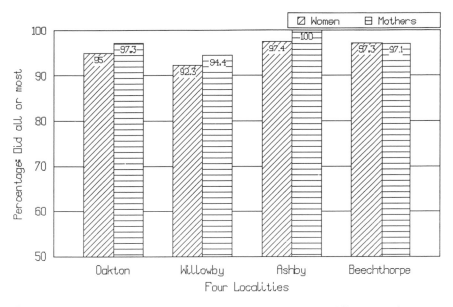

Figure 5.1.3 Domestic division of labour, 1987 survey: differences between generations – washing clothes

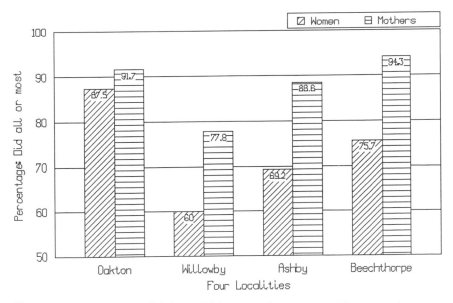

Figure 5.1.4 Domestic division of labour, 1987 survey: differences between generations – cooking for the family

Table 5.15 Male respondents' intentions given more leisure time, 1987

Percentages intending to:	Mining households	Non-mining households
Do more domestic production	34.3	16.4
Give more time to children	22.9	20.0
Entertain friends at home	11.4	14.5
Play more sport	2.9	18.2

– see Introduction and Chapter Four). In 1987 we also asked respondents to estimate the amount of domestic work done by their mothers and fathers. This suggested that there had been a slight shift from a highly segregated domestic division of labour, into one in which more sharing was apparent, although the traditional segregation had by no means disappeared. This is illustrated graphically in Figure 5.1, where the differences between the four localities are shown.

In displaying the information by localities, we can also observe another tendency, which was that in Willowby, the locality with the highest proportion of mining households, male unemployment and low net incomes, the domestic division of labour was not so strikingly segregated as in the other three localities. This held for both generations, too. It was in the more middle-class locality, Oakton, that the tendency to segregated household tasks seemed to be the greatest. This seems to contradict to some extent the findings of earlier studies of the household division of tasks that middle-class households are less segregated than working-class households (Bott, 1957).

Male respondents were asked in the 1987 survey, in the presence of their partners, what they would do if they had more time off paid work, or more leisure. Table 5.15 shows their answers.

These answers seem to reflect the different material circumstances of mining households, and possibly some male guilt about the fact that women in both sets of households still are largely, even if not exclusively tied to the domestic domain and its work. We also asked about the norms concerning the division of labour in the household in the 1987 survey, and it was clear that there was a strong preference for the woman to do most of the cleaning and child care and for the man to be responsible for generating income.

Using data from the 1986 survey, we can see that the division of labour in the household is variable according to the occupational status of the woman partner. Table 5.16 shows this, though even fully employed women are responsible for much of the domestic work. Unemployed as distinct from non-employed women seem most likely to carry the heaviest responsibility for housework. It does seem to be the case that there is more sharing of domestic work in households where women are in full-time employment, particularly in child care. As we have seen men do contribute more in the

Table 5.16 Domestic division of labour: variations according to the occupational
status of women partners, 1986

| | Women's occupational status | | | |
| | In paid employment | | Unemployed | Non- |
	Full-time	Part-time		Employed
Percentage of households where women did all or most of:				
1. Laundry	77	87	80	88
2. Tidying and cleaning	59	67	85	57
3. Domestic production	47	43	55	53
4. Child care	10	52	56	50
5. Food preparation	45	59	95	63
6. Shopping	40	46	21	44
7. Home maintenance	14	18	35	32
8. Home improvement	0	4	0	0
Number of households	22	46	20	35

spheres of home maintenance and improvement ('do-it-yourself' activities).
Further we also found that where men are unemployed, there is a tendency
towards a more egalitarian distribution of household work.

So the first hypothesis has to be modified a little, although there is in
many of these households a marked domestic division of labour. Changes
in the external labour market do have some effect on it, and there are no
significant differences between mining and non-mining households. This fits
with the summary of recent evidence drawn together by Lydia Morris about
household work generally (1988).

Household decision-making

The second hypothesis, that women are dominated by their male partners,
is on the face of it more clearly refuted. There is little evidence that the
domesic division of labour is entirely a consequence of male dominance,
though clearly we have to have a conception of power that goes beyond
mere observable domination. As Murphy says in his text on social closure
(1988: 136), power to some extent resides in being able to sit back and
profit from others getting on with the job, in the knowledge that things
are likely to work in the interests of those who are not intervening. Male
power may at times be like that. Women in their responses to a question
on how far they accepted the domestic division of labour, indicated by a
majority of sixty-five percent to thirty-five percent that they did not dissent
from it. A slightly higher percentage in mining households in fact said they
agreed than in non-mining households. We also asked a number of questions

Table 5.17 Factors which influenced women most when deciding to take paid employment, 1987

Percentage of women respondents claiming to be influenced by:	Mining households	Non-mining households
Household's need for income	94	98
Wanting to stay in the area	73	78
Doing work I enjoy	69	91
Having to look after children	34	42
Partner's views about my work	33	46
Partner's job	18	22

about decision-making in the households, and there is sufficient indication to support the view that the male partner is not assumed to be making all the decisions.

The influences recorded in Table 5.17 are placed in rank order given by women in mining households, and that for the other women is slightly different. The women in non-mining households are influenced more by their partner's views of what they should do, than women in mining households. Both sets place other factors, such as their common economic position (generally below the national average in household income) and wanting to stay in the locality, high on their lists. The intrinsic interest and enjoyment to be gained from work is also rated very highly, especially by the women in non-mining households. Other factors were also offered in the interview, like looking after elderly relatives, the possible loss of welfare benefits and the household's tax position, but these were rated as of less importance than the six ranked above. The responses indicate that few women feel that they are dominated by their male partners in what will be a crucial sphere of choice with implications for both of them.

The management of household finances has been the subject of research in recent years. Jan Pahl (1983) has suggested a typology of four household financial management systems: the whole wage system (where one partner manages all the income and expenditure), the allowance system (where a partner manages on an allowance given by the chief earner), the shared management system (where partners join in generating and managing income and expenditure) and the independent system (where partners keep their finances separate). In 1987, we asked our interviewees about their household financial management, knowing that in *Coal is Our Life*, the tendency for households to have an allowance system was said to be most prominent. Among our respondents thirty-six percent said that they used a whole wage system, twelve percent, an allowance system, forty-five percent, a shared system, and less than one percent, an independent system. Six percent had a variant of these approaches. In the poorer households the tendency was for the allowance system to be more common than in wealthier households, but either the whole wage system or sharing were in all localities and types of household more frequently reported than other systems. In the poorer households financial management by one partner, more often the woman, tended to be more common than sharing. The opposite was the case in more affluent households. Sharing the financial management seemed to be associated with women's employment status. Sharing was more frequently found in households where women had some paid employment than where they were non-employed or full-time housewives. Overall on financial management, women seemed to be either mainly responsible for, or shared with male partners in, important decisions.

Some things, however, were perhaps not discussed, and this could be to the disadvantage of women. The respondents and their partners in the 1987 survey by a big majority said that the sharing of unpaid work in the household 'seemed natural' (seventy-two percent of the original respondents and sixty-six percent of their partners). About a fifth of both respondents and partners said that such sharing of domestic work 'changed from time to time' and only one-tenth of them maintained that in their households the best way of dividing the work had been discussed. There was variation, however, and over twice as many partners in full-time employment compared with those who were non-employed claimed that they had talked about it. This was substantiated by the male respondents.

We also asked women in 1987 what kind of considerations would weigh with them when deciding to take employment, if they had a child still at school. They were asked to comment on a number of possible considerations. Their male partners' views came more into prominence, on this basis, and almost two-thirds said that they would count very much or at least to some extent compared with smaller percentages for the 'availability of satisfactory child-care facilities', 'the availability of a part-time job' and the 'household's need for income'. They gave most weight, however, to 'my views of what was best for my children' and seventy-three percent of women said that would count very much and another seventeen percent, at least to some extent. This fits with the norms of the domestic division of labour which we noted above. Women see themselves as home-minders and child-carers rather than income generators.

It may be that male power is after all not dinted very far in these mining localities, but the women are tending to enter into paid employment more, and this is perhaps the key to change in the unequal division of labour in the household. We have noted that where women are in paid employment, household financial management is shared, and there is discussion about sharing the unpaid work and a tendency for women to do less of it.

Women and paid employment

The traditional image of the mining community is that women stay by the kitchen sink and men are the breadwinners. This was probably never entirely true, though substantially so for partners of colliers in the late nineteenth and early twentieth century. The third hypothesis is clearly refuted now, however, and in three recent surveys in our research localities, about half of the women had some paid employment. Elaine Evans (1984) in a small survey found sixty percent of women had a full-time or part-time job. In our 1986 survey forty-seven percent of women had paid employment and about nineteen percent said they had second jobs or casual work in addition. In 1987 we did not ask about such second jobs, but fifty-eight percent of women had some paid employment.

Sixty percent of women in non-mining households and fifty-eight percent of women in mining households had paid jobs, though more of the former had full-time employment. For both sets of women, most of the work was clerical, factory or shop work, with another concentration in personal services, such as hairdressing, cleaning and catering. The few relatively high status jobs held by women in teaching, nursing and other professional areas were mainly held by women in non-mining households. The classification is illustrated in general terms in Table 5.13.

Not all women of course, are in partnerships. In 1987, twenty-six women, or fourteen percent of all our women respondents, were in 'single' households, often with dependent children or other relatives. Using information from the 1987 survey about all, including the single, women, Table 5.18 has been constructed to show their occupational status.

This distribution serves to reinforce the view that women in partnership mining households do not tend to share the same standard of living as women in non-mining partnerships. They are on the whole less likely to be in high status employment than women in non-mining partnership households. All women in partnerships are less likely to be non- or unemployed than the single women, though the single women as a set are more polarised. A higher proportion of them are in high status employment than women in partnerships, but there is a corresponding higher likelihood of them being either non-employed or unemployed.

Women in partnerships are more likely to have paid employment the higher the status of their male partners, and this is slightly more true for women in mining than non-mining households. In Table 5.19 we have collapsed the occupational status categories of male partners into four classes, salariat, intermediate, working and not employed (that is non-employed or unemployed). This is a reworking of the information given in Table 5.13.

The differences between the proportions in each class category in Table 5.19 are not significant, and, despite the slight differences between mining and non-mining partnerships, all in the same direction, we can assume that

Table 5.18 Occupational status of women in mining and non-mining partnership households and in single households 1987

| | Partnership households | | | | Single households | |
| | Mining | | Non-mining | | | |
Occupational status	No.	%	No.	%	No.	%
Employers	0	0	1	1.1	0	0
Administrators/managers	2	3.0	4	4.3	2	7.7
Professionals	6	9.0	13	13.8	6	23.1
Supervisors	4	6.0	4	4.3	1	3.8
Clerical	2	3.0	9	9.6	0	0
Sales staff	4	6.0	7	7.4	1	3.8
Skilled manual	2	3.0	4	4.3	1	3.8
Semi-skilled	3	4.5	8	8.5	2	7.7
Unskilled manual	16	23.9	7	7.4	0	0
Non-employed	26	38.8	35	37.2	11	42.3
Unemployed	2	3.0	2	2.1	2	7.7
Total	67	100.2	94	100.0	26	99.9

the same opportunities and constraints apply to women according to their partners' occupational status. As we have said, women in partnerships are more likely to be employed the higher the status of their partners, and are least likely to be employed when their partners are not in paid employment. The polarisation which we noted among the single women seems to occur among women in partnerships. Non-employment or unemployment is much more likely to be the situation of women in partnerships where the man is in working-class employment or is not employed at all. This would suggest that households taken as a whole are not as strongly dominated by the traditional culture of mining communities as they may once have been. Nevertheless, as we showed in relation to the discussion of decision-making, women are constrained by expectations that they should be household managers and child carers, rather than income generators. Employment among women tends to be of a periodic nature, and the work histories of women contain a large number of 'events' (starting and stopping paid jobs). This is more likely for women with working-class partners and single women than for those who are more middle class (Allen, Littlejohn and Warwick, 1989).

Women's employment varies also according to locality. Table 4.2 summarises the differences which can be seen between Oakton, the more middle-class locality, and Willowby, Ashby and Beechthorpe with lower net incomes, higher levels of male unemployment, and higher proportions of mining households. Willowby, with the highest percentage of mining households and men not in paid employment, has the smallest percentage of women in paid jobs and in full-time employment. Ashby and Beechthorpe

Table 5.19 Women's employment by the occupational status of their partners, 1987

| | Employed women in mining households | | Employed women in non-mining households | |
	Number	Percent in class	Number	Percent in class
Occupational class of male partner				
Salariat	5	83	23	79
Intermediate	6	75	12	71
Working	20	67	18	56
Not employed	8	35	4	25

Note: The class designations are explained in Table 5.13, but Not employed is a combination of Non-employed and Unemployed

tend to have more opportunities for women's employment in the locality, as a consequence of the siting of small clothing and food processing factories there. They are, however, mainly part-time jobs. This is possibly also the reason why partners of non- and unemployed men have a better chance of being employed in Ashby and Beechthorpe (thirty-six percent in both cases) than in Willowby (twenty-seven percent). In general, however, across the localities, the rule that the higher the status of a male partner's occupation the greater the chance of the woman being employed, still holds.

Gender, cultural activities and consciousness

In *Coal is Our Life*, the authors depicted the separation of men's and women's lives, in consequence of men's pit work and women's lack of employment outside the household, as one that virtually created two worlds. This was adopted by Bulmer (1975a) as one of the main characteristics of the traditional mining community. Given the changes which have occurred with regard to women's employment, how far can this gender segregation still be said to hold? We have already indicated in the previous chapter that in Ashby things were changing. In the 1986 survey we asked women and men what their preferred social activities were. Table 5.20 indicates the rank order of their replies:

This Table indicates two things. First, there is much that men and women do in common; and second, there are things that they tend to do apart. It is the case that sporting activities, pubs and clubs tend to be more commonly attended by men, while going to church and visiting relatives are more likely to be female activities, but none of these is exclusively a one gender only event.

Some of the cultural institutions of our localities obviously cannot be understood without reference to their role in countering the stigma which

Table 5.20 Preferred social activities of men and women by households, 1986

| | Mining households | | Non-mining households | |
	Women	Men	Women	Men
1.	Pubs	Pubs	Pubs	Pubs
2.	Visiting	Sports	Eating out	Clubs
3.	Clubs	Clubs	Visiting	Sports
4.	Shopping	Eating out	Shopping	–
5.	Holidays	Meals with friends	Holidays	–
6.	Eating out	–	Meals at home	–
7.	–	–	Church/Clubs	–
	N = 38	N = 20	N = 62	N = 7

Note: Other activities were mentioned but these lists are comprised of activities which were mentioned by at least ten percent of the respondents in any of the categories

many of our older, as well as some of the younger, respondents felt attached to the 'pit village'. The display of trophies on the living room sideboard, reported in one of our biographical extracts above, was clearly related to pride felt about sporting achievements. Claire Williams noticed this in her study *Open Cut*, though she defined it more narrowly in her reference to sport, by suggesting that union leaders might be able to bolster their self-respect, after suffering the degradation of some long-drawn out industrial conflict, by resort to the male sporting sub-culture. Sport has perhaps always been a key institution in this respect in industrial societies.

Sport can obviously, however, play a role for a whole locality, and can indeed be the basis of creating a sense, even if only temporarily, of communion. During the course of our research, the Rugby League team in Ashby reached the final of the Rugby League Challenge Cup and won against very strong and fancied opponents. Most of Ashby went to Wembley, men and women, though during the season as a whole we estimated that among spectators at local matches, only one in six was a woman. After winning the Cup, there was tremendous euphoria, and this extended across the research area. The team was feted and were driven in an open top bus for six miles through the district, being cheered all the way, by crowds of local men and women. The greatest cheers were to be heard in Ashby itself, and the Team Coach was reported to say 'we have a tremendous community spirit in this village'. There is no strict gender segregation culturally in these mining localities.

Similarly with regard to consciousness, there is obvious overlapping rather than separation in regard to political and economic questions. Table 5.21 indicates how far men and women agreed with the 1984/5 miners' strike in 1986.

The difference between mining and non-mining households is not perhaps

Table 5.21 Stated levels of agreement with the miners' strike of 1984/5, 1986

Percentages:	Mining households		Non-mining households	
	Females	*Males*	*Females*	*Males*
In agreement	56	48	41	30
Neither agree nor disagree	8	9	11	20
Disagreement	36	43	48	50
N =	48	21	75	10

Note: All respondents were asked an open-ended question about whether they were in agreement or disagreement with the strike of 1984/5. This summarises their responses (See Chapter Seven)

as large as might have been anticipated, but the range of responses from men and women in mining households adds more evidence for refuting any notion of totally different gender consciousnesses. What is clear is that there are differences of approach to the question of the miners' strike both from men and women in our localities. This would be expected given the different views expressed by our interviewees concerning local values and beliefs, which were indicated in the previous chapter. We will deal more fully with this in Chapter Seven. The question of political consciousness is discussed below, but what our discussion of the hypotheses is leading to, in fact, is that our localities certainly do not conform to the ideal type of traditional mining community, though in certain respects there are some reminders of that in particular forms of social organisation, its processes and institutions.

Kinship and other social networks

The traditional mining community is said to have strong social networks. Our own evidence indicates that kinship networks continue to be a very strong part of the social structure of our localities and that they operate to influence both men and women, despite the fact that our localities cannot really be seen as traditional mining communities any longer.

As we saw from the biographical studies in the previous chapter, being local and knowing people locally seemed a very important part of the local cultural capital. In fact from the moment we started collecting data in our mining localities, the significance of local kin was very evident. In Ashby, we frequently heard people say, 'everybody is related' and 'everybody knows everybody else'. Names like Smith, Brown and Jones are not just common surnames, which they are, of course, but they are indications of living kinship. In a survey in 1981 of as many Smiths as we could locate in Ashby, using the Electoral Register, we spoke to sixty-four out of seventy-two on the Register. Fifty-three percent had been born in the town, and sixty-six

Table 5.22 Percentages of respondents with local kin, by locality and sex, 1986

	Oakton	Willowby	Ashby	Beechthorpe	All
Women	70	90	90	87	84 N = 122
Men	75	100	75	50	74 N = 31

percent had relatives living there too. Of the incomers, eighteen were born in parishes contiguous with Ashby, and only one was not English. He claimed Welsh origins.

In our 1986 interviews we asked all our respondents whether they had relatives living locally. Table 5.22 indicates their responses.

There is a little difference between mining and non-mining households. Of women in mining households ninety-one percent claimed local relatives and, in non-mining households, seventy-nine percent. The meaning of 'local' can vary between respondents. In 1986 we asked a number of questions about local kin, friends and neighbours, some being open-ended, some asking for place-names. When we asked respondents about their parents and grandparents, we sought specific place names. Using two classifications we have indicated in Table 5.23 the percentages of those with parents and grandparents who lived or had lived in the same electoral ward as the respondent or partner, and of those who lived or had lived within our research area, a somewhat less stringent definition of 'local'. In the interview, we asked both men and women for this information, but as we have indicated, in our 1986 survey, we contacted fewer men in each locality. In Table 5.23 we use the responses of the women respondents.

Table 5.23 suggests that roots in the locality are very strong. Many of the grandparents referred to by older respondents were born in the nineteenth century, possibly of parents who were themselves 'locals'. We have certainly traced a number of local families through from the 1871 and 1881 Census Enumerators' Reports. The differences between the localities verge on the statistically significant levels, but in general the major distinction is that between Oakton, the more middle-class locality and the other three, where the roots seem more deeply laid. With the local economy having been dominated by coal mining through the last one hundred years, and as a consequence of young women leaving the area to find work in the past, we might have expected to find that male lines were much stronger than those of the women. This is not the case, though Ashby, where deep mining has dominated the local economy for the longest time, tends to meet the expectation. There are no indications that patrilocality of marriage homes is an exclusive tendency. Men have moved to their wives' locality on marriage and vice versa, but above all there is a high degree of inter-marriage, particularly in Willowby, and Ashby. The variablity probably relates to another fact of coal mining, that miners have not tended to associate themselves with one pit for life, and this of course

Table 5.23 Percentages of parents and grandparents of women respondents and their partners ever living in (A) the same electoral ward and (B) the research area, by localities, 1986

(A) Percentage of relatives living in same electoral ward

	Oakton	Willowby	Ashby	Beechthorpe	All
Women respondents:					
Own parents	43	59	40	47	48
Own mother's parents	14	34	23	24	24
Own father's parents	22	33	31	19	27
Partner's parents	25	59	45	40	42
Partner's mother's parents	25	26	36	42	27
Partner's father's parents	24	41	36	42	36

(B) Percentage of Relatives living in research area

	Oakton	Willowby	Ashby	Beechthorpe	All
Women respondents:					
Own parents	61	78	63	47	63
Own mother's parents	32	53	47	35	42
Own father's parents	48	53	52	26	45
Partner's parents	50	66	71	60	62
Partner's mother's parents	33	48	71	36	48
Partner's father's parents	40	48	56	50	49
For (A) and (B) N =	28	32	30	30	120

Note: The research area consists of all four localities and the neighbouring wards/parishes which make up a single geographical area and parliamentary constituency

has been an increasing tendency with pit closures and reorganisation of the management of the coalfields. Hence our data on the roots of family life in the localities do not show that mining households have stronger roots than non-mining households (see Table 5.24).

We also asked our respondents how many local relatives they had, and found that forty percent had ten or more. There were no differences between mining and non-mining households.

In the 1987 survey we asked different questions, in line with the other research teams. However, women's responses to the question 'was your family living in X (the place of interview) when you were born?' give similar indications, shown in Table 5.25, of the extent of local kinship as in our 1986 survey.

In this case the difference between Oakton and the other three places appears even more significant than in the 1986 data. The women in mining households were, as in the previous survey, no more likely to have been born locally than those in non-mining households. Thus in

Table 5.24 Percentage of parents and grandparents of respondents in mining and non-mining households ever living in (A) the same ward and (B) the research area, 1986

	Mining households		Non-mining households	
	(A)	(B)	(A)	(B)
Women respondents'				
Own parents	43	60	52	65
Own mother's parents	21	42	27	42
Own father's parents	23	42	30	48
Partner's parents	47	65	38	59
Partner's mother's parents	29	46	21	50
Partner's father's parents	35	45	36	52
N =	48	48	72	72

all localities, the possibilities of kinship interaction are likely to be quite strong.

Not surprisingly, links between kin are also seen as important. They see their nearby relatives frequently, and if they do not see close relatives during the week, they tend to telephone them. In our 1986 survey over half our women respondents saw their own siblings and their own children who had left home at least once per week or more. Higher proportions of women saw their own or their partners' parents if they were still alive. Seventy percent of the women respondents said that they telephoned a relative weekly or more frequently. We asked them to tell us of whom among relatives, friends and neighbours they saw most. Here there were significant differences between men and women, and between the localities. They are shown in Table 5.26.

The differences between men and women suggest that women still regard the links between them and their kin as crucial, whereas for men there is a relatively equal chance that friends and neighbours will be as important as kin. This possibly reflects the old patterns of work and sociability for men, in which men interacted at work with both family members and neighbours, and maintained friendship activities outside work. The emphasis which women put on relatives seems to replicate Bott's finding

Table 5.25 Percentages of women respondents whose parents lived in the research localities when they were born, 1987

	Oakton	Willowby	Ashby	Beechthorpe	All
Percent women born in locality	21	48	51	62	45
N =	39	40	37	39	155

Table 5.26 Respondents' indications of whom they see most, 1986

	Relatives	Friends	Neighbours	All equally	N
Percentages of:					
Women	54	24	19	4	123
Men	27	43	30	0	30
Percentages of Women in:					
Oakton	53	33	3	10	30
Willowby	38	22	34	6	32
Ashby	74	10	16	0	31
Beechthorpe	50	30	20	0	30

three decades ago that women, particularly working-class women, regarded the task of maintaining the kinship network as important to the security of their household (Bott, 1957). The differences between the localities suggest that while for all women kinship is important, and more important than links with friends and neighbours, the situation depends on local culture. Interestingly what we have said about Ashby on the basis of the biographical data seems to be borne out in the 1986 survey. In Willowby, the poorest locality, maintenance of links with friends and neighbours is seen to be almost as important as with kin.

Using the information about the relative importance of kin, and further answers to questions about how close they were, we estimated that thirty-two percent of households had close kinship networks, fifteen percent had much interaction with kin, but did not see them as very close, and the rest did not rate their kinship networks very highly. In the 1987 survey, we asked questions about the meaning of kin and friendship networks. Four hypothetical situations were suggested in the interviews. We asked respondents whether they would rely on someone else, and on whom would that would be: first, if they were feeling depressed, second, if they needed someone to keep an eye on their house, third, if they needed to borrow money urgently, and fourth, if they needed help in finding a job, either for themselves or for one of the family. Their responses gave us an indication of the willingness to call on others. Almost all respondents said that they would rely on others to keep an eye on their house, and generally they would call on local friends rather than relatives. Some said both. On the other hand less that half said they would rely on either friends or relatives when it came to job hunting. Among those that did, in Willowby and Ashby, relatives would be more important, but in Oakton and Beechthorpe, friends would be chosen rather than relatives. If respondents were to feel depressed, four out of five would to turn to others for support, and generally they would choose relatives rather than friends, though not by a large margin. Again relatives were more important in Willowby and Ashby than in Oakton and

Table 5.27 The relative importance of kin and friends: when respondents need to rely on someone (A) to borrow money urgently and (B) to help find a job, 1987

(A) Need to borrow money urgently

Respondents:	Oakton %	Willowby %	Ashby %	Beechthorpe %
Would rely on someone	80	66	78	59
Would rely on local friends	11	16	13	11
Would rely on local relatives	48	48	63	36
N =	44	44	46	44

(B) Need help in finding a job for self or family

Respondents:	Oakton %	Willowby %	Ashby %	Beechthorpe %
Would rely on someone	48	47	40	39
Would rely on local friends	25	13	21	37
Would rely on local relatives	19	34	24	20
N =	48	32	42	41

Note: Respondents are heads of households, mainly males, and in some households no responses to the questions were given. Respondents were asked about friends and relatives separately, so that some said both or neither

Beechthorpe. About seven out of ten respondents would be willing to turn to someone if they were in need of money urgently. Here it was kin to whom they would turn in the majority of cases, in Ashby by a big majority, and in the other places somewhat less so. The data for the two situations in which most variability of response occurred is given in Table 5.27.

There is no strict comparability between our 1986 and 1987 data on relatives and friends. The data in Table 5.26 is based on men and women separately, but here in Table 5.27 we are showing data from heads of households, mainly men. There we were asking whom do you see most, and here on whom would you rely. Thus, not surprisingly, locality differences which we saw in 1986 were not entirely replicated. Generally, however, the importance of local social networks, particularly those based on kinship, is shown. There were few differences between respondents in mining and non-mining households, but respondents in mining households were much less likely to seek help where money was concerned, than those in non-mining households. Possibly this was related to the fact that many of them had already had to do this during the miners' strike of 1984/5. Kin were said to be much more important in supporting strikers than friends or neighbours during that year (see Chapter Seven, p. 192).

It is possible to overestimate the benefits of networks of kin and friends. Lydia Morris (1988) has summarised, as we indicated earlier, all the recent literature and research on the relations between employment, the household and social networks. As she has inferred, the effects of belonging to social networks are not unambiguously beneficial. There are costs as well as benefits. It is evident in our 1986 data that in the thirty-two percent of households with close kinship networks there is less sharing of domestic tasks between partners than in those where kin networks are less important. This was particularly the case with child care, where women did all or most of it in sixty-three percent of households with close-knit networks, compared with only forty percent of households with more loose-knit networks. This replicates Bott's main hypothesis that greater segregation of gender roles in the household occurs where partners are members of close-knit networks of kin (1957).

Our evidence is not entirely clear on the difference of meaning of traditional social networks to men and women. The ideal–typical construct of mining communities suggests that the segregation of men and women will extend to their membership of social networks. From our 1986 data, in Table 5.26, we might infer, in their lesser stress on kin, some tendency on the part of men to form networks through their employment which are not as fully shared with their partners. On the other hand, from the 1987 data, given in Table 5.27, it would seem to some extent to depend on the circumstances, as to whether men see kinfolk as crucial and call upon them for support.

The hypothesis that traditional social networks are strong in the coal-mining localities is not refuted, but it has to be modified to take account of the possibility that both men and women share their networks and see them as very important, depending on the situation.

There is again much support therefore for criticisms of the belief that, with the advance of modernity, traditional social networks would disappear. We have already indicated that other recent evidence gives weight to this criticism. We would suggest that the concern about families and kinship declining in Britain and the need for the strengthening of such bonds by legislative action, on the part of recent right-wing governments, has been exaggerated. The problem for contemporary social policy, which ought to be faced in the post-Thatcher era, is that of finding the right balance of emphasis on traditional social networks and not expecting them to do more for their members than their resources permit, while giving public agencies like education, health and social services appropriate government support and funding. The question should be, not what social networks do better, but what kind of society do we want to create. We seem to have been polarising our society and this has clearly affected our localities. This is a point to which we will return in Chapter Six.

Table 5.28 Respondents' expressed voting intentions, 1987

Percentages	Con	Lab	All	Other	D/K	N
Mining households	3.2	87.3	6.3	1.6	1.6	63
Non-mining households	18.6	52.3	20.9	1.2	7.0	86
All households	12.7	65.5	15.8	1.2	4.8	165
Oakton	18.2	45.5	25.0	–	11.4	44
Willowby	8.7	78.3	4.4	4.3	4.3	46
Ashby	11.1	72.2	14.0	–	2.8	36
Beechthorpe	12.8	66.7	20.6	–	–	39
1987 General Election result	17.2	67.0	15.8	–	–	(on a 76% poll)

Note: The respondents are men and women heads of households for whom complete data are available. There were no significant differences between men and women overall in their expressed voting intentions. The 1987 General Election result is that for the constituency in which the research area is situated

DISTINCTIONS BETWEEN MINING AND NON-MINING HOUSEHOLDS RECONSIDERED

Before that, let us come back to the similarities and differences between mining and non-mining households. In presenting the Tables above, illustrating some of the evidence already seen, it is clear that in some respects there is much overlap between the two sets of households. Each set is caught up within networks of interaction which will tend to draw them together within common cultural experiences. There are nevertheless variations which involvement in different occupational structures and localities may well explain. The different levels of agreement with the strike are an example (see Table 5.21). Another of a similar kind is exemplified by the intended voting patterns at the time of the 1987 General Election (Table 5.28).

Undoubtedly the differences between mining and non-mining households indicate quite strong variations in political consciousness, in so far as voting intentions can be said to refer to political consciousness. There are significant statistical differences in the distribution of intended votes between them. This is likely to relate strongly to the different occupational class composition of each set of households. As we have seen (Table 5.4) among the men in our mining household sample 8.6 percent are in the 'salariat', whereas in the non-mining household sample 19.2 percent of the men are in the 'salariat'. However, it will also relate to locality and political socialisation, as Heath, Jowell and Curtice show (1985).

We asked our respondents for information concerning their parents' voting

Table 5.29 Voting intentions of respondents compared with voting habits of their parents by localities, 1987

Percentages

	Con	Lab	All	Other	D/K	N
Oakton:						
Respondents	18.2	45.5	25.0	–	11.4	44
Fathers	14.6	62.5	2.1	4.2	16.7	48
Mothers	16.7	56.3	2.1	2.1	22.9	48
Willowby:						
Respondents	8.7	78.3	4.4	4.3	4.3	46
Fathers	6.3	68.8	–	2.1	23.0	48
Mothers	4.3	73.9	–	–	21.8	46
Ashby:						
Respondents	11.1	72.2	14.0	–	2.8	36
Fathers	7.0	81.4	2.3	–	9.3	43
Mothers	6.8	77.3	2.3	–	13.6	44
Beechthorpe:						
Respondents	12.8	66.7	20.6	–	–	39
Fathers	7.0	72.1	–	–	21.0	43
Mothers	12.5	65.0	2.5	–	20.0	40

Note: Some respondents refused to reveal their voting intention but were willing to suggest how their parents used to vote

habits. The distribution of these is shown in Table 5.29 with reference to localities.

If we can take these indications at face value, we can suggest that Oakton respondents have become slightly more Conservative, much more 'centrist' (Alliance or Liberal and Social Democrat supporters) and less Labour oriented than their parents. In Willowby, with slightly higher percentages not knowing their parents' voting habits, generalisation is a little hazardous, but respondents seem to vote somewhat more strongly for Labour than their parents. In Ashby and Beechthorpe, similar tendencies to those in Oakton have occurred though not as strongly. Ashby and Beechthorpe

Table 5.30 Class composition of the four research localities, based in the occupational status of male respondents, 1987

	Localities Percentages			
Class category	*Oakton*	*Willowby*	*Ashby*	*Beechthorpe*
Salariat	42.2	6.9	21.2	18.1
Intermediate	22.2	4.7	19.1	13.7
Working	31.1	51.1	31.0	40.9
Not employed	4.5	37.2	28.5	27.2
N =	45	43	42	44

respondents still seem quite strongly oriented to Labour, but not as strongly as their parents seem to have been. In Willowby, the locality which has the highest proportion of mining households, we see the strongest commitment to Labour. Ashby and Beechthorpe have seen large reductions in the proportion of mining households, and this to some extent correlates with the inter-generational decline in Labour's strength. Oakton's more middle-class population was socialised by parents who themselves were more Conservative than those elsewhere.

As we have said, locality effects on voting are acknowledged by Heath, Jowell and Curtice (1985), but they argue that this is largely explainable in terms of the class composition of the locality. Taking our male respondents in 1987, Table 5.30 indicates the class composition of the localities, using the four-fold division into 'salariat', 'intermediate', 'working' and 'not employed' categories, described above (see note to Table 5.13).

This is not an entirely adequate way of characterising the class composition of the four localities, because it overlooks the twenty-six single women, whose responses with regard to voting intention are partially included in the heads of household data in Tables 5.28 and 5.29. If, however, we take the above as an indication of the differences between the localities, then some of the variation in voting intention or political consciousness is clearly attributable to the class character of each locality. Willowby, with the highest percentage of working-class and not-employed males, has the highest support for Labour, and Oakton with lowest percentage of working-class and not-employed males, offers the lowest support for Labour. The differences between Ashby and Beechthorpe in support for Labour are not related to their class composition.

Thus we would argue that the situation of households by locality has some effect on their social and political orientations. Taken as a whole, mining households are different from non-mining households in respect of security of employment and occupational status, and this has some consequences for their income, standard of living and social and political outlook. Further, they tend to be concentrated spatially in ways which will add to the differences. We find a large group of non-mining households in Oakton, which is predominantly middle class, and the high concentration of mining households in Willowby occurs in a predominantly working-class locality. That said, there are many aspects of non-mining and mining households which are shared, such as similar patterns in the domestic division of labour, in decision-making, in women's wish for and entrance into paid employment, in cultural pursuits and in involvement in social networks.

In general there are clear grounds for updating our understanding of mining communities, their households and the gender relations within them. It would seem that Bulmer's (1975a) ideal–typical model of the traditional mining community is not a very adequate guide to the contemporary reality of the localities which we have researched.

CONCLUSION

This chapter has focussed on four localities in the West Yorkshire coalfield, in which jobs in the mining industry were reduced from seven thousand in 1982 to four thousand in 1986 (O'Donnell, 1988). Since then there have been even further reductions, so that there are less than two thousand jobs now. There are differences between our localities in the proportion of households which have ever been involved in the mining industry. Oakton has a small set of mining households (twenty-two percent), but it is also characterised by a larger group of middle-class households (forty-two percent) where one member, a male, at least had high status employment in administration, management or the professions. In three of them (Willowby, Ashby and Beechthorpe) nearly fifty percent could be categorised as mining households in 1986. Only one, Willowby, had more than half its households which could be classed as mining households by 1987. Unemployment was well above the national average in mining households, and in Willowby in all households. Mean net annual income was below £7500 in all but Oakton.

We have also shown that we must update the sociological interpretation of gender relations and the domestic division of labour both in mining and non-mining households. There is no strict segregation of roles in such households, but male dominance still exists, even if it is not accompanied by the necessity for women to be completely imprisoned in the household. Women do participate in the labour market, though the opportunities vary from one locality to another. Furthermore, the opportunities for and constraints on paid employment for women in partnership households are very much related to the occupational status of their male partners. The chances of a woman having paid employment, both in mining and non-mining households, are highest if her partner is in the salariat. They are lowest if the partner is unemployed or not in employment. Where women are in full-time paid employment, there is some indication that domestic work is more evenly shared, than where they are not employed.

Our research has enabled an exploration of significant social and cultural aspects of change in four mining localities, which are rapidly being consigned to historical memory as centres of primary production of coal on which previously Britain's industrial power had rested. The bases of 'solidarity' and 'segregation' in our mining localities are probably much more complex than they were in the 1950s. The sense of class consciousness and its significance is different from that which obtained when *Coal is Our Life* was written.

Changes under way in the coal industry and in the economic structure of Britain when that book was written have obviously had a major impact on 'occupational' communities such as those which were situated in the coalfield of West Yorkshire. The ideal–typical model of the traditional mining community which was formulated as a basis for that research recalls social processes and institutions which are now more a memory than a reality.

Nevertheless, there are still many echoes of those processes and institutions formed at the height of the capitalist exploitation of coal seams, and these are part of the cultural capital of our research localities.

None of the localities is any longer a single-industry community, though Willowby is perhaps the nearest to having survived as such. There is still a sense in which the industry and its division of labour casts a long shadow over the localities, through the mining households, where men over fifty are largely redundant, and sometimes without skills to enable easy moves to other forms of employment. The local culture is still very much that which was shaped when the mining industry was more salient than now.

There is still a strong tendency to support the labour movement and there are still many reasons for political action to improve public facilities, health and education in the search for increased quality of living. The gregarious sociability of the old pit villages is still remembered and enjoyed in the contemporary pubs and clubs. Professional and amateur sport, gardening and the keeping of pigeons and animals in allotments are still the focus of much male leisure activity. There is, however, much evidence of the penetration of a mass culture generated elsewhere, and the privatisation of entertainment through television and video viewing which has reduced participation in local social activities like church and chapel going, brass bands and other musical activities. There is a domestic division of labour which carries memories of the old male dominance, and changes still have not led very far down the road of gender equality in the home or in paid employment. Traditional social networks linking households with kin, friends and neighbours, provide resources and constraints in a manner not unlike those of earlier communities, and a basis around which community identity is still maintained. The sense of the 'friendly' village or town is celebrated in numerous conversations wherever the researchers have gone, though not all are willing to concur.

The mining localities have changed, and if there is any wide sense of isolation it is different. The stigma attached to the dirt and smokiness of a mining community is still felt, even though it is now caused by open-cast working rather than deep mined shale heaps and coke ovens. This produces a reaction in locals not unlike that which their predecessors felt, when cut off from urban markets and services, in the days before extensive development of public and private transport. Predominantly, however, the extension of state and local authority services, some welcomed, others decried, some fought for and others resisted, has subjected the mining localities to networks and relationships which have reduced the independence and self-management of individuals, primary groups and associations, even if at the same time they have widened for some the possibilities of more affluent living.

If there is still some sense of two worlds, it is perhaps no longer just one for men and another for women, but one for the securely employed and one for the not securely employed and those without employment. Again this is not a rigid division, but there is some evidence that this has a locality dimension with the concentration of less secure employment and unemployment in Willowby and of more secure and high status employment in Oakton. In Chapter Six we look at this situation, and consider whether this is the most prominent polarity in our localities. We shall do this with reference to state and local authority services, education and health. They are parts of the web, perhaps the most significant parts, of support to citizens in order to overcome the divisions which seem to exist.

Chapter 6

Contemporary social divisions
Tenure, education, health and social polarisation

INTRODUCTION

We have reached the point of recognising that our four localities have virtually passed through a phase of domination by the mining industry. The collective memory of being mining localities is very strong and there are still mineworkers. Two pits still have a tenuous existence, and the mining industry still offers more jobs than any other single organisation, in Willowby, Ashby and Beechthorpe. Their number, however, is declining. We have seen, too, that while paid employment in numerical terms had not declined in the District as a whole in the first half of the 1980s, new jobs were either in construction or in professional services. The construction industry has been recently very much hit by high interest and mortgage rates, and jobs therefore have been in jeopardy. For some skilled and most unskilled manual workers there has been very much more difficulty in finding new paid employment, even though the Wakefield District Council, through its Economic Development Unit, has encouraged the setting up of new enterprises to use such labour. There are several sites within the research area where new industrial and commercial buildings have been built, but they do not provide enough employment to provide work for all who are unemployed and seeking work. New forms of training are available, and a Resources Centre has been set up to give people the chance to try out new economic activities. These do not create employment on the scale that the old industry did.

This seems to have consequent effects in our localities. Secure and well-paid employment is increasingly the preserve of well-qualified and skilled persons. For a large minority, which has grown in size in the 1980s, unemployment and insecurity are much more salient. This is tending to be the most significant basis of social divisions in our localities, and it links with the findings of sociology in Britain and other old industrial societies during the last decade, that tendencies to social polarisation have been reinforced. This results in a relatively distinct spatial division of labour, in a spatial distribution of disadvantage and in the possible creation of an 'underclass' of citizens who have much less than a fair share of opportunities and quality of life than ought to be their reasonable expectation.

In focussing on the needs of Urban Priority Areas, the Archbishop of Canterbury's Commission Report, *Faith in the City*, (1985) noted that

> [T]he process of polarisation is a general one in Britain today . . . [It] divides the UPAs from the rest of Britain [and] it involves a triple process of decision: by individuals competing for advantages in jobs, housing, schools and services; by governments offering mortgage relief [to owner occupiers] and witholding investment from blighted districts; and by enterprises rationally investing where consumer power is greatest and growing.
>
> (1985: 23–4)

The report also added that 'the poor are not confined to the urban priority areas; poverty reflects the structural inequality of the nation. . .' Indeed this general fact was noted and amplified in a paper by Goldthorpe and Payne (1986), using data from studies of social mobility in their 1972 and 1983 surveys. They were in fact arguing that their data refuted the claims of 'labour process' theorists such as Braverman (1974) and Zimbalist (1979) that polarisation was a result of the 'deskilling' of labour within the capitalist organisation of production, and that

> the return of large-scale and long term unemployment [has created] new risks . . . of downward mobility into a condition of serious social deprivation . . . [This is because of] the elimination of work opportunities of any kind for large numbers of the active population, heavily concentrated among those who had previously been within the ranks of manual wage-earners.
>
> (Goldthorpe and Payne, 1986)

This general condition is sometimes discussed in terms of an 'underclass', a concept which seems to have arisen from studies of the condition of the urban poor and ethnic minorities in American cities (Dahrendorf, 1987). Meegan (1989) uses it, for instance, in his study of Merseyside's outer estates, where he says:

> Such a class is generally distinguished by its experience of a combination of various forms of disadvantage – unemployment, poverty, low levels of education and literacy, 'unstable domestic circumstances' – and its inability to cope with this situation.
>
> (Meegan, 1989: 225)

He also notes that there are signs that 'if an "underclass" is being formed in these areas it is not without a substantial degree of resistance', and traces such resistance to tactics and strategies of community organisations based in social networks in the estate localities (ibid.).

Townsend, Davidson and Whitehead (1988) have also noted that the disadvantaging extends very clearly to health. They note:

> Striking regional disparities in health can still be observed. Death rates were highest in Scotland, followed by the North and North-West regions of England, and were lowest in the South-East of England and East Anglia, confirming the long-established North/South gradient. What is becoming increasingly clear from fresh evidence, though, is the great inequalities which exist between communities living side by side in the same region. Numerous studies at the level of local authority wards have pinpointed pockets of very poor health corresponding to areas of social and material deprivation.
>
> (Townsend et al., 1988: 352)

We have found the same situation in our localities, in which there are contrasts, as we have already indicated, between Oakton and Willowby.

In this chapter we wish to underscore this feature of the internal polarisation of mining localities, as an example of the new forms of social closure and differentiation which are occurring in contemporary Britain and elsewhere. It is not that we disagree with the sense of polarisation which is captured in the notion of the North/South divide. As Smith (1989) says:

> there are prosperous areas and towns in the North, and disadvantaged parts of the South . . . just as there are places of considerable opulence and prosperity in otherwise poor countries such as India. But the fact remains that there must be something about the South which results in it having more than its fair share of thriving towns and well-to-do individuals.
>
> (Smith, 1989: 5–6)

As anyone who travels through our area on an Inter-City express will note, and it is usually unavoidable because trains on the main line just south east of Wakefield are frequently slowed down because of land subsidence caused by earlier mining, there is a vast difference in the look of it compared to that from Grantham southwards. Spatial differences between North and South Britain are very clear. Our research area is very firmly part of the North, and even though the image is perhaps softened by the recent closure of pits and the highly subsidised farming which occupies part of the unbuilt landscape, a look at the domestic, industrial and public architecture will soon convince the sceptic of our point.

We will first attempt to provide data with which to evaluate the contention that polarisation is affecting the four localities. Then we will examine fields in which the relative deprivation of some of our localities is very clear, namely education and health.

Table 6.1 Occupational classification of men and women in four West Yorkshire
           localities, 1987

Occupational class	Oakton		Willowby		Ashby		Beechthorpe	
	% Men	% Women	% Men	% Women	% Men	% Women	% Men	% Women
Salariat	42	31	7	8	22	15	18	19
Intermediate	22	20	5	6	19	19	14	23
Working	31	13	51	29	31	26	41	23
Non-employed	0	33	7	48	10	38	9	34
Un-employed	4	2	30	8	19	2	18	0
N =	45	45	43	48	42	47	44	47

FOUR MINING LOCALITIES: EVIDENCE OF POLARISATION

We have already presented evidence of variation in the four localities on the
basis of census data from 1981 and survey data from 1986 and 1987. There
is a general description of this information in Chapter Four, some references
to the four localities in Chapters Five and Seven. In 1989 we attempted
to contact each of the households which were interviewed in our 1987
survey with a much shorter schedule, containing questions about economic
situation, smoking and health. The hope was not only to replicate certain
items in the 1987 schedule, but to add objective test data on respiratory
symptoms to more subjective responses which we had obtained in 1987.
There was a high refusal rate. Only ninety-three households out of the two
hundred were contacted and willing to be interviewed again. The reliability of
the responses is questionable, simply because of the refusals, but we present
some of the data from the 1989 survey in this chapter where it adds to the
data series.

The class status of households in the four localities indicated by the
occupational classification of the males was given in Table 5.30 in the
previous chapter. In Table 6.1 we add the classification of the women's
occupations for each of the localities.

The classification follows the definitions of occupational class which we
indicated above in Chapter Five. We have included in the salariat a small
number of employers, who strictly speaking may not be paying themselves
a salary. The differences between localities are statistically significant, and
of course this is accounted for by the strong variations between Oakton
and Willowby, with Ashby and Beechthorpe taking middle positions. We
can compare the distribution with that given for social classes using the
Registrar General's categories in the 1981 Census. That is based entirely
on heads of households, which includes some single women, and is not
strictly comparable with our information for men and women separately.
However, it is very clear that the differences which we have found in

Table 6.2 Localities and the not-employed men and women, 1981 to 1987

| | Oakton | | Willowby | | Ashby | | Beechthorpe | |
	Men %	Women %	Men %	Women %	Men %	Women %	Men %	Women %
1981 Census	13	46	27	54	19	47	24	52
1986 survey	10	46	59	64	34	31	38	50
1987 survey	4	35	37	56	29	40	27	34

Note: The 'not employed' includes all who are not in paid employment whether defined unemployed, non-employed or sick and disabled, and men and women of every marital status. The data for 1981 refer to those aged sixteen to sixty-four, and are from OPCS (1984). The 1986 survey includes data on sixteen to sixty-four-year-old members of one hundred and twenty-four households. That for 1987 covers all twenty to sixty-four-year-old respondents and partners in two hundred households

our 1987 survey were already to some extent in place in 1981. Oakton had twenty-eight percent of heads of household in the Registrar General's classes I and II, Willowby had seven percent, Ashby, sixteen percent and Beechthorpe, thirteen percent. Given the possible errors of estimation from our small sample, it is probable that we can assume that there has been little change in the position of the salariat as a proportion of the employed in our four localities. The changes that are indicated, that is a probable increase in the proportion of the employed in salaried jobs in Oakton, Ashby and Beechthorpe, are in line with the increase in jobs in professional services which has occurred in the Wakefield District in the 1980s.

It is when we compare the situations in the localities with regard to those not in paid employment that evidence of change appears. Table 6.2 above, by comparing the 1981 Census data for the non-employed and unemployed men and women, shows fairly clear indications, despite the relatively small samples in our 1986 and 1987 surveys, and despite the general problems of unemployment which increased between 1981 and 1986 both locally and nationally, that the proportion of those not employed in Oakton has declined, while that in Willowby has increased. The situation of men in the three localities which had most mining households, Willowby, Ashby and Beechthorpe, in terms of unemployment and non-employment, has perhaps improved since 1986, but not to the levels of 1981.

It would thus seem more than possible that there has been a growing proportion of disadvantaged persons in Willowby, even given the slight improvement between 1986 and 1987, while the opposite is the case in Oakton. In Ashby and Beechthorpe the situation of men and women has varied. That for men has got worse, while for women it may have improved. We can assume that this largely relates to the incidence of unemployment since 1980 with the closure of pits, but we have already noted that Ashby and Beechthorpe have suffered as much, if not more, decline than Willowby in this respect (see Table 5.1). Ashby and Beechthorpe, however, are nearer

Table 6.3 Comparison of household financial situation in four localities, 1987 and 1989

	Oakton		Willowby		Ashby		Beechthorpe		All	
	A	B	A	B	A	B	A	B	A	B
	%	%	%	%	%	%	%	%	%	%
A lot better	28	27	4	4	17	16	11	12	15	14
A little better	32	41	18	30	30	37	36	24	29	32
Much the same	26	9	47	26	24	26	30	40	31	26
A little worse	13	23	20	22	9	16	15	20	14	20
A lot worse	2	0	10	19	20	5	9	4	10	8
N =	47	22	49	27	46	19	47	25	189	93

Note: A is the comparison made by respondents between 1987 and their financial position in 1986; B their comparison between 1989 and 1988

to some of the new developments undertaken by the local authority, and this may well have contributed to the higher levels of employment than is the case in Willowby. What we said in Chapter Five about women's employment, however, should caution us. Women tend to have a more variable work history than men. They change from non-employment to employment relatively frequently, and much of their employment is either temporary or part time. A higher level of employment among women, especially in manual work, is not likely to bring significant improvements in households where the men have become unemployed or non-employed. This constitutes the first, very tentative, evidence that polarisation is occurring in our localities.

Further evidence comes from comparing our 1987 and 1989 data which comes from asking respondents about their financial position compared with a year earlier. Relative household income levels in the four localities, were shown in Table 4.2. Willowby had more than three-quarters of its households with less than the national average household income at that time, Beechthorpe was close to that and Ashby had two-thirds of its households at that level. Further, a third or more of the households only had half the national average income level. Ashby had a slightly higher proportion at this level (thirty-five percent) than Willowby (thirty percent). Beechthorpe had twenty-five percent of its households at less than half the national average income and Oakton had only eleven percent. We have no comparison with earlier years in the decade, since this data was only collected in 1987.

We asked in 1987, and again in 1989, about whether they felt worse or better off than a year previously, and these subjective responses have been summarised in Table 6.3.

The differences in the distribution of responses for 1987 across the four localities are statistically significant at the ninety-nine percent probability level, and approach the ninety percent level in 1989. The 1987 information relates to the years immediately after the miners' strike. The highest proportions of those worse off are in the localities which had the highest number of mining households, with Ashby having the highest proportion of those feeling a lot worse off, but Willowby again somewhat higher if we include both those a little, as well as a lot worse off. By 1989, Willowby has a much higher proportion in both categories than the others. Interestingly, Oakton, the locality which has fewest households in the lower income ranges, nevertheless has an increased percentage in the feeling worse off category. We can only speculate on this, but it could be problems related to mortgage interest repayments. In 1989, only one of the respondents in Oakton was a tenant. There have been increasing problems concerned with repayments since the housing price boom in 1988 and the increasing levels of interest on loans. This could account for some of the sense of being worse off across the localities, given that there has been an increase in owner-occupiers and a corresponding decline in tenant householders.

We will return to the question of tenure, for this seems perhaps the most significant indicator across the localities of the difference between the relatively secure and insecure, but it is interesting to note first the variation in coping strategies. In 1987 we also asked a question about making ends meet. Twenty-eight percent of all respondents said that they were currently finding it quite or very difficult to do this. The differences between the localities were very close to being statistically significant at the ninety-five percent level. The contrasts were between Oakton on the one hand with only seventeen percent experiencing problems, and the other three localities, with Beechthorpe and Willowby having a third or more of their households in difficulty. Their coping strategies varied from ones that would cause, perhaps, the least difficulty, such as going out less and not going on holiday, which were the most frequently mentioned, to actions which clearly might create much more household conflict and even stigma, such as going into debt and borrowing money. Seventeen percent of all respondents said that they had got into debt, but Willowby households were much more likely to mention this than those in the other localities, with twenty-seven percent there compared to fifteen percent or less in the others. Sixty-three percent of households in Willowby said that they had given up plans for going on holiday, compared with forty percent or less in the other places. This adds up to a conclusion that households in Willowby were very much more likely to be experiencing frustrating social conditions than those in Oakton, and even in Ashby and Beechthorpe, which on some indicators are not much more disadvantaged.

Whether the term 'polarisation' actually captures this locality variation adequately is perhaps disputable, but it is clear that even within our research area, there is some tendency for the social differences which have been there through the decade, to have been strongly reinforced. It is likely that the citizens of Willowby sense a considerable degree of enclosure within a locality where many expectations of citizenship, particularly the right to work and to share a reasonable quality of life, are not adequately met.

This was the locality in which one of our interviewers was told, when yet another refusal to grant a two-hour interview was given, 'Now you know what a closed community is.' The sense of closure may also have been reinforced by the new house builder who, having erected and sold a set of about twenty small dwelling houses in the middle of Willowby in 1987, then built a high wooden fence around the estate, which more or less prevents visual communication either way, inwards or outwards.

TENANTS AND OWNER-OCCUPIERS: INDICATORS OF SOCIAL INEQUALITY

If there is any clear indicator in our localities of the locus of disadvantaging social conditions, it is that of house tenure. It is likely, too, that this has become even more apparent as the policy of selling-off tenancies to occupiers continues to take its effect, and local authorities are prevented by government policy from undertaking new house building, despite a growing shortage of accommodation. Using the 1981 census and our recent surveys, we illustrate the change in Table 6.4.

It is possibly a little accidental, given the relatively small samples of households in each locality in 1986, 1987 and 1989, that there is such relative co-linearity about Table 6.4. Yet the situation is that there has been an increase in owner-occupier households and a decrease in tenant households. There are still variations between the localities, which in fact correspond to the differences which existed at the beginning of the decade. Willowby remains the locality with the largest proportion of tenants, and Oakton the one with the least.

In terms of conditions such as employment, income, and health, we have seen particularly in the 1987 survey, confirmed again by our smaller survey in 1989, that there are statistically significant differences between owner-occupiers and tenants. Those who remain tenants, with some exceptions, are likely to be among the poorest and most disadvantaged households. Among the one hundred and ninety-one householders for whom complete details were available from their responses to our 1987 interview schedule, two-thirds of the owner-occupiers and only two-fifths of the tenants were in full-time employment. Nine percent of the owner-occupiers were unemployed compared with twenty-eight percent of tenants. In our 1989 survey, again nine percent of owner-occupiers were unemployed, but forty-five percent of tenants said they were. (Even if there were some problems of reliability with that survey data, because of non-response, this still marks out a significant difference.) Ten percent of tenants in 1987, but only four percent of owner-occupiers, were permanently sick and disabled. Among male tenants twenty-nine percent reported bad respiratory symptoms, compared with twelve percent of males in owner-occupier households. Women reported lower incidence of such

Table 6.4 Changes in house tenure in four localities, 1981 to 1989

		1981 %	1986 %	1987 %	1989 %
Oakton	Owner-occupiers	67	83	83	96
	Tenants	33	17	17	4
Willowby	Owner-occupiers	17	47	58	63
	Tenants	83	53	42	37
Ashby	Owner-occupiers	42	45	67	68
	Tenants	58	55	33	32
Beechthorpe	Owner-occupiers	51	73	75	84
	Tenants	49	27	25	16
All	Owner-occupiers	49	62	71	77
	Tenants	51	38	29	23

Note: The 1981 data is taken from 'Key Statistics for Urban Areas: The North', Census 1981, Office of Population Surveys. The rest is from research surveys, already described, in the localities

symptoms, but among tenants twice as many as among owner-occupiers reported them.

Among tenants in 1987, household income was significantly lower than among owner-occupiers. Only thirteen percent of tenant households, compared with forty-five percent of the others, had more than the national average household income of £850 per month. Thirty-nine percent of tenants had less than half the national average, roughly twice the proportion found among owner-occupiers. They also were much more likely to feel that they were less well off than they had been a year before – forty-two percent compared with fifteen percent of owner-occupiers. (There was an increase in the proportion saying that they felt worse off in 1989 than they had been a year earlier, and this applied to both tenants and owner-occupiers, although there were proportionately twice as many tenants as owner-occupiers feeling worse off. This corroborates our earlier remarks about the impact of interest rates.) This sense of relative dissatisfaction was confirmed when we asked them for their feelings concerning the level of pay they received in employment. Only nine percent of tenants, as against thirty-two percent of owner-occupiers, declared themselves satisfied with their pay. Tenants and their partners tended to be slightly older than the others, so that their relative poverty could not be ascribed to position in the life cycle. Younger householders have more expenses, especially with children, than their older counterparts. Tenants were, however, much more often in single households, thirty-six percent compared with only nine percent of owner-occupiers. Associated with this, owner-occupiers were significantly more likely to be married with a partner than tenants. Thirty-eight percent of tenants were single, widowed, separated or divorced compared with fifteen percent of owner occupiers.

There are distinct differences of outlook between householders in these two categories. Among males, tenants claimed to be Labour Party supporters significantly more than owner occupiers (eighty-three percent to fifty-six percent) and this was very much the position among women. Yet there was little support for the idea that this was a consequence of political socialisation in their family of origin. Both categories suggested that about sixty percent of their fathers had voted Labour, and about sixty-five percent of their mothers. Respondents who said that they had Conservative parents were relatively few (just over ten percent), but they were more likely to be claimed by owner-occupiers than tenants. It would seem that apart from the fact that all these voters tend to live in localities within a Labour held constituency, the significant differences have to be explained in terms of shifts of outlook related to the form of house tenure which they choose or are constrained to take up. (This would seem to confirm the predicted electoral outcome of a policy of selling off Council houses claimed by the Conservative Party.)

In addition to differences of political outlook, tenants and owner-occupiers tended to be significantly different on their views of where government might increase its expenditure, particularly, and not surprisingly, on council housing and unemployment benefit. Tenants expressed themselves significantly more vehemently with regard to the treatment given to Supplementary Benefit Claimants, the amount they received and the length of time they were made to wait. The self-image of some tenants also tended to be much less positive than that of owner-occupiers. Thirty-five percent of male tenants said that they felt respected by others in their locality compared with sixty-two percent of owner-occupiers.

On the other hand, there were some issues where differences within the categories were more significant than between them. For instance on an indicator of racism, based on their attitudes to increasing financial help given by government to ethnic minorities, both sets were polarised between support and dissent. The tenants were more likely to express strong support or strong dissent than owner-occupiers. There were also within-group differences on the National Health Service. On treatment by General Practitioners, about one in six of both tenants and owner-occupiers was dissatisfied, but a half of both expressed satisfaction. Similarly, when being treated at hospitals as outpatients there is general satisfaction with the medical care, but one in five of both categories is dissatisfied with the time they had to wait, compared with one in four who was satisfied.

Tenants and owner-occupiers, however, do have significant differences

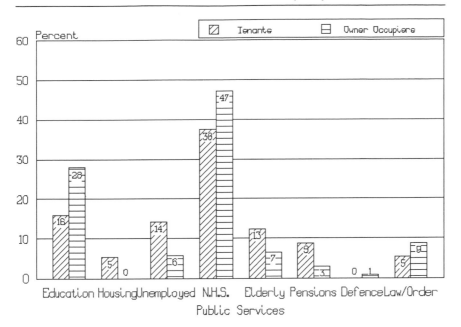

Figure 6.1 Priorities in government spending, 1987 survey: tenants and owner-occupiers

when it comes to their views on the priorities which government ought to place on services in the locality. Their rank ordering of priorities does not look very different. Both put the National Health Service first, followed by education. Both would give some priority to spending on the elderly and on unemployment benefit, but it is the proportions supporting particular public services which vary significantly. Owner-occupiers would put more emphasis on 'law and order', the National Health Service and education, than the tenants who give much more support to housing, unemployment benefit, the elderly and pensions. Figure 6.1 indicates these differences.

A majority in both sets agrees that if the government is to spend more, it should increase tax on the 'rich' and reduce expenditure on 'defence'. Neither set wishes to have government support given to private education or private health schemes, but the owner-occupiers are less likely to oppose it than the tenants (sixty percent oppose government support, compared with seventy percent of tenants). In these respects there is a strong element of anti-Thatcherism among all our respondents, and this presumably relates to their sense of justice living in an area which has more than its fair share of disadvantage. Public services are still seen to be the major means of resolving social and individual problems. This accords with more general surveys of opinion such as the *British Social Attitudes* reports, which have shown since

1983 that support for collectively organised welfare services, particularly health and education, has grown (Jenkins, 1990).

Let us now focus on how far two of these services, education and health, have impinged on the mining localities.

EDUCATION

The research area was served by the West Riding County Council as far as educational provision was concerned from the end of the nineteenth century until 1974. A major reorganisation of local government in that year abolished the West Riding and set up the Wakefield Metropolitan District Council as the local education authority. Prior to the 1944 Education Act, the area was served by a number of elementary schools, many of which were voluntary aided or controlled, that is managed to some extent by the churches. Many of these were built in the nineteenth century as deep mining extended into the area and population grew. They tended to provide schooling either for infants to the age of seven, or juniors to the age of eleven. A smaller number of larger schools in each locality provided some education up to the age of fourteen which was the statutory school leaving age. Secondary education to the age of sixteen and beyond was offered only in grammar schools to fee payers and County scholarship holders, and there was only one grammar school, in the centre of the area. Otherwise, children who passed their scholarship examination at the age of eleven had to travel to the secondary schools in towns like Wakefield, Normanton and Pontefract, which were outside the area. Few could afford grammar school fees. (This has been mentioned above in the biographical summaries of respondents in Ashby.) There was one mixed independent school in the area, which provided secondary education for day pupils and boarders, but again few local pupils found their way there because of the necessity to pay fees. Technical education was also only available outside the area at Whitwood and Wakefield, or to the south and east, at Barnsley and Doncaster.

Some of the meaning of the early twentieth-century educational provision to people living in our mining localities has been gained from a small number of interviews on childhood experience in part of the research area, near to and in Willowby. Members of a Workers' Educational Association class in the area in 1986 and 1987 were asked to undertake such interviews with elderly relatives or friends. Five such interviews were completed. They covered size and membership of households and kinship in the locality, arrangements for the birth and rearing of infants, the transition from infancy to childhood and going to school, school experiences at junior and senior level and other aspects of childhood socialisation. The responses on schooling, though few, are relatively consistent. Teachers were expected to be tough, school buildings were somewhat austere, lessons were taken as serious parts of life, playtimes could be anything from a great relief to a repetitive trial, when children worked off their energies and could hurt one another, and above all 'success', seen as passing a scholarship to a grammar school, was not expected. The following seemed typical:

> The teachers were very strict and always seemed to be old. We sat two to a desk, the rooms had large high windows, the walls were panelled halfway, and the paintwork was brown. The teacher's desk and chair were very high and not on the same level as our own. I liked needlework, but not maths, geography and history. We had games, netball and rounders. At playtimes girls were separate to the boys, and we played skipping, buttons and hopscotch. There was not much naughtiness or fighting. There were epidemics most years. My brother got scarlet fever and had to go to the isolation hospital. We all had to leave the house while it was stoved; it smelled terrible and we went to the bull fields to play while it was done. Boys and girls weren't treated differently at school. If a girl did anything wrong, she was caned. I never did the scholarship examination.
>
> When I went to senior school, the teachers were very strict and it was much the same. The cane was used as punishment. No-one dared to play truant or smoke. We still had games. I can't say my school years were a pleasure. I was glad to leave.
>
> (L.F. born 1920, a miner's daughter, lived in Willowby).

Two of the five respondents took the scholarship examination but did not pass. Generally the experience of school was not hated but seen as largely irrelevant because it was a competition in which they were not expected to succeed. One respondent, a man born in 1920 and son of a local butcher, said that he 'was grateful for the character building', which was no doubt one of the justifications used by the teachers for their work with him. Like many others he could remember them very well.

Provision of secondary education without payment of fees was the achievement of the 1944 Act. The West Riding increased the provision of scholarship places, but no new grammar schools were provided in the area. Some schools were renamed Secondary Modern Schools, and pupils followed secondary courses to the age of fifteen, which became the statutory leaving age after the Act in 1947. In the 1950s it was quickly becoming apparent throughout the whole country that fewer pupils were attaining educational credentials after secondary education than had been anticipated, following the 1944 reform. Some reform of the examination system took place, but it was a report commissioned by the Minister of Education in 1954 from the Central Advisory Council for Education on *Early Leaving* which led to more important changes (Minister of Education, 1954). This revealed that working-class pupils were far more likely than middle-class pupils to leave secondary courses as soon as they possibly could, and therefore not attempt examination courses. It was also shown that leaving was not always related to lack of educational ability. A whole series of research programmes began to look at the social and psychological components of what came to be known as wastage of ability (see for instance Halsey, Floud and Anderson, 1961). The key to altering the situation was thought by many to be the introduction of non-selective secondary education, by allowing pupils to transfer from what was now called the primary education stage to the secondary stage without the barrier of tests at the age of eleven. Instead of different types of secondary school, grammar, technical and modern, there were to be comprehensive schools. It was a strongly contested idea, however, and there were many long debates before reorganisation of secondary schools took place in local authorities.

In a memorandum to members of the West Riding Education Committee in 1958, Sir Alec Clegg, West Riding's Chief Education Officer wrote,

> In the last forty years, vast new industries have arisen . . . which have to be manned and serviced by people who are much more highly trained than those who manned the nineteenth century economy. In these circumstances, it appears to be the height of folly to waste ability as we are wasting it in South Yorkshire.

(Hargreaves, 1986)

This was argued after a survey of comparative educational achievement in the northern and southern parts of the West Riding, which showed that children in the coalfield areas of the southern part were achieving well below their potential. Reform in school organisation towards a non-selective secondary comprehensive system was offered and eventually agreed to be the key to changing this situation. Within the research area this eventually arrived in the late 1960s, with the opening of a new large high school near Beechthorpe, with the changing of the one grammar school to be a comprehensive school and with the eventual provision of another high school in Ashby in the 1970s. They took pupils at thirteen from feeder schools called middle schools which catered for the nine to thirteen age group, and these in turn provided entry for children from first schools which dealt with the five to nine-year-olds. This involved some new buildings, but more often the transformation of existing schools, to fit the new types. One voluntary secondary school remained outside this local authority reorganisation, as did the independent school.

Pupils were able to follow the whole of their education in schools more or less within the localities up to the age of sixteen, which became the statutory leaving age in 1972. Two of the high schools provided courses beyond sixteen. School buildings, old or new, were brightened up considerably during the 1960s. By this time, the old two-seater desks had been removed and tables and chairs introduced. A more relaxed atmosphere was encouraged, if not always achieved, and younger teachers were trained in colleges and university departments of education, which for a time espoused 'progressive' methods, despite the continued criticism of traditionalists. The transition to comprehensive secondary schooling was argued as a 'progressive' revolution which required new approaches from teachers and a school environment to match. Pupils and students were not simply to be seen as receptacles into which knowledge had to be poured, but encouraged to be willing and self-directed learners starting on education for life. Teachers should be communicators and not mere controllers. The West Riding was a local education authority which was reputedly very much in the van of such thinking as a consequence of Sir Alec Clegg's professional leadership (see Hargreaves, 1986; Clegg, 1974).

The system has been transformed again, however, since the abolition of the West Riding County Council. A decline in child population in some of the area and in the Wakefield District generally in the 1980s has led to the abandonment of the middle school stage and a return to the primary/secondary split, though without selection. Some redundant schools have been converted to other uses, such as the Resources Centre, which is sited not far from Beechthorpe. The provision of post-sixteen education is being increasingly transferred to what is called a 'Tertiary College', which is centrally organised in Wakefield, but with 'out-stations', one of which is located in our research area.

The research we have undertaken allows us to make some comments on whether Sir Alec Clegg's hopes for a reduction in the wastage of ability and an increased evaluation of education as a significant part of life for all, not just the middle class, in the coal-mining localities have been fulfilled. In 1979 one of our colleagues undertook a number of interviews with twenty male secondary school leavers in Ashby and, for comparison, with thirteen boys in the same sixteen-year-old age group in the High School of a neighbouring village just outside our research area, also a mining locality. In each group the respondents were chosen to reflect the spread of educational achievement at that stage. There were no significant differences between the two groups. School and locality differences did not seem to be marked. The neighbouring village had become more suburbanised than Ashby had done, and the sense of it being a mining locality had weakened as the local pit was about to be closed. Ashby at this time was still very much dominated by its local pits. We were able to follow up the group interviewed at Ashby during 1984, with the help of one of the teachers at Ashby High School, who was also a member of a WEA class. The original interview covered likely job or course after leaving school, the qualities and achievements thought likely to aid success in employment and life generally, class and political consciousness, attitudes to violence, race relations, the mass media, their own education and their locality. In the follow-up we asked about employment and the school gave us the results of any secondary examinations which they had taken.

Of the twenty school leavers in Ashby, a half thought that they would find jobs in mining and seven of the others thought they would do some form of manual work. They were asked to rank education, ambition, intelligence, effort, knowing the right people, personal character, social background and luck as aids to success in employment. Education with six first choices, ambition with five and intelligence with four, were put above all the others and social background, in terms of parents class or status, was hardly ranked as important. Counting second choices, ambition seemed slightly more important overall to respondents than education. Most were willing to talk about social class, though they were very vague about how to define working, middle and upper class. There was a tendency to treat money as the guide, and some seemed to believe that miners' wages put them in the middle class.

Fifteen out of twenty said that they were likely to vote Labour in a General Election, which is similar to the proportion of respondents in Ashby in our 1987 survey (see Table 5.28). In discussing racial tension, a minority, six of the twenty, made remarks which were anti-immigrant or racist, and a similar number suggested that they did not share such views. They said that this had been discussed in school. Most said that they were aware of roughness and violence in the streets of local towns, often between groups of young men from different localities. This also occurred they said in discos. 'Football hooliganism' was also mentioned both at soccer and Rugby League matches. They put it down to territorial rivalry and the need for excitement. Ashby was not thought to be a very exciting place, but most thought they had reasonable facilities at school. Six out of twenty thought that they would want to stay and live in Ashby and of those who were prepared to leave, several mentioned that they would want to come back.

Their comments on the school and their education revealed much variation. Only two said that they had enjoyed their schooling though neither of them were to do well in their examinations. There was much ambivalence, especially from the ones who did well in the examinations. Three, not necessarily the lowest achievers in the examinations, indicated that they had disliked school. The most condemnatory remark was of teachers; 'I hate 'em all; they make you do things you don't want to do.' The highest achiever in the examinations thought that education was not so vital and was not enthusiastic about his schooling, though he said that he had enjoyed himself. Another relatively high achiever thought that 'the only reason for coming to school is to learn to mix with other people'. A third high achiever said, 'I feel that school is all right as such . . . but the people here would rather not be. I am in a minority. Intelligence is what counts.' His view was echoed but also shown to be somewhat faulty by a leaver whose low achievement was concerning him.

'Well! I think this is a bit dreadful really, but I've looked back and at times I've been a bit ignorant, really. I haven't seen what people are doing for me and I've tended to waste their time and my own. In general, I think people react badly to school – you know, people my age – they think it's a waste of time . . . I start to realise that I've wasted my education, really, or a lot of it.'

(S.G. a sixteen-year-old boy in Ashby)

In general there was acceptance that school-leaving qualifications were important as a means of validating claims to certain levels of employment. School had been wasted if there were no examination passes to show at the end of it. There was not much evidence that education for life and as an interest in itself, the kinds of goals which 'progressives' might set for teachers and schools, had been accepted by all of these boys. They generally accepted 'vocationalism' – the view that education and schooling should be about preparing people to enter into employment – which has become a very widespread view in the 1980s. There was however no clear indication that this meant any more than doing well in tests and examinations.

Four of the twenty had no educational credentials at the end of their course at Ashby High School. Using a simple points system, two for a pass at age sixteen in 'O' level or CSE grade one, one for a CSE at less than grade one, and nil for a fail or an ungraded mark, the mean score on the sixteen plus examinations of these twenty was 6.1. The highest score was eighteen, and four had a score higher than ten. Their educational qualifications had differentiated them with regard to employment. Ten of them sought work between 1979 and 1984 with the Coal Board, and six of them were working at nearby collieries. Being the son of an existing employee of the Coal Board was probably more important than an educational credential as far as getting a job was concerned, but certificates differentiated between members of teams of face-workers and skilled craftsmen. Four of the original respondents described themselves in 1984 as miners or face-workers, and two of them as skilled craftsmen, an electrician and a fitter. The miners had average or less than average results. The two skilled craftsmen had scores above average.

Five of the twenty were unemployed and seeking work in 1984 and of these three had scores of nil in their examinations. The other two unemployed had less than average results. Of the four with scores higher than ten, one was a trainee metallurgist in a firm making engine bearings, another was at university taking computer studies, a third was a Coal Board skilled craftsman, and the fourth a driver's mate delivering locally made soft drinks. Largely their expectations had been fulfilled, except that four who had wanted to work in the coal-mining industry had been disappointed. The industry was recruiting on a much reduced basis in the 1980s. Of the fourteen employed eleven were in manual work. In terms of occupational status, their early years of seeking and getting work seemed to be reproducing the differences among them which we have seen in the adult generations in Ashby. How far the five who were not employed and seeking work in 1984 have been able to find work, we do not know. There is a hint however of how lack of educational success as well as decline in chances on the labour market may contribute to the creation of an 'underclass'. It would be difficult to speculate on the basis of this evidence whether the school had contributed to their disadvantage, or whether it was a combination of social background, motivation, ability and luck. The low achievers themselves put weight on education when they were asked to rank the factors that contributed to success in employment, and one of them said he liked school. Only one of the unemployed had put 'social background' in his top three of the factors contributing to success. Can we simply say with Bourdieu that this was a case of 'misrecognition' and that social reproduction goes on behind our backs (Bourdieu and Passeron, 1977)?

We can widen the analysis of the effects of local educational provision with reference to data which we collected in 1986 and 1987. In 1986, we asked the adult respondents about educational qualifications and we can compare their responses with those of a national sample of adults in England and Wales. The *General Household Survey* (OPCS, 1987) indicates that forty-five percent of men and thirty-nine percent of women, aged between twenty-five and seventy years, in England and Wales, have educational qualifications at 'O' level or above. It is not clear how far these have been obtained during school years and immediately afterwards, and how far by later education in adulthood. The qualifications of the sample of men and women in our four localities, shown in Table 4.2, are those obtained in full-time school attendance. About half of the sample attended some form of adult or further education and of those just less than a fifth obtained a qualification which would be equivalent to 'O' level or above. Overall in our four localities, according to our sample, sixteen percent of the men and seventeen percent of the women have the equivalent of 'O' level or above. Most of those who got a late qualification of that kind were adding to existing qualifications rather than starting out from scratch in adult education.

The mining localities are still, it seems, showing the effects of the situation surveyed thirty years ago by Sir Alec Clegg, but it is necessary to note that most of the respondents in our survey are adults who completed their school years before comprehensive reform. In line with the findings of the *General Household Survey (OPCS, 1987)*, which shows that fifty percent of the under forties have educational qualifications (at 'O' level or above) compared with forty percent of the over forties, a higher percentage of younger members of our sample have similar credentials. In terms of qualifications obtained at school or later, twenty-seven percent of those under forty and nine percent of those over forty years have them. The improvement between the younger and the older set is much greater than that registered nationally, but of course starting from a lower base-line. This may mean some credit should be given

Table 6.5 Women and schooling: school leaving and educational qualifications in four mining localities, 1986

Percentage of respondents who:	Year left school		
	Up to 1944	1945–1969	1970 onwards
Left school by statutory leaving age:	82	78	80
Attained 'O' level equivalent or higher:	7	14	40
Gained a school award of any kind	11	27	50
Total N =	28	64	30

Note: We have included CSE results lower than grade one, clerical and commercial qualifications, plus internal school certificates in the third row of the Table

to Sir Alec Clegg's policies. Nevertheless, the distribution of opportunities seems to have been more readily taken up in our more middle-class locality, Oakton, than elsewhere. There, at least a third of all men and women have educational qualifications at 'O' level or above, whereas the proportion is only half of that or less in Willowby, Ashby and Beechthorpe.

The information we gained in the 1986 survey is based on the responses of one hundred and twenty-three women and thirty-one men. Using the educational data for the women, it is possible to show there has been an increase in educational achievement among women, even though the 'early leaving rate', that is the tendency to leave school as soon as statutory leaving age is reached, has not changed. Table 6.5 illustrates this.

Thirty-one percent of the women in our sample had achieved an educational credential of some kind at school. Among the thirty-one male respondents, seventy-three percent of those aged forty or younger left school by sixteen, and ninety-five percent of the older men. Fifty-five percent of the younger men had achieved some award, but only ten percent of all the men's awards were at 'O' level or above, and they belonged to three younger men in Oakton. We have seen from the small sample interviewed in 1979 in Ashby, that only four out of twenty sixteen-year-olds had no school leaving qualification, and four others had a good spread of passes, suggesting again that an improvement in educational standards is occurring.

Forty-five percent of our women respondents had attended some form of further education, and there was a significant difference between women who had left school by 1944 and those who left later. Only twenty-three percent of the earlier group compared with fifty percent of the post-war school leavers had gone to some further education. Among the most recent school leavers, that is those who had left school since 1970, there was a slight drop in further education, but among them there was a higher attainment rate. Fifty-three percent of those women had attained a qualification, compared with seventeen percent of the pre-war school leavers and forty-one percent of those who left between 1944 and 1970. Of those who had taken classes, over seventy percent were in local evening classes. Only thirty-two percent of those women who had attended some further education said that it was employment related or based in training at work.

As Table 4.2 shows relatively high proportions of men, except in Willowby, had had some further education after school. Seventy percent of our male respondents were in this category, of whom almost nine out of ten (eighty-eight percent) had got it through employment related courses. As we noted in our discussion of employment in Chapter five, 'training' has assumed much importance since the 1960s. This is reflected among the men, in that ninety percent of younger men claimed some form of qualification from further education, whereas among the over forties it was only fifty-nine percent. Overall, women in our 1986 survey tend to have stayed at school beyond school-leaving age more than men, and have gained more higher level educational qualifications than men in these localities. Men, however, have had significantly more training, especially employment related training, and men are more likely to have gained post-school qualifications than women.

The general position is that men and women in our four localities are much less well qualified than adult men and women in England and Wales as indicated by the *General Household Survey* published in 1987. There has, however, been a tendency for local educational development policies to be relatively successful. Younger respondents are better qualified than those who are older. Whether the qualifications obtained will translate into better job opportunities for those that have them is disputable. The jobs have to be there, and qualifications do not always make the holder someone sought after by an employer. In a recent study of employers in Leicester, Sunderland and St Albans, only a half of the employers thought that qualifications were useful yardsticks of ability (Ashton et al., 1982). Nevertheless, it depends on the occupational category, and in a recent survey of employees in a relatively burgeoning part of the English economy, the Northampton area, twenty-six percent of both men and women workers in full-time jobs said they had to have further educational qualifications (equivalent to at least 'A' level) and a further forty-two percent said they required 'O' levels or equivalent. Levels of pay correlated with qualifications, but even so there were significant differences between men and women in pay levels even controlling for educational qualifications. Women received less than men, despite having the same qualifications or better (Horrell et al., 1989). This is another form of 'disincentive' effect, and we can see at various levels in localities such as we have studied, how scepticism and resistance or alienation can colour attitudes to education.

Table 6.6 Priority ranking of public services by respondents in four localities, 1987

Oakton		Willowby		Ashby		Beechthorpe	
Service	*% vote*	*Service*	*% vote*	*Service*	*% vote*	*Service*	*% vote*
Health	43	Health	41	Health	35	Health	54
Education	37	Education	18	Education	19	Education	24
Law &		Services to		Law &			
order	7	elderly	18	order	16	Unemployed	9
Others				Retirement		Services to	
less than	5	Unemployed	14	pensions	14	elderly	7
		Others				Others	
		less than	5	Unemployed	9	less than	5
				Others			
				less than	5		

Note: Housing and Defence, the only other services not mentioned in the lists above, got no more than two percent of the vote in any locality

In our 1987 survey we gathered much information about attitudes to and evaluation of local education. Figure 6.1 shows how tenants and owner-occupiers differed in their evaluation of public services, in answer to the question 'Which service would get the highest priority for extra spending?' When we look at the answers given by localities, there are strong differences. Table 6.6 summarises these by showing the percentage vote for each public service.

The variations to some extent can be explained with reference to the social differences between localities. Health has significance to all respondents and during the past decade has been seen to be under threat from government cuts. This reflects national opinion, but in this Labour held constituency, there will also probably have been extra opposition. The expression of second priority for education seems to follow social class lines. The more middle-class population of Oakton rates it more highly than the more working-class respondents of the other three localities. Willowby and Beechthorpe have the higher proportions of older respondents, and correspondingly higher votes for services to the elderly. The three localities with the highest proportion of unemployed workers, are the ones that give more priority to extra spending on the unemployed. The stress on 'Law and Order' in Ashby reflects a concern which was conveyed to us by informants that youthful deviance had increased in the locality (see Chapter Four). Our youthful respondents in 1979 tended to confirm that too. 'Law and Order' has been seen also as something of a cornerstone of government policy in the 1980s and perhaps not surprisingly in this constituency is only given a noticeable rating in Oakton where support for the government of the 1980s is highest. The low rating which housing receives indicates how much the shift to owner-occupation reflects a general trend in opinion. Only tenants give it any support (see Figure 6.1 above).

That education receives second place voting across the whole set of localities does indicate that scepticism and alienation are not complete, but when we asked respondents about whether they were satisfied with the teaching and resources of local schools, one reason perhaps for the second ranking was revealed. Quite large proportions of respondents in each locality thought the question not applicable because they had no school age children. Further, by those who were prepared to judge, dissatisfaction was more clearly shown than satisfaction, though with an exception in Beechthorpe where teaching was considered satisfactory by as many as thought it unsatisfactory (see Figures 6.2 and 6.3).

Perhaps we should be wary of reading too much into such opinion poll like data, for the possibility is that we cannot identify all the forces which shape public opinion. The schools and the teachers in a locality are not entirely homogeneous. The responses, however, do tend to follow expected trends. Together with the data we gathered in 1986, the opinions expressed in 1987 seem to suggest that, despite doubts about the especial relevance to the area's needs of educational services, education and schooling have not served the localities well. There is some hint, too, that lack of educational credentials, however we explain that phenomenon, does contribute to the polarisation of the people in the localities. Some change may be taking place, however, and we have traced indications of overall improvement. It is possible to be very sceptical about educational provision and reform, but the evidence is mounting that the reorganisation of secondary education on comprehensive lines in the 1960s and 1970s has had some influence in countering other polarising and differentiating forces in British society (McPherson and Willms, 1987). Unfortunately the current educational reforms following the 1988 Education Act seem likely to negate the good that may have been done.

HEALTH

Whereas educational provision can only hope to make things better in the longer term, health services are expected to put things right that are obviously wrong, such as the spread of disease, as rapidly as possible. As J.D. noted (see Chapter Four), however, improved medicine could only be one factor in many that contributed to such an end. Working conditions, household income, personal care, diets and housing are all involved in the incidence of health and disease. A society which is polarised is one which experiences major inequalities in health.

The social and political changes which brought about educational change have also been accompanied by changes in medicine, health and disease. This had meant a growing professionalisation of medical services, enlarged

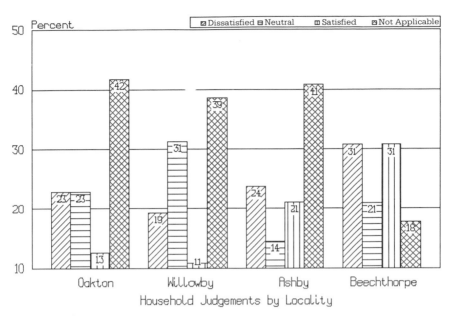

Figure 6.2 Quality of schools and teaching, 1987: four mining localities in West Yorkshire

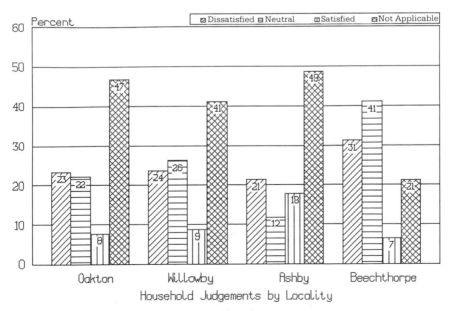

Figure 6.3 Quality of resources in schools, 1987: four mining localities in West Yorkshire

Table 6.7 COF3M and SBREATH by locality and sex, 1987

Percentages	Oakton	Willowby	Ashby	Beechthorpe	All
With COF3M					
Men	6	31	14	15	16
Women	12	11	10	3	9
All	9	20	12	9	12
With SBREATH					
Men	6	18	18	12	13
Women	17	38	36	21	27
All	11	28	25	16	20

organisations with administrative hierarchies, changes in the expectation of life and health and an eradication or great reduction in the incidence of some diseases. Nevertheless, there are many questions about health relating to the mining and former mining districts of West Yorkshire. One which we wish to focus on here, and on which we are able to offer some explanation is: Why are standardised mortality ratios for respiratory diseases in these districts double those in the rest of the UK?

Studies of the health of people in mining areas show them to be subject to illness and ill-health with much higher prevalence than is the case regionally or nationally. In the Pontefract Health District, which includes our research area, and drawing on data from the Yorkshire Regional Health Authority for the years 1984–86, the standardised mortality ratio was 197 for men and 167 for women, and for heart disease 115 for men and 130 for women (UK = 100). Taking deaths from chronic bronchitis and emphysema alone, the ratios in the Wakefield and Pontefract Health Districts are twice the average for the Yorkshire Region. For these two diseases, the standardised mortality ratio is 54 in Harrogate, 103 in Leeds East and 210 in Pontefract. Contrary to the situation in Harrogate and Leeds East, the rates are higher for men than for women in the Pontefract District.

Earlier evidence drawn from a large study undertaken in the 1960s in South Wales showed that 'chronic bronchitis is two or three times more common among coal miners than among non-miners living in the same district' (Lowe, 1969). There is some debate about how far this is a consequence of environmental, occupational and personal activities and conditions, and in what relative proportions. In our 1987 survey, in partnership with the Chest Consultant at Pontefract General Infirmary, we collected data within households on respondents experience of respiratory symptoms, using Medical Research Council validated questions. We asked both respondents and their partners about the incidence of coughing, phlegm, breathlessness and wheezing, and then about smoking, industrial experience and forms of heating used in the household. Two symptoms are crucial indicators of potentially chronic chest diseases. These are coughing frequently on most days for as much as three months in the year, an indicator which we have labelled COF3M, and shortage of breath experienced when undertaking various forms of activity, which we have labelled SBREATH.[1] Table 4.2 indicates the prevalence of severe coughing (COF3M) in each locality. Table 6.7 shows the reported incidence of these symptoms in the four localities.

The immediately obvious fact is that rates tend to be higher in the localities which have a higher proportion of mining households. There are also differences between the men and women, so that with the exception of Oakton, men have much higher experience of COF3M and women of SBREATH. Overall the prevalence ratios are reversed. Men are about twice as likely to experience COF3M and women about twice as likely to experience SBREATH. These points are illustrated in Figures 6.4 and 6.5.

As we have noted above, there are debates about how far the extent of respiratory disease is a consequence of environmental, occupational and personal activities and conditions. We have examined the possibilities as systematically as our data will allow and these are published (Littlejohn et al., 1990). Here we will summarise the findings briefly and add some discussion of these in the light of the data collected in 1989. The smallness of our sample means that we are examining the reported incidence of thirty-four cases of COF3M among two hundred and seventy-one men and women for whom we have complete data, and fifty-five cases of SBREATH among two hundred and seventy men and women. When these are divided for analysis into more than three or four categories, the percentage variations begin to lose reliability, and when we wish to examine the interrelationship between a number of independent variables, again we quickly run into similar problems. Our analysis for this reason has to be seen as preliminary rather than exhaustive. The main value is however to be able to bring to bear a wider variety of variables than has been possible in previous research.

We would assume that the environmental, occupational and personal can not in any real sense be separated from each other as factors in explaining the cause of respiratory symptoms. Sociological analysis has always pointed to the importance of recognising the interaction of factors in a social context of institutions and processes. Our variables are no more than indicators of the complex which makes up that social context. We have already noted that, in drawing samples of respondents from four different localities, we have found variations in the prevalence of the respiratory symptoms. There is therefore a likelihood that while the whole of our research area has high levels of respiratory disease there are crucial variations of activities and conditions within the area which should be explored. Already in summarising the socio-economic conditions, we have pointed to variations between mining and non-mining households, but particularly between tenants and owner-occupiers. These are summarised in Figures 6.6. and 6.7.

When we control for tobacco smoking, which is seen by many as the

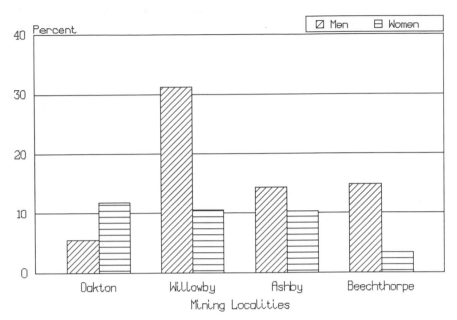

Figure 6.4 Respiratory symptoms: severe coughing by locality and gender,
1987 survey

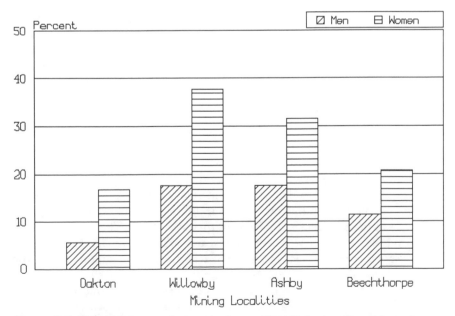

Figure 6.5 Respiratory symptoms: shortage of breath by locality and gender,
1987 survey

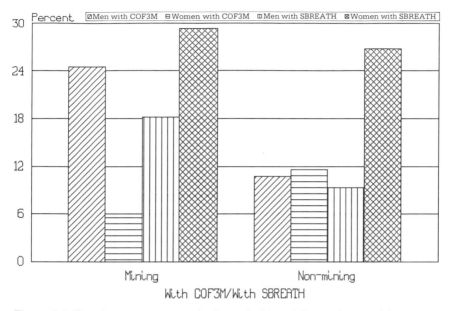

Figure 6.6 Respiratory symptoms by households, mining and non-mining, 1987 survey

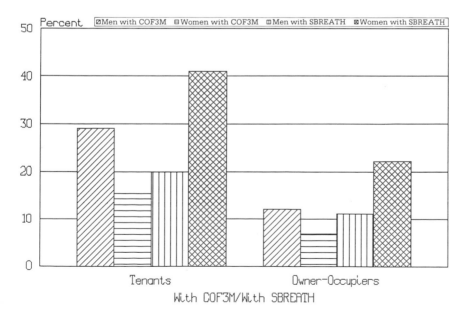

Figure 6.7 Respiratory symptoms by tenure, tenants and owner-occupiers, 1987 survey

Table 6.8 Respiratory symptoms by smoking, mining/non-mining households and sex, 1987

	Men		Women	
	Mining households	Non-mining households	Mining households	Non-mining households
Percentages				
With COF3M				
Smokers	35.29	20.69	6.69	22.73
Ex-smokers	7.69	.00	.00	5.26
Non-smokers	.00	6.45	8.33	8.89
With SBREATH				
Smokers	23.53	20.69	33.33	34.78
Ex-smokers	15.38	.00	37.50	16.67
Non-smokers	.00	3.45	18.18	26.67

prime reason for the high incidence of respiratory disorder (see Lowe, 1969), it is clear that the incidence of COF3M is higher among smokers, than ex-smokers or non-smokers, but the significant difference between men in mining households and other men remains (35.29 percent among miners who smoke regularly compared with 20.69 percent among other male smokers). The crucial significance of involvement in the mining industry is further evidenced when we note that COF3M among women smokers is lower among those in mining households (6.67 percent) than those in non-mining households (22.73 percent). Generally, smoking is not as discriminating an indicator of COF3M or SBREATH among women as it is among men. Male smokers report significantly higher incidence of both symptoms than non-smokers, but while women smokers report higher incidence, the differences are not significant. This is the case despite high levels of reported tobacco smoking in our localities. Fifty percent of the men and thirty-eight percent of the women said that they were regular smokers, compared with OPCS figures relating to England and Wales in 1984, of thirty-six percent of men and thirty-two percent of women (OPCS, 1986). Smoking is a significant feature of the local culture.

The differences in the incidence of COF3M and SBREATH between men and women are quite large, but we have not been able to assess the effect of different kinds of industrial experience (as for instance in textiles or garment making) on women, since there are no large groups of women with particular kinds of experience within the sample to make valid comparisons possible. Respiratory symptoms do generally increase in incidence for men and women with age, and it is clear that house tenure, which summarises the effect of a number of social and cultural variables, affects men and women similarly. Tenants experience virtually twice the rates of both COF3M and SBREATH observable in the four localities (see Figure 6.7).

The data seem to confirm the significance of what Rex and Moore (1969) termed 'housing class', in the determination of life-style and position in the social structure. It may not entirely confirm evidence of 'polarisation' or the formation of an 'underclass', but certainly 'polarisation' seems a reasonable conclusion if we add the other evidence of changing circumstances in household income, employment and other social conditions, which are affecting those who live in the different localities.

In 1989, as we have indicated, we also carried out further research in our localities, using a spirometer to estimate respiratory functions, as well as checking on employment, house tenure, relative affluence and smoking since the previous research. The spirometer measures the volume of air in the lungs and potential volume of flow of that air, by recording the amount blown by a person into a tube connected to the machine. It was thought that the test readings would supplement the more subjectively given responses which were used to create the variables COF3M and SBREATH, and provide more objective measures. Like, or together with, COF3M and SBREATH, spirometer readings can provide reliable predictors of respiratory disease. Three measures based on spirometer readings may be used: PEF (peak expiratory flow), FEV1 (forced expiratory flow in first second) and FVC (forced vital capacity). The second is possibly the most critical.

The measure of forced expiratory flow (FEV1) is a measure of the volume of air that is taken into the spirometer during the first second of blowing. Expected expiratory flow can be predicted according to a person's age and height. When the actual flow is measured as a percentage of the expected flow, some comparison between those tested and a standard population can be made. In 1989 we collected spirometer test readings, ages and heights for seventy-nine men and ninety-six women across the mining localities. Standardised FEV1 scores were calculated. Among the men, nineteen percent had FEV1 scores below eighty percent of expected volume. Fewer women, only 15.6 percent, had FEV1 scores below eighty percent. Nevertheless, these are both high readings and indicate damaged lung capacity, particularly among the men.

Table 6.9 illustrates some of the relationships between FEV1 in standardised form and the other variables we have used in the analysis.

There is a problem of reliability, of course, because of the relatively low numbers of respondents. In general, however, the distribution of FEV1 confirms, in expected directions, variations which we have already noted from the 1987 data. The relationship between low FEV1 scores, COF3M and SBREATH is much clearer and statistically significant for men, than it is for women. Indeed the relationship between FEV1 and SBREATH among women is unexpected. This may result from the lack of stringency in the variable SBREATH (see note 1). (It would also suggest again that the conditions which produce respiratory malfunctions in women are different from those for men. One factor which we did not measure was weight, but

Table 6.9 Respiratory function, FEV1: relationship to other survey variables, 1989

| Percentage of: | Forced expiratory flow | | N |
	Below 80 percent	80 percent and over	
All men respondents	19.0	81.0	79
All women respondents	15.6	84.4	96
Men with SBREATH	44.4	55.6	9
Men without SBREATH	15.6	84.4	64
Women with SBREATH	14.3	85.7	28
Women without SBREATH	17.7	82.3	62
Men with COF3M	45.5	54.5	11
Men without COF3M	14.5	85.5	62
Women with COF3M	37.5	62.5	8
Women without COF3M	13.4	86.6	82
Men tenants	36.4	63.6	11
Men owner-occupiers	16.2	83.8	68
Women tenants	15.8	84.2	19
Women owner-occupiers	15.6	84.4	77
Men: ever in mining who worked:	20.8	79.2	48
underground	24.3	75.7	37
on surface	9.1	90.9	11
Men: never in mining	19.0	81.0	42
Men: smokers	18.6	81.4	43
ex-smokers	25.0	75.0	16
non-smokers	15.0	85.0	20
Women: smokers	23.1	76.9	39
ex-smokers	12.5	87.5	24
non-smokers	6.5	93.5	31

Note: FEV1 is here presented as two categories of its standardised form, above and below eighty percent. The test reading is expressed as a percentage of the respondent's predicted score (based on height and age)

observations indicate that many women in the mining localities are somewhat overweight, in terms of age and height. This seems to be a consequence of a diet containing high levels of sugars and fats, which seems to be another strong feature of the local culture.)

The differences between tenants and owner-occupiers, both men and women, are in expected directions, but not significant statistically for women. Men's involvement in the mining industry is not a clear predictor of lower FEV1 scores until we discriminate between surface and underground workers. Even so the obvious differences (twenty-four percent of underground and nine percent of surface workers with low FEV1 scores) are not statistically significant in a sample of this size. We also found that underground workers were more likely to have COF3M, though not SBREATH, than surface workers, but the differences were not statistically significant.

The use of more objective tests of respiratory function has to some extent confirmed the tendencies which we noted from our 1987 survey using self-reported symptoms. When we control for smoking, dividing our sample into smokers, ex-smokers and non-smokers (those who claim never to have smoked) there is a clear and consistent relation between smoking and low FEV1 scores among women, but not among men. This again suggests, as the analysis of the self-reported symptoms did, that smoking is not the only, or the most significant correlate of, respiratory disorders. A higher percentage of tenants who are smokers has low FEV1 scores than owner-occupiers.

When we look at the distribution of FEV1 scores across the four localities, we again note the clear fact that Oakton is the place with the lowest percentage of respondents, both men and women, with readings of less than eighty percent of the expected rate. The variations by locality are different, however, for men and women. Among men, while the differences are not statistically significant, in the Oakton sample only fifteen percent had low FEV1 scores, compared with between eighteen and twenty-two percent in the other three places. When we examine the forced expiratory flow of women, in Oakton only five percent of the sample had low scores, Ashby had nine percent, but Willowby with nineteen percent and Beechthorpe with twenty-five percent both had significantly more. This may reflect different employment patterns among women, and it may also relate to our suggestion that the causes of respiratory disorder in women are not the same as those for men. Nevertheless, it is the localities with lower levels of affluence and employment which have poorer health indicators.

Those localities in which the mining industry has played a salient role as far as the labour market and the local economy is concerned have been and still are centres of social disadvantage. Willowby seems to be particularly 'cross'd with adversity', and is the locality which overall experiences the highest rates of respiratory symptoms. The locality is, among the four that we researched, the one that most nearly fits the character of a traditional mining commnity. The economic, social and cultural aspects of its environment predispose its inhabitants towards the highest rates of respiratory disease. The collapse of the mining industry in the area will, however, be a doubtful blessing, for although it may remove some of the causes of ill-health, without the reconstruction of the local economy, it will merely allow other predisposing agents to assume greater significance.

Further research will be necessary to assess the real significance of these findings, since our samples have been rather small. Nevertheless, there are pointers here to the fact that public policies with the aim of raising the levels of life-expectation and standards of living would be a sign not only of caring, but also of social justice. It is not surprising that answers to our question about priorities in public expenditure should have revealed that our respondents would give the highest priority to health (see Figure 6.1).

CONCLUSION

This chapter has attempted to show that a process of social polarisation, which has been acknowledged as a significant feature of contemporary British society, as well as other old industrial societies, is at work in the research area, and is creating social divisions within the mining and former mining localities. The policy of encouraging the sale of council and other rented housing to tenants, much favoured by governments during the 1980s in Britain, in an attempt to create 'a property owning democracy', while not objected to by significant proportions of the electorate, has had the undoubted countervailing effect of concentrating disadvantage in some areas where unemployment, ill-health and relative poverty make house purchase an impossible choice. We have seen, indeed, that there is a dwindling proportion of tenants in comparison with owner-occupiers, and that it is increasingly the division between these two categories which indicates the cleavage between citizens who still have clear means of participating in democracy, and those who are being pushed into what some call an 'underclass' for whom participation becomes difficult if not meaningless. We have also suggested that a public policy which puts at risk the general widening of educational opportunity, through encouraging, as the 1988 Education Reform Act does, private competitive control and the diminution of locally elected Council control of schooling, will not be of great benefit to the people of these mining localities. There are signs that educational achievement has grown recently, but that is something which needs positive encouragement. Above all, it would seem that there needs to be a much clearer policy about employment and income guarantees, to meet the disadvantage which increasing social division has created.

Such divisions were fully understood by the leadership of the National Union of Mineworkers and the National Coal Board in the early 1980s. It was conflict over the disadvantaging of some localities and some of the households within them as a consequence of Coal Board policies which created the strength of feeling and led to the year-long strike in the British mining industry. It is to that which we now turn.

Chapter 7

Four mining communities, the miners' strike of 1984/5 and the future

INTRODUCTION

In the previous chapters we have examined the basis of community formation in the context of the coal-mining industry and social change in the nineteenth and twentieth centuries. In the four localities we have seen evidence of the processes and institutions which together helped to create something like traditional mining communities in at least three of them, but we have also seen reason to doubt the existence in any unambiguous way of homogeneous working-class community identity and consciousness. The countervailing effects of 'centripetal' and 'centrifugal' forces and the other oppositions and contradictions, which Dennis, Henriques and Slaughter detected in their study of 'Ashton' (1956) should have been incorporated more clearly in Bulmer's ideal–typical account (1975a). In our localities, history and biography have combined to create a consciousness of skills, knowledge and sensibilities, which may amount to what we can call a local cultural capital, with means of reproducing that by key individuals and groups. There have, however, been different formulations and shades of meaning attached to that and to the notion of a mining community.

Change from what might have been taken to be single occupational communities in the early twentieth century has meant that, although the mining industry still casts a long shadow over our localities, there are different senses of division and coherence. There is a heterogeneity of occupational experience and there have been changing attachments to and interventions by the state and local authorities. Women are now much more likely to have paid employment than in the early twentieth century, and this has an effect on the domestic division of labour. There is still a marked gender division in terms of employment opportunities and in domestic work, but this is not tantamount to a hard and fast men's sphere and women's domain.

As we have argued, if there is a growing sense of two worlds, it is that which divides those who are relatively secure and affluent from those whose insecurity and lack of affluence is marked. This seems to have both spatial and social reference within our research area; spatial, in that there seems to be a clear division between the more affluent locality, Oakton, and its near neighbour, the much less affluent Willowby; and social, in that it is particularly expressed through housing tenure, with the growing number of owner-occupiers seeming, by and large, to have much more security than the decreasing number of tenants. The late 1980s, with high rates of interest on mortgages, have seen some growth of insecurity among owner-occupiers, and the dichotomy has to be taken cautiously. There is evidence, however, of social polarisation within our research area. Undoubtedly, it can be seen on a much bigger scale in larger urban areas and in Britain (as well as other states) as a division between inner city and run-down tenanted estates on the one hand and relatively prosperous suburbs on the other. It can also be seen as regional differentiation, such as North versus South, in the case of nation states. This has been promoted by the decline of, and reduction of investment in, old industries such as coal mining, contrasted with re-investment and spatial reallocation of new economic activity elsewhere.

This, at its most drastic, for the people who are based in declining areas, can mean unemployment, insecurity and poverty, and the threat of the 'loss of community'. Social protest and social movements to counter such trends, as we indicated in Chapter One, have been evidenced in many parts of the world, and, because of the fragmentation of large-scale production which tends to have accompanied the trends, have more often been organised on a locality, rather than on an occupational, or trade union basis (Castells, 1983). On the other hand, the sense that these trends are world-wide, has also created a global dimension, so that at one and the same time a locality struggle is often clearly a global issue. Trade unions and the labour movement created and institutionalised in modernising societies have often been slow to recognise both the localisation and globalisation of their concerns. The National Union of Mineworkers undoubtedly came to recognise the trends as early as any other branch of the labour movement. It has always had a strong local base in mining communities, but it has also had a sense of the international dimension of coal and other mineral extraction.

In some ways, then, we can say that the year-long strike of 1984/5 among Britain's miners was symbolic of the new forms of social protest. They are often long and inconclusive, frequently have far more power stacked against them than the protesters can muster, are commonly expressed most strongly in a number of localities, have a complex set of issues at their centre affecting patterns of consumption as well as production, community identities and citizenship rights, and usually have international as well as national involvement. Nevertheless the historical memory of earlier strikes and industrial conflict also gave the 1984/5 strike many links with the past, and the tactics and strategies of the NUM and its branches may have been more attuned to the past than to the present and to social change. What the strike indicated most of all was a response to the changes occurring in the mining industry, especially pit closures, and in industrialised societies, in particular to the social polarisation which these changes are effecting.

Fundamentally for the NUM leadership the strike was concerned with future employment and the future of the working class. The social trends which we have outlined have meant a decline in manual working-class jobs, and pit closures were the embodiment of those trends. First, therefore, the strike had a class dimension. As we have seen, however, the mining industry and its localities had a gender dimension. Few women were employed in the industry but many women were involved in paid employment often close to their own household in the community. 'The closure of a pit means the closure of a community' was a slogan which had both economic and social implications for women as well as men. The trends which made the miners strike also led the women to protest. The issues of class and gender were to some extent unified within the strike, although there were separate issues, also, because of the gender division of labour both in employment and in the household. It has always been the case, though not clearly recognised, that strikes not only involve withdrawal of labour from employment, but also withdrawal from the mainstream economy and the necessity generally to manage a subsistence economy. A strike implies that households are managed differently, and arrangements have to be made to cope with the stress of reduction of earnings.

Now it is these issues of gender and subsistence which have often been overlooked in analyses of strikes. Further, we have already noted that the gender issue tends only to be seen stereotypically in the model of the traditional mining community, as an issue of men's world versus women's world. The interrelatedness of these two worlds, rather than their separation, is especially clear in a strike and it is on these issues that we conducted our research in the mining localities.

This chapter therefore will focus first on women and women's involvement in the strike. As we have also said, the strike had local dimensions, and it will be to the implications of the strike for the localities that we will turn second, examining its effects during the strike and the future prospects. This will lead us finally to turn to class and general issues.

WOMEN AND THE STRIKE

Our research in the localities had begun in the late 1970s, and we were able to collect interview data from a small sample of households in Ashby during the strike itself. These were selected so as to have a number of mining as well as non-mining households, and in the event we interviewed forty men and forty women, in twenty-five mining and eighteen non-mining households. In the interviews we asked about their domestic arrangements, their views on the strike and on women's action in it, along with some classificatory questions about age, income, house tenure, employment, trade union and political party support.

In the late summer of 1984, with the strike some five months old, the mining households were having to cope with income at about a third or a quarter of previous levels. In some cases it had fallen much more, especially for those who found themselves isolated from kin and neighbours who shared their beliefs and interests. One couple, for instance, had recently come to Ashby from another district, and the miner worked in a pit some distance from Ashby. They were doubly isolated, not having contact with kin or with a local union branch. In nearly all mining households, however, it was still the women who were responsible for managing the domestic economy, and their reactions to the situation were varied. Some had carried on much as before the strike, relying on relatives, friends and neighbours. Women's groups had been formed and a few of our respondents had joined them.

The wife of a welder at the local pit told us that she had had sleepless nights worrying about how to pay the bills. She had never before got into debt. Now she felt 'like a criminal' because she was not able to pay the electricity bill. She was getting support from a sister and declared that she would cope largely because she could cook and bake, and knew how to make meals out of 'nearly nothing'. Further she said, 'we have always been a close family and we are helping each other out . . . and after you've been so long [on strike] you can carry on as long as it takes'. She had not, however, joined the local women's group, for 'my husband never wanted me to go or get involved'. Her husband acknowledged very much his indebtedness to his wife. 'I would be in a right bloody state if it wasn't for my wife. . . I've already lost thousands [of pounds] in wages', but, he added, 'when you've lived in Ashby all your life, you're part and parcel of some social thing . . . you accumulate a lot of close friends'.

Others saw the situation a little more light-heartedly. A local school cleaner, the wife of a face-worker, agreed that they were living only on a day-to-day basis. Responding to our question on income before the strike she said,

> when you reckon it up, you'd about £80 a week and it still went on food and that. But now you're still getting through, on next to nothing, and it's making you wonder what did you do with all that other money. A lot of people say the same thing. I'm wondering what I did with that £50 odd, that I don't have now, each week. I mean, we're not getting the meat we used to have, and we don't go out for food. . .

She was another who had not got involved with the women's group (or groups) in Ashby, largely because of her employment. Her husband, however, who had very strong views about supporting the strike and, because at fifty he thought he was a bit old for picketing, went to help out in the meals kitchen which a women's group had organised. 'There's still a need for Unions, t'Labour Party and rallying around, helping each other', he said.

A home help who was the wife of a pit mechanic had found the women's group to be very useful and said,

> I have become more politically aware, but I think a lot of women are just not interested. I had to go out of curiosity and I was also feeling depressed . . . and needed somebody to talk to beside my husband. . .

He, a Union branch committee man, had said to us,

> I wonder who recharges Arthur's batteries . . . cos it's a drain. Lads that you talk to . . . you have to nudge them a bit: you have to keep hammering at them that we're not settling [the strike on 'their terms']. Then take t'situation with t'police: when you're brought up as a law-abiding citizen and you see this happening, it has a disorientating effect on you. It opens little doors in your mind that you didn't realise were there. . . Who protects you from the 'protectors' when they're getting at you? That disturbed me a lot. I went off for a couple of days on my own to the caravan. . .

So she had gone to the women's group for help.

> It really got to him and I began to think it was my fault. . . I was upset thinking he wouldn't come back. . . After going [to the group] I felt a lot better, thinking that we weren't fighting alone. . . My mother [also a miner's wife] told me when she was younger how they all used to live in streets and all got together. They all rallied round. I just thought that I'd never experienced anything like that. We'd always lived in our own little boxes and gardens, not in a terrace, and I'd never experienced any neighbourliness apart from my immediate neighbour – I thought we'd never get the same sort of . . . good relationships going with us all, but it has done, really has done.

She also noted that the incident of him going off was just a reflection of the situation which had existed for a long time. He never did any of the household management and could just go off. Nevertheless she added, 'he's not bad really' and she would be trying to change things. She later repeated that she had also become more politically aware since the strike had begun and that she intended to join the local Labour Party when it was all over. She would be going out, too.

This was also the intention of one of the founder members of the first women's group to form in Ashby. The Party, she reckoned, had not been concerned enough with supporting the strikers and it needed to be 'woken up'. She thought that what the women gained from their experience of the women's group meetings was the conviction that the real struggle was in the economic and political area, and not in the household and the community. The men needed support now and women should give it from the basis of their domestic management experience. After the strike was over women should move into what had been the men's world of economics and politics. She did not feel that there was an important gender issue. Her idea of politics was that it was very much about party and class, and gender really did not come into it. When we asked her if the women's group was 'political', she therefore interpreted 'political' in party terms and separated the meaning of the strike from that of the women's group. She said that the strike was the consequence of a 'bad' party leader, known for her obstinacy, pitted against the miners, also known for their obstinacy, and went on

> No, I don't think it's [the Group] political. . . It is with the men. Women are more concerned with getting through it, paying bills, running that place [the meals kitchen] for those lads. It's not a politically moti-vated thing.

This was borne out, too, when we asked how the women's group had started. It had not been a result of experience of other women's meetings, she claimed, nor on hearing about the formation of such groups in other localities across the coalfields. There had been a need to face the difficulty of coping with a household on next to nothing. So it was a matter of providing meals collectively, or the where with all to make meals through food parcels, and of boosting the morale of the women who had to do the coping.

There were, however, differences of view about the women's groups in Ashby. We asked all the people we interviewed in 1984 an open-ended question: 'What is the value of the women's groups, do you think?' Their responses were first coded into nine categories, but it does not do too much damage to them to reduce them to four basic categories. Some of the respondents gave complex answers which contained more than one category and seven respondents did not give answers to the question. The totals therefore for men and women come to more than forty. Tables 7.1 and 7.2 list the women's and the men's response categories.

The responses of the men and women reveal no significant differences, but show that the major tendency was to value the women's groups for their contribution to household and community survival. The emphasis in the responses in this category was to agree that women were extending their household management work into a collective situation. Nevertheless, there were those who recognised that women were involved in the economic and political issues, either in the specifics of the strike itself, or more generally. A small number of responses indicated the view that there was a gender issue involved. Women were coming out, and it was not entirely to do with the strike alone. Two men respondents mentioned the concurrent women's protest at the Greenham Common Missile Base, and said that they saw similarities between the women's peace initiatives and the women's groups

Table 7.1 Value of women's groups during the strike: men's and women's views, 1984

Range of responses	Men	Women	Basic category	Men	Women
	Number			Percent	
1. Women should stay at home	0	1	Sceptical		
2. They don't do much	3	6	or	11	17
3. Don't like their methods	2	1	negative		
4. They are good and necessary for their families	10	10	Household and community survival	32	32
5. They show community solidarity	5	5			
6. They are helping the men fight for their jobs	2	3	Support for men's struggle	15	25
7. They show support for the men	5	9			
8. Women are becoming political	6	4	Politicisation of women	15	11
9. They show women are oppressed	1	1			
Non-response	13	7	Non-response	27	15
Total	47	47		100	100

here. Not unexpectedly, there were some sceptical or negative responses from both women and men. There was less overt scepticism among the men's responses, but the men were more non-responsive than the women and this could mean an unexpressed opposition.

We attempted to analyse the variations in the responses according to some of our classificatory interview questions. Table 7.2 summarises some of the significant variations.

There were differences which were statistically significant between respondents in mining and non-mining households and between those who gave unambiguous and positive support for the strike and those who were less than positive. The differences between the over-forties and the younger respondents approached statistical significance. The older respondents were much more emphatic about the women's groups being concerned with household and community survival, and the younger ones were more likely to express the view that the groups had a wider meaning. The younger generation were also a little less sceptical. The existence of different ideological outlooks in Ashby is suggested by this variation and even more by the differences between the mining and non-mining households and the positive and less than positive supporters.

In Table 7.2, there are very clear differences between the mining and

Table 7.2 Value of women's groups during the strike: categories of response by age, type of household and support for the strike, 1984

| | Basic response categories | | | | Percentages | |
	Sceptical negative	*Household community*	*Support men*	*Politicis-ation/ women*	*N/R*	*N*
Age						
Women up to 40	16.7	23.3	26.7	16.7	16.7	30
Women over 40	17.6	47.1	23.5	0.0	11.8	17
Men up to 40	8.0	28.0	20.0	20.0	24.0	25
Men over 40	13.6	36.4	9.1	9.1	31.8	22
Type of household						
Women: mining	10.7	42.9	28.6	14.3	3.6	28
Women: non-mining	26.3	15.8	21.0	5.3	31.6	19
Men: mining	0.0	24.1	13.8	17.2	34.5	26
Men: non-mining	23.8	38.1	14.3	9.5	14.3	21
Support for strike						
Women: positive	4.0	32.0	36.0	20.0	8.0	25
Women: not positive	31.8	31.8	13.6	0.0	22.7	22
Men: positive	3.7	29.6	22.2	14.8	29.8	27
Men: not positive	20.0	35.0	5.0	15.0	25.0	20
All men and women	13.8	31.9	20.2	12.8	21.3	94

Note: N/R means non-response

non-mining households as to the importance of the groups. First, respondents in the non-mining households were more sceptical and, second, they tended to put more emphasis on the more particular relation between the groups and the locality. The men and women differ in both mining and non-mining households quite significantly, however, and this suggests another factor, that there was in some households evidence of conflicting views. In one mining household the husband, who was a face-worker and a member of the local branch committee, told us that 'the strike's caused a bit of aggro because my wife's not one hundred percent behind it . . . we've had some really awful arguments . . . she is t'only worker and she's also a workaholic around the house.' In a separate interview with his wife, who had some part-time employment, she said to us that the argument with her husband was more about how to run the household than over the principles and meaning of the strike. She had, in fact, been to two major women's demonstrations in favour of the strike. Here was a case of faulty communication, perhaps being a cause of conflict.

Among those who supported the strike very positively, as among the younger respondents, there was much more sense of the groups having a link with the economic and political aspects of the strike, and much less scepticism than among those who were ambivalent or against the strike. When we analysed the sources of the support using the classificatory data from our interviews, there were significant variations according to social class determined by occupational status, house tenure and being a 'local' versus an 'incomer'. In social class terms, thirteen of our respondents were in the salariat, and only eight percent of them expressed positive support. Fourteen were in the intermediate class position, and forty-three percent of them said that they supported the strike fully. Forty-five were working class, and of them seventy-one percent expressed full support. Eight were not employed and half of them were supporters. There was a clear class gradient of support. Given what we have said about tenants earlier, it is not surprising, perhaps, that the highest level of support was found among tenants. Seventy-four percent of tenants, compared with forty-six percent of owner-occupiers were in support of the strike. 'Locals' were far more likely to be supporters than 'incomers', sixty-three percent of the former compared with forty-one percent of the latter. Finally, sixty-seven percent of respondents in mining households were fully in support of the strike compared with thirty-four percent in non-mining households.

WOMEN'S SUPPORT GROUPS

The 1984 interviews were not carried out on a randomly selected basis, and in 1986, we were able to interview respondents selected randomly in four localities. We asked about the existence of women's groups during the strike in each place and we asked all the respondents for their views on them, within the context of questions about the strike generally. From the above survey, and from the literature which emerged on women's groups (see Gibbon, 1988) in the strike, four main views have been expressed:

1 They were a product of a feminist consciousness at work.
2 They emerged as a consequence of women participating in a class struggle. (For these see Campbell, 1986.)
3 They were forms of community defence. (See Samuel et al., 1986.)
4 Women in mining households had to organise subsistence during the strike collectively. (See Hudson, 1986.)

We went into our interviewing with these as our hypotheses and what follows is a summary of the findings from our household survey in 1986 along with data from nineteen special interviews given by former members of support groups, contacted during the course of the main survey.

There were twelve active support groups in our research area during and after the strike. There was a group in each of the localities, and in some, two or more. Not all women, however, heard about the groups, and thirteen percent of the women claimed not to have been aware of their existence in the 1986 survey. In the same survey only two women out of one hundred and twenty-three interviewed said that they had belonged to such a group, but almost a quarter of the sample said that they had been active in support of the strike or strikers in some way.

There seemed to have been three major stimuli to the formation of women's groups initially. First the local Labour Parties and the National Union of Mineworkers branches stimulated the formation of such groups, no doubt moved by historical memory of previous struggles. Second, women supporters of the strike in the research area were incensed by the sight on television of women opposed to it calling for men to return to work, and determined to provide active support for the strikers. Third, individuals and groups of women already concerned for the state of the coal industry sensed the need to do 'something' to help striking miners and their families. It is also possible to see that there was some kind of 'snowball' effect as women in the mining localities heard of groups forming and recognised their probable value as household incomes were reduced in the early weeks of the strike. There was variable support and opposition in the localities, and varying reasons for involvement, which could explain the formation of more than one group in some localities (see p. 187).

The groups varied in size from about six to fifty members. Each tended to have a core of more active members who were or became deeply committed. The members were drawn largely but not exclusively from mining households. Most of the nineteen specially interviewed informants had been employed, typically as factory workers, shop assistants or clerical workers. Two had been canteen workers in the pits. Two others had been nurses. Very few of them had any paid employment at the time of the strike, and so had time available for support group activities. As we have indicated above, active support by women was conditional upon support being given to them, and in the 1986 survey we asked women who had not joined the groups why they had not. Their main reasons turned on their domestic responsibilities or their employment.

The groups had to be organised for their activities and there were variations. The Labour Party and NUM sponsored groups tended to adopt formal organisational approaches, electing a chair, secretary and treasurer, holding general meetings and delegating members to do different jobs. Other groups were in some cases formed by women with no previous experience of committees and formal meetings. They used meetings as a general forum for discussion and decision-making. They developed more haphazardly, and this too was sometimes a cause of new groups forming in the localities. We heard of three cases of groups forming as splinter groups, taking on separate functions.

Primarily, in the view of our nineteen interviewees, the groups were formed to give practical support to striking miners and their families. Their tasks were distributing food and household necessities and vouchers, setting up kitchens and making meals for pickets and others, organising social gatherings, concerts and parties and giving advice and providing moral support to families. Some of the members wished to participate in the strike activities and went picketing, joined rallies and marches and spoke at public meetings. Many were involved in raising funds to make all these activities possible. This brought them into contact with their communities via collections, raffles and fetes. It also led to visits to other parts of Britain and abroad. They thus came to be linked in numerous support networks, which at times assumed the reality of a vast social movement, mobilised to advance the cause of the miners, and the cause of women too.

When we asked the respondents of the 1986 household survey, again in an open-ended question as in 1984, what they considered the value of the support groups to be, we received a wide range of answers. These have been categorised in ways that hopefully do not do an injustice to their meaning, but somewhat differently from those of 1984, for the range of responses was not entirely like that in the previous research. They are summarised in Table 7.3.

There were quite significant differences between women in mining households and others, and there are differences between the four localities. In mining households and also in Willowby, which has the largest concentration of mining households, the emphasis was on the practical support and its necessity for keeping the strike going, whereas in the non-mining households and the other localities there is a greater emphasis on its community aspect and providing moral support. In some ways, then, we see a replication of the two aspects of involvement, the ideological and the material referred to above, this time in terms of emphasis given by women more or less involved in the strike. We had asked the same question in the 1984 survey and the major difference recorded in 1986 was a decline in responses which suggested that women's groups had little or no value or which suggested that there was a feminist meaning attached to them. Otherwise the emphasis then as in 1986 was on the practical and moral support, with women in mining households differing from others in the same way as in 1986.

At the end of the strike, the nineteen women from the support groups told us that there was sadness, even anger, among the members of the groups, when they realised that the pit closures and redundancies would not cease. Participation had seemed to offer some possibility of control, as well as a wide range of experiences not likely to be repeated. As we indicated at the beginning of Chapter One, one group organised had told us (here a fuller quotation):

Table 7.3 Value of women's support groups in the 1984/5 miners' strike: women's views by household and locality, 1986

Women's groups	Women in Mining h'hlds	Non-mining h'hlds	Oakton	Willowby	Ashby	Beech-thorpe
Gave practical help to men and families	35	20	9	45	23	23
Gave practical help to communities	26	20	17	10	31	31
Gave moral support	9	25	26	14	23	12
Kept strike going	14	13	9	28	8	8
Helped women's cause	0	5	13	0	0	0
Sceptical or negative responses	2	5	0	0	4	12
Other	14	13	26	3	12	15

Percentages — *Women in localities*

This strike was different. Before they've all been about money. They usually got what they wanted in the end when the strike was about money . . . the women used to push them back to work. This was totally different – it was about jobs and communities – it was for the young ones - jobs. With so many millions on the dole already, women can see further into the future than men – I think women were determined this time.

Two others in conversation with the interviewer said when they were asked if they had noted any changes among the members:

A. Well, some a lot more than others. . . For some, I think it were a good thing . . .
B. It was for me. I wouldn't have wanted it to happen, but I'm glad it did for me . . . I'd never have thought I'd have gone to Belgium for two weeks and spoke to Trade Unionists over there. Or you'd [speaking to *A.*] never have gone to the Soviet Union and met Trade Unionists and argued your case . . . I think . . . you can't go through all that and not become more aware . . .
Interviewer. And what about women, awareness of women's position?
B. I think that's a more difficult one, because you've got to remember this is a community that's built on very strict divided sex roles, and it's very difficult to break them down. When the pit wasn't working, it was different, but when the pit's working . . . the structures are there, the attitude's there, the culture's there.

When we consider such a set of responses and return to the four explanations of the women's action in the strike, it would seem that none of them is irrelevant. Being 'practical' or giving 'moral support' in the communities, gave opportunities for wider issues to be raised. Among our nineteen key informants about the groups, six said that they had become more politically conscious, nine, more self-confident and ten, more socially informed. Some said, with a tone of confidence in their existing consciousness, that they had not changed at all. The outcome of participation also remains unpredictable. An additional kind of resource based in the networks emerged in the strike among some women and this could be useful in facing the problems of social and economic change which are affecting the mining localities of West Yorkshire. Members of some of the groups continue to meet, and at least one group turned its attention to trying to bring more resources to its locality in the form of a community centre. Others have joined informal educational groups supported by local authority funds. Undoubtedly, a strong component in the formation of the women's support groups was thus the desire to give practical support to striking miners and their families, rather than to express in any conscious way class or gender solidarity.

We have noted in this discussion of the gender issue that the strike also had many implications for institutions and processes in the four localities. Our 1986 research began with an attempt to assess the relationship between variations in community integration, the degree of mobilisation and the organisation of women's action during the strike and this led us into interviewing a random sample of respondents in four mining communities (see Chapter Four). After a series of pilot interviews, our colleague Claire Peterson developed ten hypotheses concerning the implications of the strike and we now turn to these.

TEN HYPOTHESES ON THE IMPLICATIONS OF THE STRIKE

Traditional social networks and support for the strike

1 *Miners (and mining households) with extensive family and friendship ties (traditional social networks) in the community, and especially those who have lived all or most of their lives in the community, were more active in their support of the strike than miners without extensive local support systems.*

We use two indicators to measure support for the strike. The first tapped the respondents' 'agreement with the strike', and we treated this as a trichotomous variable, because some expressed neither full agreement nor outright opposition. Among our respondents, forty-seven percent were in agreement, forty-two percent disagreed and eleven percent were in the 'undecided' category. The second indicator relates to activities of any kind in support of the strike and those on strike. We asked, for instance, whether they had picketed or raised funds, attended meetings, organised help for

Table 7.4 Attitude to the 1984/5 strike by support activities, 1986

| | | Active support | | | |
		Yes	No	Total	Percent
	Yes	17	54	71	47.0
Agreement	Yes and No	4	12	16	10.6
with strike	No	16	48	64	42.4
	Total	37	114	151 *	100.0
	Percent	24.5	75.5	100.0	

Note: * There were three respondents who did not answer one or other question and could not be included

strikers in their own work-place, or given direct help to households of striking miners. The responses are categorised in Table 7.4 as a dichotomy, allocating respondents as having engaged in at least one of these activities, or not having done any. Twenty-five percent had given some active support while the rest of our respondents had not. These indicators are also used separately, because there is no statistical association in the distribution of the responses. (Chi-square equals zero in Table 7.4.)

We found in our localities, that being born and bred in, that is being a 'native' of, a mining village or town seemed to count more than length of residence. There are many jokes about 'having passports' to come and go, and of these being conferred as of right to 'natives', but to 'incomers' only after twenty-five years, or so. In mining households, there was no significant difference in either of our two variables of involvement in the strike, among 'natives' and 'incomers'. In general the tendency was to confirm the hypothesis, however, in that agreement with the strike was higher among both men and women who had lived longest in, or were natives of, the localities (Sixty percent to forty-six percent) and active involvement was greatest in 'native' households (twenty-nine percent to seventeen percent).

The first hypothesis concerns the relation of social networks as well as length of residence in the localities to involvement in the strike, in mining households. As an indicator of traditional social networks, we used the number of local relatives cited by each respondent for themselves and their partners. We divided the respondents into two categories: those with ten or more local relatives, and those having less than ten. In mining households thirty-nine percent of respondents said they had ten or more local relatives. Among those with a bigger kinship network, a higher percentage said that they agreed with the strike, than those with a smaller network. The difference was statistically significant among the men but not among the women. There was a very clear relation between active involvement and number of local relatives, with thirty-three percent of those with a larger kinship network claiming to have been active, compared with sixteen percent of those with a smaller network. The difference was particularly significant among the women respondents (thirty-seven percent to eight percent).

Thus overall we would claim that the evidence supports the first hypothesis. Among respondents in mining households membership of larger kinship networks, being 'native' and having lived in a locality for a length of time are characteristics which related to differential involvement in the miners' strike, particularly to active involvement.

Differences between mining and non-mining households

2 *Miners, and those whose partners or other family members have spent a large part of their working lives in the mines, were more active in their support of the strike than non-mining families.*

The second hypothesis is concerned with whether there is something unique in character about mining households compared with non-mining households. We have distinguished these as in Chapter Five. Mining households are those where a current member of the household has employment in mining or, because of the number of pit closures which occurred in the 1980's, recent employment in mining. Those without such members are non-mining households. We have already noted in Chapter Five that there are differences as well as overlaps between such households. Analysis of their involvement with the strike suggests the same conclusion.

Comparing mining households with the rest, we find that there is a distinction between them on one of the two indicators of involvement in the strike. In mining households, fifty-four percent of all our respondents said that they agreed with the strike, but only forty percent in the other households. (The difference does not reach the ninety-five percent level of significance.) The level of active support for the strike was slightly, but not significantly, lower in mining households (twenty-two percent) than in the others (twenty-seven percent). We relied mainly on women's responses for our data in the 1986 sample of households. In a quarter of the households, however, we also interviewed a male partner. Among men in mining households twenty-nine percent were actively supportive of the strike, compared with twenty-two percent in the other households. A higher percentage of women in the other households claimed to have been active in support of the strike than in the mining households twenty-seven percent compared with nineteen percent). This is shown in Table 7.5.

The data can most safely be interpreted as not giving clear support for the hypothesis, though there is some evidence that there are differences between mining households and the others in expected directions. The evidence which runs counter to expectation, namely that women in mining households seemed to have been less 'active' than those in the other households, might

Table 7.5 Support for the strike: gender differences by households

| | Percentages | | | |
| | Mining households | | Other households | |
Respondents who:	Females	Males	Females	Males
Agreed with strike	56.3	47.6	41.3	33.3
N =	48	21	75	10
Gave active support	18.8	28.6	27.4	22.2
N =	48	21	73	9

well be explained by the fact that in most cases they were taken up with making ends meet in their own households on a reduced income, and were not able to give much active public support for the strike, unless they had support from a large social network. Interestingly the relationship between membership of local social networks and involvement in the strike also held for the non-mining households, suggesting that support for the strike was not based simply in occupational attachment, but also in social and cultural location. For both mining and other households, levels of agreement with and active support for the strike were higher among the 'natives' and those who had lived longest in the localities, and among those with the larger kinship networks, than among the others. With regard to active support for the strike, the differences between those with large and small kinship networks reached statistical significance.

The discussion of the first two hypotheses suggests that involvement with the strike was not merely a matter of occupational attachment, but also of membership of local social networks.

The relation between support for the strike and views of the extent of support in the community

3 *Respondents who supported the strike themselves have different views regarding the extent of active community support for the strike than respondents who did not support the strike.*

During our research, we asked all respondents a year after the strike ended what they thought people locally felt about the strike. 'Were they in support, neutral or opposed?' We specified particular groups, such as their neighbours, the miners in the locality, the local pit managers, local shopkeepers and local newspapers (to get a view of the media presentation of support). In Table 7.6 we present the findings.

Those who claimed to be in agreement with the strike were significantly more likely to judge 'community' support to have been greater than those who were not. This even holds for the pit managers, whom the large majority nevertheless did not consider to have given support to the strike. These

Table 7.6 Support given to the strike, as judged by groups of respondents, divided by involvement in the strike

| Respondents: | Percentages Support shown by: | | | | |
	Neighbours	Miners	Pit managers	Shop-keepers	Local papers
In 'agreement with strike' (N = 72)	75.0	75.0	21.1	57.7	49.3
Not in 'agreement with strike' (N = 64)	39.1	39.1	6.3	47.6	33.3
Gave 'active support' (N = 37)	56.8	54.1	14.3	69.4	48.6
Not-'active' (N = 112)	59.8	59.8	15.2	46.4	38.4

Note: The table records the percentage of respondents in the four categories who indicated that support was given by the above groups or the press in their local community

findings would validate the hypothesis that supporters of the strike had a different way of seeing or defining the situation. However, using the other indicator, which relates to the giving of active public support, there is only one significant difference between the judgements of the 'actives' and the non-'actives' – That is in their views of support given by local shopkeepers. Certainly, we were given many reports by respondents and other informants in our research, that some local shopkeepers did give discounts, prepared special offers and helped those who ran kitchens to supply meals to strikers, and 'active' supporters would have been likely to know more about these, perhaps, than non-'activists'. Otherwise, the 'activists' did not necessarily judge the degree of local support differently from non-'activists', and did not have widely disparate ways of seeing the support for the strike from other respondents.

Generally, therefore, the two indicators, which are seen in Table 7.4 not to be statistically associated, are tapping different aspects of support for the strike. The 'agreement' indicator seems to link with attitudinal or ideological orientations, whereas the 'activism' indicator, in linking closely with membership of large kinship networks, relates to material factors, suggesting that 'active' supporters felt the sheer necessity and/or the possibility of giving support, and did not necessarily 'agree' with the strike ideologically. This difference between the indicators also holds when we examine the data in relation to hypothesis four.

Mass communication as sources of information and support for the strike

4 *Active supporters of the strike were more likely to have read union publications and to feel that the media were biassed in their presentation of strike-related news.*

The majority of our respondents, sixty percent, claimed that television broadcasts had been their chief source of information and comment on the strike. Second, and a long way behind, came what we have called informal networks, including workmates, family, friends and neighbours, with twenty-seven percent claiming them to have been their chief source. Radio broadcasts and newspapers were only secondary sources of information. Television broadcasts and commentaries on the strike were thought to have been biassed against the strikers by forty-seven percent of our respondents, and radio broadcasts by twenty percent.

There were significant differences between those who said they agreed with the strike and those who disagreed, on their judgements of the fairness of broadcasts. Radio broadcasts were judged to be biassed against the miners by thirty-four percent of those in agreement, and by thirteen percent of those who disagreed. Television broadcasts were similarly judged biassed in favour of opponents of the miners' strike by sixty-three percent of those who agreed with the strike, and by only thirty-three percent of those who were not in agreement with it. Similarly, sixty-three percent of those in agreement said they read trade union papers, compared with only twenty percent of those who disagreed. There were no such differences between the 'activists' and the non-'activists'. (We also asked our respondents in 1986 what daily newspapers they read during the strike, and whether they thought they were fairly balanced in their presentation of the strike. Table 7.7 shows some of the results.)

This evidence adds weight to the suggestion that support for the strike was based to some extent in ideological orientation, and to some extent in terms of necessity and of having resources to make it possible. The different ideological orientations made for tendencies, not only to adopt different ways of seeing the situation, but also to derive information and make judgements upon it in varied ways. The evidence also supports those who argue that the media of mass communication do not possess unequivocal power to influence opinion and judgement, and that audiences perceive messages according to their own prior definitions of the situation, which may well derive from membership of particular occupational communities.

In terms of support for the strike, our respondents varied not so much according to their involvement in the mining industry, but in terms of their membership of social networks in their localities and their definitions of the situation, based in ideology (or consciousness). Those in mining households

Table 7.7 Most popular daily newspapers read during the strike and judgements of their fairness

Newspaper	Percentage of respondents (N = 135)	
	Reading	*Readers claiming it to be fair in reporting strike*
Daily Mirror	39	56
The Sun	22	23
Daily Express	11	15
Daily Star	9	50

were more likely to express their agreement with the strike than those in other households but, as we saw, the differences were not quite statistically significant at the ninety-five percent level. Being active supporters of the strike was clearly related to having strong network support, and not to being in a mining, as distinct from another kind of household.

Variations in support for the strike by sex, age, education and social class

5 *Respondents' membership of mining households was a more accurate predictor of their level of support for the strike than other factors such as sex, age or education and social class.*

We have already commented on the differences by gender when discussing the differences between mining and other households, but it is important to look further at these, not least because in the assumptions drawn from stereotypical views of mining localities, men and women are seen to inhabit separate social and cultural worlds. The greatest variations which we have observed so far, some of which are statistically significant, are linked to the indicator of agreement with the strike. We have suggested that this links to ideological differences or variations in consciousness. We therefore examine it in terms of gender differences and three other variables, age, educational qualifications and social class, which are known to be key determinants of social and cultural difference.

The lack of any significant differences among our male and female respondents, when we take the whole sample together, is very obvious in Table 7.8 on both indicators, and membership of mining households was a much clearer discriminator, despite the fact that the differences do not reach a rigorous level of statistical significance. (See Table 7.5.)

When we introduce age difference, we are making assumptions that life-cycle situation with its varying constraints is likely to lead to different ways of defining reality. With relatively small samples of respondents, categorising them into more than two or three sets makes meaningful

Table 7.8 Support for the strike and gender differences

| | | Percentages | |
		Females	Males
	Yes	47.2	45.2
Agreement with strike	Yes & No	11.4	6.5
	No	41.5	48.4
	N =	123	31
	Yes	24.0	26.7
Active support in the strike			
	No	76.0	73.3
	N =	120	30

comparison difficult, and so we use a dichotomous variable for age, turning on being over forty, or being a member of the pre-war or war-time, as distinct from the post-war, generation. Table 7.9 presents the data on support for the strike, by gender and age group.

None of the differences reach a stringent level of statistical significance, but age did obviously make some difference to outlook and participation in the strike. Younger women were more likely to have agreed with the strike than older women or younger men, and the fact that younger women were likely to have been less 'active' than older women probably relates to the earlier point, made about women in mining households. Younger women are likely to have had greater domestic responsibilities, such as more child care. In general it conflicts with our earlier conclusion that there are no major differences between men and women. Clearly, the overall figures on support by men and women may conceal important differences between men and women, when they are grouped by household type or age. When we examine the support for the strike by age and membership of mining or other households, irrespective of gender, a further point becomes clear.

Agreement with the strike seemed to decline with age, but active support tended to increase. The differences between mining and other households were mainly ideological. There was less agreement with the strike in other households, but if anything there was more active support.

Turning to education, we have another variable which relates to differences both in consciousness and social status. The data which we collected on education in the mining localities suggests that though our younger respondents had more years of schooling and more educational credentials than older ones the overall level of educational achievement was lower than the national average. This can largely be explained in social class terms, but it may also be a consequence of educational change and locality, too (see Chapter Six and Table 4.2). Using the possession of any nationally

Table 7.9 Support for the strike: gender and age differences

| | Percentages | | | |
| | Females | | Males | |
Respondents who:	Up to 40yrs	Over 40yrs	Up to 40yrs	Over 40yrs
Agreed with strike	54.5	41.4	33.3	50.0
N =	53	70	9	22
Gave active support	21.6	25.7	12.5	31.8
N =	51	70	8	22

Table 7.10 Support for the strike: households by age

| | Percentages | | | |
| | Mining households | | Other households | |
Respondents who:	Up to 40yrs	Over 40yrs	Up to 40yrs	Over 40yrs
Agreed with strike	57.9	52.0	48.8	33.3
N =	19	50	43	42
Gave active support	21.1	22.0	20.0	33.3
N =	19	50	40	42

validated educational award, at 'O' level or above, as the criterion, in Oakton, thirty-seven percent of our female respondents and thirty-three percent of the males had educational qualifications, whereas none of the other places had any male respondents with such qualifications on leaving school. In Willowby and Ashby, six percent of the women had qualifications, and in Beechthorpe, seventeen percent. Overall, sixteen percent of the women respondents and thirteen percent of the men had such qualifications. Using a less stringent definition of educational qualification, and including locally

Table 7.11 Support for the strike: gender and educational differences

	Percentages			
	Females		Males	
	With		With	
Respondents who:	ed. quals	None	ed. quals	None
Agreed with strike	37.2	50.5	33.3	52.6
N =	35	87	12	19
Gave active support	20.6	25.6	16.7	33.3
N =	34	86	12	18

Note: Educational qualifications includes all nationally accredited certificates, plus school awards for merit

Table 7.12 Support for the strike by gender and social class/occupational status of heads of household

Percentage of respondents in	Employed by class			Not employed	
	Salariat	Intermediate	Working	Non-employed	Un-employed
Women who					
Agreed with strike	22.2	51.9	59.5	30.4	57.1
Gave active support	27.8	22.2	28.6	17.4	21.4
N =	18	27	42	23	14
Men who					
Agreed with strike	25.0	42.9	58.3	0	40.0
Gave active support	25.0	28.6	66.7	0	20.0
N =	4	7	12	2	5

Note: Social class allocations have been made on the occupational status of the heads of household, as in Table 5.13 above

awarded certificates, twenty-nine percent of women and thirty-nine percent of the men had some credentials. In Table 7.11 we show the relation of the possession of these qualifications to support for the strike.

Again none of the differences reach statistical significance, but here they are all consistent, and if we take the possession of credentials to be class related, we may conclude that support for the strike was based more among the working class than those of intermediate or middle-class status. Another finding which supports the class interpretation arises when we examine the relation between house tenure and agreement with and 'activism' in the strike. Among owner-occupiers there were lower percentages of those in agreement and those who were 'active' than among tenant householders, though the differences did not reach statistical significance. In fact there was a strong direct relationship between social class, indicated by occupational status of the head of household, and support for the strike. This is shown in Table 7.12 and it applies both to women and men.

The indicator of expressed agreement with the strike shows that the working-class men and women gave far more support than those in the salariat. They tended to be more active, though in the case of women, only by an insignificant margin. Those we have classified in the intermediate social class position tended to have been intermediate in support also, though that is not the case for women who gave active support. Women in the salariat gave more active support than those in the intermediate class. This is probably added confirmation of the analysis above, that active support tended to relate to having the material resources to make it possible. The figures seem to suggest a significant difference among those who were not working at the time of our 1986 survey. Among the retired and redundant, not seeking work, ('non-employed' in Table 7.12), there was much less support, either ideologically or materially, than among the unemployed. The levels of agreement among the unemployed seem to be similar to those of working-class respondents. Their active support was lower than among the working class, again suggesting material factors at work. Clearly the occupational status of the head of household was of great importance. The position and consciousness of the non-employed were such as to reduce support for the strike. A number of respondents in the non-employed households indicated their sense of lack of involvement and this would perhaps suggest the effect of cultural as well as economic factors. This would be an interesting area for further study.

At this point, the testing of our hypotheses leads us to suggest that while belonging to a mining household made some crucial differences to involvement in the strike, particularly in terms of expressing agreement with it, other factors were at work. These were membership of social networks that were able to give material or other support, class background indicated by the occupational status of the head of household, as well as by education and house tenure, and the sense of community support. Position in the life cycle and gender were not such clear bases for difference. If we turn to look at the localities separately, then we find a source of other variations and these probably indicate some shared material and cultural conditions which to some extent cut across the more general factors and suggest the importance of what we have termed local cultural capital.

Variations by locality in support for the strike

6 *There were differences between localities which cut across the other factors which related to support for the strike. There was evidence of variations in local cultural capital, which is based on the idea that persons in relatively integrated communities develop a shared set of information, skills and values which they use in defining and acting in particular situations.*

This hypothesis is based on the assumption that the shared sense of community identity, belief and knowledge, which constitutes the cultural capital of each locality (see Chapter Four) will be reflected in their differing levels of support for and active involvement in the strike. We would assume that the localities can be ranked from most supportive of the strike to least supportive:

1 Willowby – site of a local pit in 1986 and the greatest occupational homogeneity at the time of the study.
2 Ashby – resident miners worked in several pits as well as at a large local pit up to 1985, when it closed.
3 Beechthorpe – still includes many miners working in nearby pits even though Beechthorpe pit was closed twenty years ago.
4 Oakton – has fewer mining households and a larger proportion of middle-class residents than the other localities.

Table 7.13 Levels of support given to the strike, as judged by groups of respondents, divided by locality

Percentages of respondents in:	Neigh-bours	Miners	Level of support shown by:			N*
			Pit managers	Shop-keepers	Local papers	
Oakton	32.4	41.7	5.7	28.6	45.7	(37)
Willowby	76.9	64.1	13.2	71.8	53.8	(39)
Ashby	71.1	74.4	23.1	55.3	33.3	(38)
Beechthorpe	52.6	55.3	13.2	50.0	35.1	(38)

Note:* There were slight variations from the total of respondents in each locality on some of the judgements, because of non-response in a few cases

Table 7.14 Support for the strike by locality: respondents' own expressed views

Respondents in	Percentages				
	Oakton	Willowby	Ashby	Beechthorpe	All
who: Agreed with strike	39.5	64.1	35.9	44.7	46.1
N =	38	39	39	38	154
who: Gave active support	27.7	33.3	15.8	28.1	24.5
N =	36	39	38	38	151

The data relevant to assess this is shown in Tables 7.13 and 7.14. The differences between the expressed support by locality are statistically significant (with probabilities on the chi-square test greater than or equal to ninety-five percent) in three out of the five judgements, (neighbours, shopkeepers and local papers), and nearly so in the other two (miners at ninety-three percent and pit managers at eighty-five percent).

Table 7.13 shows an almost consistent and significant difference between respondents in Oakton, the more middle-class locality, and those in the other three. If we summarise the five support ratings into a mean across the five, then Willowby had highest support rating at fifty-six percent, Ashby was second with forty-nine percent, Beechthorpe third with forty-one percent and Oakton last with thirty-one percent. This fits with our earlier assumption.

A slightly different picture also emerges if we divide the respondents on our two support measures by locality. Table 7.14 shows the differences, which almost reach statistical significance. What emerges is a variability between the localities which is not quite that shown in Table 7.13. Willowby remains, in strike support and activism, ahead of the other localities. Ashby, however, whose respondents gave high ratings of community support, second to those of Willowby, now falls behind both Beechthorpe and Oakton.

There is of course no necessary contradiction between these findings. We asked the respondents to judge the support of others and then to indicate their own view of the strike, and we would claim that our respondents, having been selected randomly, are representative of their localities. On many items within our 1986 and 1987 surveys there were significant variations between the localities, for instance on the importance and strength of kinship bonds, on being born and brought up in a locality, on the number of mining households, on aspects of health, and on social class as indicated by education, house tenure and occupational status. Each had a distinct historical pattern of development. These suggest subtle and important variations in the social structure of each locality, which would support the notion of different local cultures, not necessarily completely integrated and coherent but containing the possibilities of both community and conflict. We saw in Chapter Four that in Ashby there were ambiguities and oppositions within what we defined as the local culture, and this is possibly reflected in the different rank order of support given to the strike in the localities in Tables 7.13 and 7.14.

The remaining four hypotheses are concerned with the implications of the strike for the people in our research area and for the local economy and culture.

Changes in values and beliefs: differences between mining and other households

7 Miners and their partners more often changed their values and beliefs and other aspects of their lives as a result of the strike than non-mining households.

We asked respondents about changes they had made in their lives since the strike, focussing particularly on their daily work and on changes that had taken place in women's lives, their identity and their political consciousness. In addition we asked what changes had taken place in the way they interpreted industrial relations, police tactics and the news offerings of the media as a result of events that occurred during the strike.

On *paid employment*, the principal concern was the decline that had been taking place in the labour market since the strike and mining households were experiencing higher rates of unemployment than other households. Not surprisingly, more women from mining households than other households said that they had changed their views about seeking paid employment since the strike (thirty-seven percent compared with twenty-eight percent). Getting a paid job would help if and when a partner's income was cut, but some also noted that earning their own income would give them a sense of autonomy.

When they were asked if it had been increasing male unemployment or factors such as the miners' strike and the sense of activism among women during that time which had changed their views toward paid employment, twenty-three percent of the women in mining households compared with eleven percent in other households said it had been the former.

With regard to *industrial relations*, we asked respondents in particular about whether they had changed their views on striking and picketing. The answers on striking reflected on the miners' strike itself, and there was a tendency for those in mining households to have changed more than in other households. The changes occurred in about a quarter of the former, but these split evenly between those who thought striking justified, even though they had disagreed with it at the time of the miners' strike and those who disagreed, though they had agreed with the miners' strike. In other households, about a fifth said they had changed, and overwhelmingly they now said they were against striking. On picketing fifty percent of respondents in mining households compared with thirty-four percent in other households, claimed that their views had changed since the strike. On the whole most were concerned that there had been too much violence, but nevertheless, while nearly a fifth of all respondents wanted more controls put on picketing, almost a half still saw it as a valid exercise of rights.

Closely related to this were their views on *policing*. Among women there were highly significant differences between those in mining and those in other households. In the former fifty percent of women said their views had changed, and in the latter twenty-four percent. The differences among men were minimal, but a greater percentage of men claimed that the strike had made them change their minds about policing. The majority in each case said that they now had less confidence in the impartiality of the police.

We asked also about *watching television* broadcasts. In mining households almost half of respondents said that their viewing habits had changed, and that they had watched more news and current affairs programmes, compared with before the strike. Respondents in two-fifths of other households also said the same. The changes, however, seem to have had more effect in mining households, where nearly a third claimed not to have gone back to a former pattern of viewing, compared to only fourteen percent in other households.

As we have said, our principal interest in the research project was to discover the effect of the strike on *women's lives*. Stereotypically, women in mining localities have been held to lead somewhat closed lives, dominated in a patriarchal system, and occupying a separate domestic sphere, while men have been the breadwinners and have lived in a men's world. During the strike women were seen to come out, and in the liberated atmosphere of women's groups to have forged a new role for themselves. How far had this occurred?

We have made an assessment of this in our interviews of nineteen women, but here we approach an answer by looking at a random sample of women, only two of whom had any active involvement in women's groups during the strike. All the respondents were asked whether they wanted to see any lasting changes in the lives of local women. Among women in mining households twenty-eight percent said 'yes', whereas in other households it rose to fifty-seven percent. This was a very significant difference. Among men there was less difference, but again the men in mining households were more conservative with forty-four percent wanting change compared to fifty percent of the men in other households. For the women this seemed to contradict the set of responses on the question of women's paid employment, especially when that was linked to some extent with achieving more autonomy. When we asked whether they thought there were likely to be changes, women in mining households were still more conservative in their judgements than those in other households, though not significantly (forty-two percent to fifty percent thought there would be changes). Among men, those in mining households were slightly more willing to believe there would be change (fifty-three percent) than men in other households (forty-one percent). Thus in mining households the tendency seemed to be to think that changes were going to occur but, presumably, since there was also a smaller desire for change, the changes were not thought likely to be beneficial. The largest response category among those who said why they did not want changes in women's lives was 'we prefer it as it is' or something very similar. The small leap we have to make here is to remember one of the most prevalent slogans of the strike campaign, 'Close a Pit and You Close a Community'. This was the kind of change that was not acceptable or thought to be beneficial either to men or women. Yet it was occurring.

On questions about whether their *own lives and outlook* had changed there were differences between those in mining households and those in other households. Men and women in the former thought that they were more politically aware than they had been before the strike to a greater extent than those in other households. Among women the most marked differences were claimed with regard to their 'identity' – how they saw themselves since the strike. In mining households, thirty-eight percent of women compared with only thirteen percent of those in other households, said that they now saw themselves differently. Among men there were no differences, however, and only thirteen percent overall felt they had changed. The women who had participated in support groups not only reported being more conscious politically, they also said they were more self-confident and more socially aware. A number of women were attracted to educational and vocational courses in centres set up by the Local Authority. Interestingly when we asked whether the changes they felt would be obvious to others around them, less than ten percent thought they would.

It is clear, although on only a few items, that differences between mining and other households reach statistical significance, and there is some support for the hypothesis that there have been more changes because of the strike among respondents in mining households than in others. The changes reported and the attitudes to change are somewhat contradictory. There is a desire for more autonomy, but there is no confidence that that can be achieved through the economic hardship which is entailed in pit closures, if there are no alternative opportunities made available in the labour market.

The chief problem for many mining households when the strike was over was coping with debts which had accrued during the twelve months of much reduced or negligible income.

Traditional social networks and the problems of the strike

8 *Persons with more extensive family and friendship ties in the community, and those who were members of the striking community, received more extensive help and were better able to cope with financial hardships than the more isolated miners and their families.*

In 1986 when we asked respondents about their financial situation during and after the strike, forty percent of mining households admitted some debt. Later, in replying to questions about whether they were still burdened with debt, about half of all the respondents now said that they were. It may be that questions about debt raise issues of personal and household morality, and that respondents are constrained from giving a complete answer. Two-thirds of those who got into debt were still in that position.

The chief reason for debt was of course the absence of the mineworker's income, but in addition many households experienced income reductions as a consequence of social security benefits to which they were entitled being withheld. Again the responses of our interviewees were possibly not as full as they might have been because of the strong constraints which affect people discussing benefits and entitlements. There is still a sense of such moneys being 'charity' and of 'shame' in having to admit to receiving them. Social Security officers in any case were told to award benefits on the incorrect assumption that the strikers were receiving strike benefit from their Union. In addition nineteen percent of mining households said that they experienced further reductions in social security payments, and others had problems with invalidity and child benefits. Altogether fourteen percent of households reported problems when seeking redress about what they considered to be reductions in their entitlements. A third of households noted that they had also had to cope with variations from week to week in their income, and of these a half reported declining income during the strike.

The chief means used for coping with the reduced income was in deferring the payment of rents, mortgages, rates, electricity bills and hire purchase accounts. Further, savings were run down, insurance policies were cashed

Table 7.15 Sources of outside help for mining households during the strike

Source	Percentage of households receiving help
1. Support groups	63
2. Family	61
3. Union branches	55
4. Local authorities	55
5. Local shopkeepers	29
6. Friends	26
7. Neighbours	18
N =	38

in and items were sold. In about ten percent of households respondents said that they or their partners had managed to get some paid employment. About three-quarters of mining households received some help in the form of cash, food vouchers and/or commodities from others. Table 7.15 indicates the rank order of sources of outside help.

Overall, it is difficult to establish the relative importance of traditional social networks (relatively informally organised groups in the locality) in providing support during the strike. All our earlier evidence suggests that it is likely to have been important. Among the networks we would obviously count family and other local groups, like the support groups. We do not know in detail comparable values of help given as against the household's own budgetary and other measures, such as dietary changes, in dealing with financial problems. Table 7.15 suggests nevertheless that they were important and this accords with the general impression gained from the earlier discussion of support groups and about how families helped out in the susbsistence economy enforced by the strike.

Household debt reached a median level of £250, but as much as £1000 in some cases. Those households which had a larger kinship network reported that they had help from relatives more frequently than those with smaller networks, but interestingly were significantly more likely to have told us that they ended up in debt. 'Natives' among the respondents claimed significantly more often, than others who had lived for shorter periods in the localities, that they did not end up in debt, or, if they had, that they had cleared their debts. This might be a comment on their lack of confidence or willingness to talk about debt, or on the effect of their status in the localities. In terms of our indicators of support for the strike, those who expressed agreement were less likely to have ended up in debt than those who had not agreed (thirty-nine percent of the former and fifty percent of the latter). On the other hand slightly more of the 'activists' ended up in debt (forty-four percent) than the non-'activists' (thirty-nine percent).

There is some support, then, for the hypothesis that traditional social networks were important in the strike and afterwards in helping households to cope with debt. Those who had access to such networks had a further resource to draw upon, and did not simply have to manage in isolation.

The domestic division of labour and the effects of the strike

9 *Active strike supporters showed most post-strike changes in attitudes and behaviours. In particular, women who participated in the support groups' activities came out of the strike with much more activist self-concepts, and they and their partners adopted new views of 'women's work' and 'men's work' in the home with less clear-cut boundaries between the two than in the past.*

Among women who participated in the support groups, it was often reported that there was during the strike period a perceived change of relationship with their male partners. There seemed to be more equality in decision-making and more sharing of domestic tasks. Commentators often made the claim that this was the beginning of a permanent change for women in mining localities as we pointed out earlier. Since we were interviewing women who had stayed in the localities after the strike, we are unable to assess the level of marriage break-up which was reported as having increased by women informants active in support groups elsewhere.

We collected information from households about the domestic division of labour in both 1986 and 1987, and this is analysed in Chapter Five. As we said there, a highly gendered division of domestic labour still exists. In 1987 we also asked respondents to estimate the amount of work done by their mothers and fathers. Their replies suggested that there has been a slight shift from a very highly segregated domestic division of labour, but nevertheless the traditional segregation of domestic tasks has not disappeared.

When we asked our respondents whether there had been any change during and since the strike in their own household's internal division of labour, only twenty-nine percent of women reported that there had been. Of those who reported change, almost a half (forty-six percent) said that the strike was the cause, and the others reported reasons like ill-health, retirement and getting paid employment outside the home. The claimed changes were clustered among the women who had agreed with the strike, but not significantly so, and there was little difference between those who were and were not active supporters of the strike.

The analysis of answers to specific questions about household work before, during and after the strike, showed that there was a period of relative egalitarianism during the strike. This contrasted with the more segregated situation before and after the strike (Figures 7.1.1–8).

Our 'optimistic' hypothesis, which noted the significance of women's action and anticipated a release of women afterwards from traditional gender

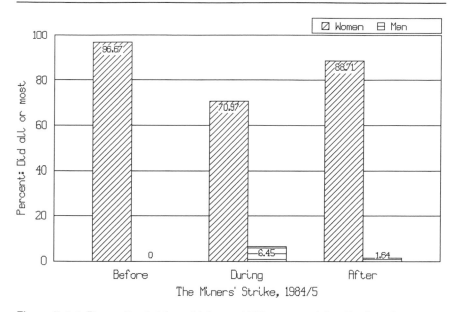

Figure 7.1.1 Domestic division of labour, 1986 survey: doing the laundry

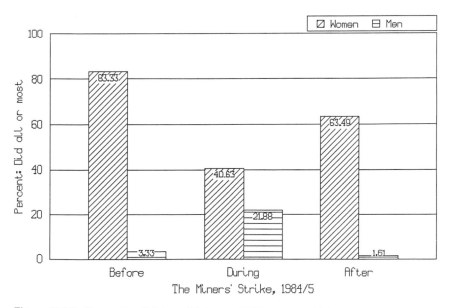

Figure 7.1.2 Domestic division of labour, 1986 survey: tidying and cleaning

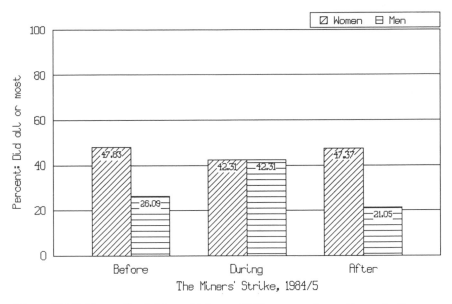

Figure 7.1.3 Domestic division of labour, 1986 survey: domestic production

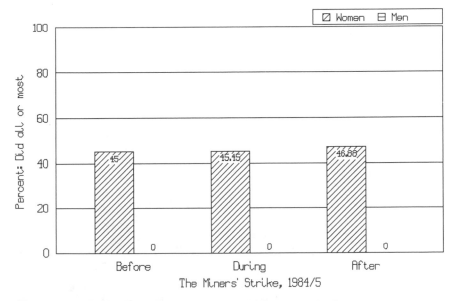

Figure 7.1.4 Domestic division of labour, 1986 survey: child care

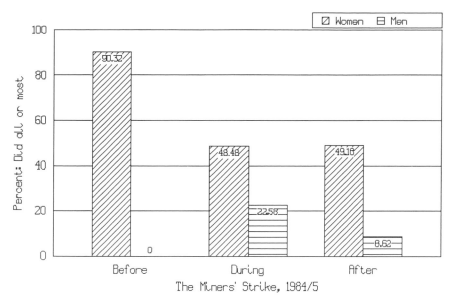

Figure 7.1.5 Domestic division of labour, 1986 survey: food preparation

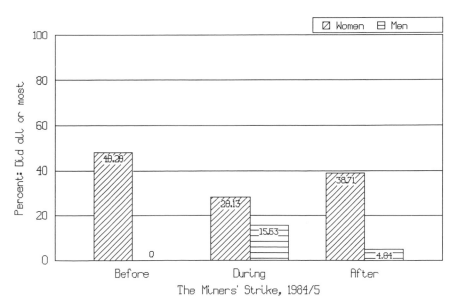

Figure 7.1.6 Domestic division of labour, 1986 survey: shopping

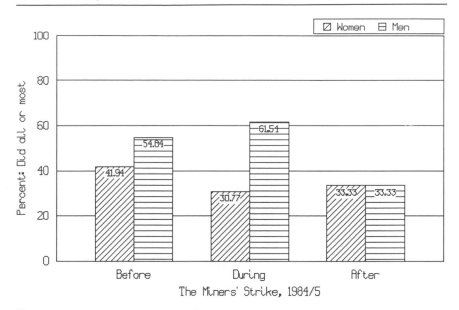

Figure 7.1.7 Domestic division of labour, 1986 survey: home maintenance

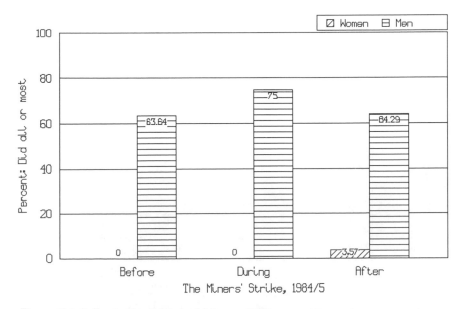

Figure 7.1.8 Domestic division of labour, 1986 survey: home improvement

roles, is not confirmed. If there are to be changes in the domestic sphere, they are more likely to be the effect of the long-term trend which we noted in the 1987 data, and of changes in the tendency of women to move into the labour market. As we said above, we found that the least segregated domestic arrangements were in those households where women were in full-time paid employment outside the home.

Future prospects for households and the local economy

10 *All respondents were pessimistic about future prospects with little or no difference between those in mining households who were active or not in their support of the strike, or between mining and non-mining households.*

In 1986 we asked a set of five questions relating to the future. These were about the prospects for children, for men, for women and for the coal industry, and their opinions on what needed to be done in the area, considering the closure of pits. The responses showed an overwhelming sense of pessimism, which had been there in the pilot interviews.

With regard to the future for the *children*, the apparent lack of jobs to replace those that were being lost in the mining industry seemed to dominate the considerations of nine out of every ten of the respondents. There was little hope for the future either in mining or other households, and no differences emerged among those who had varied in their support for the strike. Twelve percent of respondents thought that children would have to be ready to move away in search of employment.

The prospects for *men* were seen to be either bleak or worse. Again the need to move away was thought to be the only option by a significant minority (eight percent). Those who had agreed with the strike, or who had actively supported it, and those in mining households, tended to define the situation for men in worse terms than those who had not supported the strike or were not in mining households. Those in mining households were also less likely to want to think of the option of men moving away from their locality.

The most frequent response concerning *women*, given by thirty-nine percent of all respondents, was that their prospects would not be improved without the provision of more opportunities in the labour market. Among the mining households and among those who had supported the strike, there was a tendency to see this as a more important issue than in other households and among the non-supporters. Even so there was not much optimism about it happening, with the respondents in the former categories again expressing more pessimism than those in the latter. In line with the general patriarchal character of the local culture, it was not suggested that women should move away, unless of course to follow their menfolk. This attitude is not, of course, confined to mining areas.

On the *coal-mining industry*, some twenty-four percent thought that prospects were relatively good for the industry as a whole, even if not in the immediate locality. The closure of surplus capacity and the development of new 'super-pits' was seen by them as generally beneficial. This was roughly the attitude taken by British Coal in 1986. Among the rest, there were some twenty percent of all respondents with a diversity of views, which were basically neutral. The other fifty-six percent considered that the industry was being closed down or drastically reorganised for privatisation. There was no difference in the spread of these responses among mining and other households, nor among those who had or had not been 'active' in support of the strike. There were, however, significant differences between those who expressed ideologically opposed views on the strike. Generally, those who expressed the 'British Coal' point of view were those who had disagreed with the strike, and those who were pessimistic were those who had said they agreed with, or were not entirely negative about the strike. The highest degree of pessimism was found in Willowby, and the most pro-'British Coal' sentiment in Oakton.

What was to be done? There was little agreement on a preferred policy of action. In general the approach was pre-empted by the view that nothing much could be done, and if improvements were on the way, it would be elsewhere and not in these localities. Given that, however, a plea for further investment was made by seventeen percent of respondents. A further ten percent thought that it would be better to be rid of the government. A few (three percent) felt that the local authority policy of bringing of resources to the area could help. About five percent thought that it was up to individuals to make their own decisions, such as moving away from the area. 'Collective' solutions in terms of public investment were more strongly expressed in Willowby, Ashby and Beechthorpe, than in Oakton, where more 'private' solutions were indicated.

CONCLUSIONS TO BE DRAWN FROM THE DISCUSSION OF THE TEN HYPOTHESES

Our hypotheses were meant to elucidate the factors that were behind support for, or opposition to, the miners' strike of 1984/5, and the implications of that strike for the localities. We approached the collection of data in terms of an understanding of mining localities derived from discussions of the ideal–typical model of traditional mining communities and in the light of optimistic assessments of the meaning of the considerable extent of women's action in support of that strike (see Allen et al., 1987).

In assessing support for the strike, we had assumed that expressions of agreement with the strike and the tendency to be active in support of the strike and the striking miners would overlap. We found however that statements of agreement did not show any statistical association with statements about active support. We therefore used the two as separate indicators of support and in our analysis we found that they seemed to be tapping different aspects of that support. The 'agreement' indicator seemed to link with attitudinal or ideological orientation, whereas the 'activism' indicator seemed to relate to social or material factors which made that support necessary or possible. Statements of agreement were associated with quite different ways of defining the situation, for instance in terms of the amount of community support that was given to the strike, or in assessing the future of British Coal in the area. Those who disagreed with the strike tended to view the future of the industry in a more positive light than those who had agreed with the strike. Further, those who expressed agreement with the strike derived information about the strike and made judgements about its validity in quite different ways from those who disagreed with it. Statements of active support were associated with respondents who were members of large kinship networks, were 'native' to (born and brought up in) the locality or had lived a long time in it.

Our hypotheses made assumptions about the differences between mining and other households which it was difficult to sustain completely. First there was the difficulty in categorising households as mining or non-mining, because of changes over time in employment in the coal industry. We used a stringent definition for the purposes of analysis, but we found that for both mining and other households, levels of agreement with and active support for the strike were higher among the 'natives' and those with large kinship networks. There were some differences between mining and other households, and in expected directions. Belonging to social networks, being a 'native' and being in a mining household, together, were more important indicators of support for the strike than age and gender. Social class was consistently, or almost so, related on both indicators to support for the strike, and seemed to be as significant as membership of kinship networks and being a 'native'.

Some of the variation in support for the strike was also related to membership of particular local cultures. Willowby was the place which had the highest level of agreement with the strike and most expressions of active support. This was found using two approaches to assessing levels of support in the communities. Our most middle-class locality, Oakton, was the one which had the lowest levels of support, when using respondents judgements of others in the community. Nevertheless, using self-reported support as an indicator, it had a higher level of 'activism' than two of the more working-class communities. This might have been related to the relative affluence of Oakton. As we said earlier, active support to some extent depended on having the material resources to give it. Nevertheless, when we were discussing local culture in Chapter Four, with particular reference to Ashby, we noted that ambiguities and oppositions can and do occur. Local cultural differences were related to somewhat unique historical, social and economic variations.

The implications of the strike were assessed in terms of changes in economic security and in outlook on economic activity, on issues like strikes and policing which were significant during the strike, and on women's lives and the domestic division of labour. Not surprisingly there had been more changes in mining than other households. The changes reported and the outlook on them were somewhat contradictory. There was a desire for more autonomy especially among women, but there was no confidence that it could be achieved, considering the economic hardship which is entailed by pit closures, and if no alternative opportunities are made available on the labour market. The optimistic analyses of the strike period which forecast the liberation of women from the patriarchal relations of mining localities were also found not to have been justified. Though more women are entering paid employment, and where this happens tends to be associated with a reduction of the demands placed on the women's domestic roles, the domestic division of labour is still a very gendered one. Any tendency towards egalitarianism between men and women which occurred in the strike period tended to have been eroded after the end of strike.

There was a profound pessimism about future prospects. In general the consideration of what was to be done was pre-empted by the view that nothing much could be done, and if improvements were on the way, it would be elsewhere and not in these localities.

THE SOCIAL IMPLICATIONS OF THE DESTRUCTION OF THE WEST YORKSHIRE COAL MINING INDUSTRY

Our research was carried out against the background of the closure by British Coal of most of the pits that were working in our research area at the beginning of 1984. When we started our work, there were seven collieries actively producing coal, and in two of them, one in Ashby and the other in Willowby, recent multi-million pound investment schemes had just been set in train. At present, only two of the pits are still producing coal, and do not include the two with substantial investment. At least 5000 jobs have been lost in the mining industry from 1978 to 1988 (O'Donnell, 1988).

This is not to suggest that British Coal has singled out the West Yorkshire coalfield for special attention. It is part of a general policy of closures, against a background of government intention to end the nationalised control of the industry, and to slim it down into what can be seen as a more profitable shape, in readiness for privatisation. The latest plans include the closure of twenty more pits, with an output reduction of twenty-five million tonnes of coal per year over the next four years (Harper, 1989). Since the end of the miners' strike in 1985 and up to 1989, ninety-four pits had been closed in Britain, and jobs reduced from 221,000 to 92,000. A further 30,000 jobs would go if the new plans were to be implemented. There were twenty pit closures in 1989 and the 1990 workforce was below 80,000 (Wise, 1990). British

Coal has also employed hard-line management techniques and has found the Union of Democratic Mineworkers to have diminished the effectiveness of the National Union of Mineworkers. Meanwhile, in 1990, the government seemed to be intent on legislating to increase the numbers of workers that may be employed underground in privately owned pits from thirty to one hundred and fifty, as a stage on the road to full privatisation (Hymas, 1990). In areas where underground mining has ceased, open-cast working is being developed. The most significant development of this kind in our research area is at Ashby. It employs few workers and the methods of extraction using earth-moving equipment and mechanical diggers have little regard for the quality of life of the people who live nearby. Ashby has been the scene of many protests against the dust and noise pollution which has been caused.

It is possible to argue as the Wintertons have done that the destruction of the mining industry is a conscious Tory policy against the working class. For them

> the 1984 conflict could have been fought out in almost any industry because the same conditions were afflicting the whole economy . . . The coal industry became the terrain for the confrontation because of the symbolic importance of the miners in the labour movement and because the effect of Government policies was becoming acutely apparent in coal.
>
> (Winterton, 1989: 1)

They see the strategy of closure as ideologically motivated and not as a rational economic process. Alternative scenarios can be envisaged, they argue. Britain could have a very different conception of the energy market, which could be based on self-sufficiency and conservation, rather than the present process of sterilisation of reserves and use of imported fuels. Another approach could be based in planned moderate economic growth and the use of as much internally deep mined coal as possible. For the Wintertons, however, the present government is concerned little with the specifics of the coal industry, but is absorbed in an attempt to defeat the labour movement and socialism through taking on and breaking its vanguard. Some support for this position might be judged to stem from the statements of the former Prime Minister, Mrs Thatcher, when in a speech at the time of her resignation, she claimed as one of the achievements of her eleven years of office the defeat of the miners in 1985.

An account of the present situation which takes issue somewhat with the Wintertons is that of Gibbon and Bromley (1990). This follows Gibbon's earlier review of the vast literature on the miner's strike, in which he contended that 'the basis of the strike, its form of struggle, its unevennesses, not to mention "Scargillism", are deeply rooted in the specificity of the British mining industry' (1988). His account lays great stress on varying local cultures, on grassroots 'pit politics' and on the contrasts which could occur between the local, the regional and the national levels of industrial relations. We have shown evidence, in the development of mining in the nineteenth and twentieth centuries, which supports this position. In the 1980s, they argue, British Coal and the government in abandoning the corporatist approach to management exacerbated the relations between different areas and transposed 'pit politics' onto the national stage. This explained the length, the degree of resistance and the local variations in the strike.

Gibbon and Bromley go on to argue that the run-down of the coal industry

> has been a party-consensual aim in Britain since 1956 . . . and while since 1979 the Conservatives had let the brakes off further on this run-down by their increased support for nuclear power and their tax changes to encourage a North Sea oil and gas boom, the consignment of coal to the role of a minor player appears not to have been envisaged.
>
> (Gibbon and Bromley, 1990)

The ideological approach of the Thatcher governments was not linked particularly to defeating the labour movement, but to reducing the call of the industry on state expenditure, in the context of 'an energy policy in which coal was to be run down and sources of power internationalised, and an industrial relations policy in which "union power" was to be curbed' (ibid.). The strong resistance of the miners during 1984/5 merely made British Coal more dependent on the government, and forced it afterwards into having to introduce more cuts and more streamlining through upgrading management information systems and other modern management systems to keep up with government policy. In the end it has lost any power to bargain with government, and while British Coal may feel it has been 'transformed from an "institution" to a "business", the goalposts have meanwhile been shifted . . . it [is] one business among many working in the energy sector' (ibid.).

The explanation for the strike and its aftermath put forward by the Wintertons relies on evidence of consciously motivated capitalists using all resources at their disposal, including technology, planning devices, propaganda, police and military force, to defeat the working class. That of Gibbon and Bromley seems to rely more on evidence of a mixture of political and organisational innovation and opportunism within the context of a capitalist culture with all its unevennesses, divisions and local variations. Organisations are pursuing ends of profitability and growth or stability and survival and using techniques which a modern society makes available. In the competitive and often unpredictable environment, the victims are those with the least power to hold their corner.

Attractive and evocative though the former explanation tends to be, it is the latter which seems more in tune with the situation as it is defined by our working-class respondents in all four localities. Though some of the respondents in our biographical interviews in the early 1980s indicated that class conflict motivated the dominant classes and was responsible for the decline of coal mining and trade unionism, the locally dominant view of Labour Party and trade union activists, with its concern for negotiation and attempts to improve the life chances of working-class people, would have more readily incorporated the explanation of Gibbon and Bromley.

Many of our respondents saw that their economic resources are based in a declining labour market. There is a local authority policy designed to attract new industries to these localities, with new workshops and factory buildings at peppercorn rents and with resource centres for people to learn new skills. It is not making any real impact on unemployment. Two significant developments have recently been secured in the Wakefield District, a new electronics factory which is part of a Japanese corporation, and a large rail terminal for northbound goods traffic from the Channel Tunnel. It is hoped to create several thousand jobs, but they are not likely to balance the recent job losses arising from pit closures. The most recent count (March 1990) of job losses since 1981 in the mining industry, in the Wakefield Metropolitan District as a whole, shows a reduction of over 14,000. As we have indicated, three out of four of our localities have significant sections of their population with less than half the average household income. There is some evidence too that the situation is worsening, with the polarising effects of government fiscal and social policies in the 1980s.

The social and cultural resources of these communities are their kinship networks and their local skills, and memories of past individual and collaborative efforts to improve the quality of their lives, their churches, clubs and co-ops. We have noted, however, that organised attempts to improve and extend these skills, through education and health services, have major handicaps to overcome. Levels of educational achievement have been slow to improve, and the incidence of health disorders is high compared with other parts of Britain. Housing policies, at one time dominated by local authority building aimed at big improvements in rented accommodation, have shifted to the sale of council houses and private building. While this has been a relatively popular policy, it has contributed towards social polarisation, and the tendency to increase poverty and disadvantage once more, especially in Willowby.

As far as political resources are concerned, these are increasingly tied to their unexpanding rights as electors, and the alternative of union power has been drastically eroded, as the pits and large-scale industry in nearby towns and cities have closed. Inevitably their rights as citizens can be overlooked, since they have little collective voice to use, and the state has in any case withdrawn or reduced its support for individual citizenship. Some of our respondents in their biographical interviews, recorded in Chapter Four, noted this decline of local power, seeing it particularly in terms of the growth of relatively distant bureaucracies, the Metropolitan District Councils and the Coal Board. By the time of the later surveys, few of our respondents thought that either of these could or would do anything to improve the future for these localities. The pessimism is really a sense of alienation.

This is what Bauman (1988) sees as an almost inevitable product of the new conditions which prevail as old industries and old labour markets are dismantled and the globalised capitalist economy is restructured. The Thatcherite response to these conditions and the problem of 'translating human concerns into political programmes' has been to promote 'the exit of human concerns from politics . . . This dismantling of effective citizenship is presented as the triumph of freedom; as liberation . . . Politics is a nuisance. The less of it the better' (Bauman, 1988). The 1980s, the years of Mrs Thatcher's premiership, have seen an enormous erosion of civil, economic, political and social rights, which the study of these four mining communities has charted. As our colleague, Professor Sheila Allen, has noted, we have witnessed a narrowing of the legitimately recognised expectations of citizenship. A profound shift has occurred in which a formerly achieved floor of basic rights in employment and social conditions has had its foundations removed. Since 1979 measures have been introduced, through the Employment Acts of 1980 and 1984, and the Wages Act of 1986, to reduce employee rights and control collective organisation and activities in their defence. Deregulation and privatisation, in the name of competition, enterprise and wealth creation have been major mechanisms in this restructuring process (Allen, 1989c).

The mining communities which we have discussed are being restructured by such forces, largely out of the control of the people who live there. The certainty of employment in a local industry, always subject to the constraints of the market for coal, the geological conditions and the organisation of production, has now virtually disappeared. What may have been a dream, or a nightmare, for boys in these localities is no more than a fading shadow.

The local cultural capital which has been created in the four communities is likely to be eroded within a generation as the reality of coal mining as employment and that basis for social and political organisation disappears. The disadvantage which this will reinforce ought to be the subject of much more scrutiny than it is receiving. The local authorities which had or have significant employment in the coal industry, along with trade unionists and some other interested parties set up the Coalfields Communities Campaign in the 1980s. It has promoted research, produced many documents, held well-organised conferences and lobbied parliamentary and industrial representatives. Its effect on the policies of the current government seem to be minimal. There is as yet no indication that British Coal is going to be diverted from preparing the industry for a very small, privatised role in energy production in the future. British Coal, through its Enterprise organisation, disburses grants and advice to ex-miners and others who want to set up new forms of business or industry in the mining localities. Research

Plate 7.1 Dream or nightmare? (Photo by Dennis Warwick)

into these has not so far shown them to be making much impact. Essentially new policies must be created which recognise the erosion of rights which has occurred.

Economic and industrial rights as part of citizenship may be argued to be integral to the social rights on which in turn the exercise of political and civil rights depends. For the majority of the population in our West Yorkshire communities (and more widely), the aftermath of the strike has meant a radical erosion of these rights. There is greater inequality now, and, given the significance of the women in the domestic division of labour which we have noted, any such increase in inequality must fall most heavily on working-class women. The remaining resources which traditional social networks and local cultural capital may provide, important as they are, are not likely to provide much of a bulwark against the decline in citizenship. Nevertheless, in the way that they operated during the strike, with encouragement and renewal, they might become a basis for the kind of social movement which Bauman (1988) sees as perhaps the only hope for promoting democratic self-determination and raising the possibility of full rights of citizenship once more. Essentially, however, the promotion of citizenship rights requires not only an active social movement but a government that is willing to respond positively in terms of the provision of adequate economic opportunities and safeguards, and is conscious of the disadvantages to individuals, households and localities, which market-led and unplanned restructuring can cause.

Notes

3 THE HISTORICAL BACKGROUND OF WEST YORKSHIRE MINING COMMUNITIES

1 Drawing on the unpublished work of the late Jim MacFarlane of Sheffield University and through discussion with our colleague Dr Carolyn Baylies at Leeds University, it is possible to reconstruct the events surrounding 'the Featherstone Massacre', in a way that goes beyond the brief reference to it in *Coal is Our Life* (see p. 82). The account of R.G. Neville (1976) and the official report (Bowen Report, 1893) provide very full descriptions, but to differing extents start from unsociological positions, in that they do not focus on the wider context of economic, political and social relations.

2 The account of the Hemsworth lock-out is based on work carried out by members of the Hemsworth WEA Local Studies Group in 1986/7, by Ann Lewis, a former student of Bradford College (who wrote a dissertation in fulfilment of the requirements for a Teacher's Certificate, entitled 'The Hemsworth Dispute', 1976) and John Lynas, a former student at Leeds University. Points of detail have also been discussed with Dr Baylies. Sources of information include minutes of the Yorkshire Miners' Association, local newspapers, and articles in a socialist monthly, the *Labour Record*. A record of events at the time was made by a local in Hemsworth, called Wales, and many of the prints have survived.

4 RESEARCH IN FOUR MINING COMMUNITIES IN THE 1980s

1 Humour is an essential ingredient of the local culture and comes through in all the indigenous writing which has been generated recently by Yorkshire Arts Circus, an independent organisation supported by public funds. The Circus has been set up to encourage local writers. A good example is the recent publication edited by I. Clayton, A. Rhodes and T. Lumb (1990), *This is Featherstone: At home, at work and at play*. A paper presented at the British Sociological Association Annual Conference in 1978, at the University of Sussex, by A.E. Green, 'Only Kidding: Joking among Coal-Miners', is a very useful analysis of some aspects of humour. He suggests that some humour celebrates the relationship of 'insiders' to each other. It is a game, played by members to emphasise their membership and to test 'outsiders', before they are let into the group. It operates then as an aspect of social control. It may also relieve the tension of dangerous moments, industrial conflicts and risk-taking which are well known in the mining industry. 'Staffy' jokes can be seen to fit very much into this kind of context.

5 PAID EMPLOYMENT, TRADITIONAL SOCIAL NETWORKS AND THE GENDER DIVISION OF LABOUR

1 The source for the data on employment in the mining industry in 1981 was the Planning Department of the West Yorkshire Metropolitan County Council, a local authority which was abolished under legislation in 1986.
2 The Coal Industry National Consultative Council annually receives reports in the field of recruitment, education and training, and these give an indication of the wide variety of training schemes and courses, both internal and external to the industry, which clearly relate to hopes both on the part of the management and the unions involved for an upgrading of the skills and expertise of workers at all levels. Such schemes emerged particularly after legislation in 1974, setting up the Manpower Services Commission, and the Industry Training Boards, in a period of corporatist attempts to bring together capital, government, industry and unions so as to increase industrial efficiency and productivity. These have to be seen in terms of attempts by all parties to enhance their interests in a time of economic difficulty, following the oil and energy crises of the early 1970s.

6 CONTEMPORARY SOCIAL DIVISIONS: TENURE, EDUCATION, HEALTH AND SOCIAL POLARISATION

1 The indicators COF3M and SBREATH were constructed out of answers to questions which progressively indicated more serious respiratory conditions. COF3M is based in the answers to the final question in the series on coughing. It is a crucial part of the Medical Research Council definition of chronic bronchitis. SBREATH is based on the answers to the first in the series of four questions on breathlessness. Only a small number of respondents gave affirmative answers to the later questions.

Table 6.10 Frequency of responses to SBREATH questions by sex

	Total frequency	All responses	Percentage of: Males	Females
SBREATH1	68	21.18	12.90	27.50
SBREATH2	20	6.23	5.38	7.97
SBREATH3	10	3.11	3.08	3.52
SBREATH4	9	2.80	2.79	2.81
Total respondents	321			

As shown in Table 6.10, the disparity between male and female experience of shortage of breath disappears as the seriousness of the symptom increases. This is unlike the coughing symptom where the disparity increases slightly with the seriousness of the symptom, and where the incidence among men is always higher than that among women. Our use of SBREATH1 in the analysis provides an indicator which is certainly not as stringent as COF3M but is generally indicative of a somewhat different aspect of respiratory problems. Nevertheless, as with COF3M, SBREATH at any level seems to be more common among the relatively disadvantaged respondents, and the general findings for SBREATH1 are indicative of those for the other more stringent levels, as far as we can judge. For example SBREATH2 is experienced by 14.49 percent of tenants compared with 4.02 percent of owner-occupiers.

Bibliography

Allen, S. (1983) 'Waged Work in the Household: Continuity and Change in Production and Reproduction', *Sociological Review* 31 (4).

Allen, S. (1989a) 'Flexibility of Work and Working Time', in J.B. Agassi and S. Heycock (eds), *The Redesign of Working Time: Promise or Threat?*, Berlin, Sigma.

Allen, S. (1989b) 'Gender and Work in Mining Communities', Paper presented to the BSA Conference, Plymouth, March.

Allen, S. (1989c) 'Social Aspects of Citizenship', Paper given at Queen's University, Belfast, May.

Allen, S., V. Carroll and C. Truman et al. (1987) 'Women in Mining Communities', Paper presented to the BSA Conference, Leeds, April.

Allen, S., G. Littlejohn and D. Warwick (1988) *Mining Communities and Social Change*, Economic and Social Research Council, End of Award Report, September.

Allen, S., G. Littlejohn and D. Warwick (1989) 'Gender and Work in Mining Communities', Unpublished paper, University of Bradford.

Allen, V. (1981) *The Militancy of British Miners*, Moor Press, Baildon.

Archbishop of Canterbury's Commission on Urban Priority Areas (1985) *Faith in the City*, London, Church House Publishing.

Ashton, D., M.J. Maguire and G. Garland (1982) *Youth in the Labour Market*, Research Paper no. 34, Department of Employment, London, HMSO.

Austin, D.J. (1984), *Australian Sociologies*, London, Allen & Unwin.

Bauman, Z. (1988) 'Britain's Exit from Politics', *New Statesman and Society*, London 29 July.

Bedarida, F. (1979) *A Social History of England: 1851–1975*, London, Methuen.

Bell, C. and H. Newby (1971) *Community Studies, An Introduction to the Sociology of the Local Community*, London Allen & Unwin.

Bell, C. & L. McKee (1985) 'Marital and Family Relations in Times of Male Unemployment', in B. Roberts, R. Finnegan and D. Gallie (eds), *New Approaches to Economic Life*, Manchester, Manchester University Press.

Berry, L.A. and D.M. Williams (eds) (1986) *Featherstone: A Glimpse of the Past*, Chorley, Countryside Publications.

Blauner, R. (1960) 'Work Satisfaction and Industrial Trends in Modern Society', in W. Galenson and S.M.Lipset (eds) *Labor and Trade Unionism*, New York, Wiley, pp. 337–60.

Blumer, H. (1964) 'Industrialisation and the Traditional Order', *Sociology and Social Research* 48: 132.

Bott, E. (1957) *Family and Social Network*, London Tavistock.

Bourdieu, P. and J-C. Passeron (1977) *Reproduction in Education, Society and Culture*, Beverly Hills, CA, Sage.

Bowen Report (1893) *Report of the Committee to Enquire into the Circumstances Connected with the Disturbances at Featherstone on 7th September 1893*, Parliamentary Papers, Vol. XVII, London.

Braverman, H. (1974) *Labor and Monopoly Capital*, Monthly Review Press, New York.

Brook, E. and D. Finn (1977) 'Working Class Images of Society and Community Studies', in *Working Papers in Cultural Studies*, Vol. 10, Birmingham, CCCS, University of Birmingham.

Bulmer, M. (1975a) 'Sociological Models of the Mining Community', *Sociological Review*, 23.

Bulmer, M. (ed.) (1975b) *Working-class Images of Society*, London, Routledge and Kegan Paul.

Bulmer, M. (ed.) (1978) *Mining and Social Change, Durham County in the Twentieth Century*, London, Croom Helm.

Campbell, A. (1978) 'Honourable Men and Degraded Slaves: a comparative study of trade unionism in two Lanarkshire mining communities, c. 1830–1874', in R. Harrison (ed.), *The Independent Collier: The Coal Miner as Archetypal Proletarian Reconsidered*, Brighton, Harvester.

Campbell, B. (1986) 'Proletarian Patriarchs and the Real Radicals', in V. Seddon (ed.), *The Cutting Edge: Women and the Pit Strike*, London, Lawrence and Wishart.

Castells, M. (1983), *The City and the Grassroots*, London, Arnold.

Clayton, I., A. Rhodes and T. Lumb (eds) (1990) *This is Featherstone: At Home, at Work and at Play*, Glasshoughton, Yorkshire Arts Circus Education.

Clegg, A. (1974) 'A Subtler and More Telling Power', *Times Educational Supplement*, 27 September.

Cohen, A.P. (1985) *The Symbolic Construction of Community*, London, Horwood/Tavistock.

Collins, R. (1979) *The Credential Society*, New York, Academic Press.

Cooke, P. (ed.) (1989) *Localities: The Changing Face of Urban Britain*, London, Unwin Hyman.

Cousins, J. and R. Brown (1975) 'Patterns of Paradox: Shipbuilding Workers' Images of Society', in M. Bulmer (ed.), *Working-class Images of Society*, London, Routledge and Kegan Paul.

Dahrendorf, R. (1987) 'The Erosion of Citizenship: Its Consequences for Us All', *New Statesman*, 12 June.

Dennis, N., F. Henriques and C. Slaughter (1956) *Coal is Our Life*, London, Eyre and Spottiswoode (2nd edn 1969, London, Tavistock, with a new Introduction by Fernando Henriques).

Department of Employment (1987) *Family Expenditure Survey, 1986*, London, HMSO.

Duncan, S. (1989) 'What is Locality?', in R. Peet and N. Thrift (eds), *New Models in Geography*, Vol. 2, London, Unwin Hyman.

Effrat, M.P. (1974) 'Approaches to Community – Conflicts and Complementarities', *Sociological Inquiry* 43.

Engrand, G. (1975) 'Les consequences sociologiques du statut du mineur', in Centre Interuniversitaire de Récherches en Sciences Humaines, *Une Région en Mutation: Le Nord-Pas de Calais*, Cahiers du CIRSH, No. 1, Universite de Lille III.

Evans, E. (1984) 'The Place of Women Today in Featherstone: A Comparative Study', A Dissertation presented in the Examination for B.A. in Combined Studies, Bretton Hall College, Wakefield.

Featherstone Urban District Council (1901) *Report of the Medical Officer of Health*, Featherstone.

Frankenberg, R. (1966) *Communities in Britain*, Harmondsworth, Penguin.

Frankenberg, R. (1976) 'In the Social Production of their Lives . . .', in D. Leonard-Barker and S. Allen (eds), *Sexual Divisions and Society: Process and Change*, London, Tavistock.

Gallie, D. (1988) 'Employment, unemployment and social stratification', in D. Gallie (ed.). *Employment in Britain*, Oxford, Blackwell.

Gibbon, P. (1988) 'Analysing the British Miners' Strike of 1984–5', *Economy and Society* 17 (2), May.

Gibbon, P. and S. Bromley (1990) 'From an Institution to a Business?: Changes in the British Coal Industry, 1985–9', *Economy and Society* 19 (1), February.

Gibbon, P. and D. Steyne, (eds) (1986) *Thurcroft, A Village and the Miners' Strike: An Oral History*, Nottingham, Spokesman.

Goldthorpe, J. (1980) *Social Mobility and the Class Structure in Modern Britain*, Oxford, Clarendon Press.

Goldthorpe, J. H. and C. Payne (1986) 'Trends in Intergenerational Class Mobility', *Sociology* 20 (1).

Goodchild, J. (1978) *The Coal Kings of Yorkshire*, Wakefield Historical Publications.

Hall, B. (1987) 'Te Kohurau: Continuity and Change in a New Zealand Rural District', Ph.D. Thesis, University of Canterbury, Christchurch, New Zealand.

Halsey, A.H., J. Floud and C.A. Anderson (eds) (1961) *Education, Economy and Society*, New York, Free Press.

Hargreaves, A. (1986) *Two Cultures of Schooling*, Brighton, Falmer Press.

Harper, K. (1989) 'Twenty Pits Face Axe in Coal Break-up', *Guardian*, 7 August.

Harrison, R. (ed.) (1978) *The Independent Collier: The Coal Miner as Archetypal Proletarian Reconsidered*, Brighton, Harvester.

Havighurst, R.J. and A.J. Jansen (1967) 'Community Research – A Trend Report', *Current Sociology* 15 (2).

Heath, A., R. Jowell and J. Curtice (1985) *How Britain Votes*, Oxford, Pergamon.

Horrell S., et al. (1989) *Unequal Jobs or Unequal Pay*, SCELI Working Paper No. 6, ESRC.

Howell, D. (1983) *British Workers and the Independent Labour Party*, Manchester, Manchester University Press.

Hudson, J. (1986) 'Holding it Together' in V. Seddon, (ed.), *The Cutting Edge: Women and the Pit Strike*, London, Lawrence and Wishart.

Hymas, C. (1990) 'Safety Clash Fails to Stop Pits Go-ahead', *Yorkshire Post*, 10 January.

Jenkins, J. (1990) 'The Lady Never Turned Us', *New Statesman and Society*, 16 November.

Kamenka, E. (ed.) (1982) *Community as Social Ideal*, London, Arnold.

Kelly's Trade Directory (1889) *West Yorkshire*.

Kerr, C. and A. Siegel (1954) 'The Inter-industry Propensity to Strike: An International Comparison', in A. Komhauser et al. (eds) *Industrial Conflict*, New York, McGraw-Hill, pp. 189–212.

Lee, D. and H. Newby (1983) *The Problem of Sociology*, London, Hutchinson.

Leonard, D. and M. Speakman (1986) 'Women in the Family: Companions or Caretakers', in V. Beechey and E. Whitelegg (eds), *Women in Britain Today*, Milton Keynes, Open University.

Littlejohn, G., M.D. Peake and D. Warwick et al. (1990) 'Socio-economic Conditions and Aspects of Health: Respiratory Symptoms in Four West Yorkshire Mining Localities', in P. Abbott and G. Payne (eds), *New Directions in the Sociology of*

Health, Brighton, Falmer Press.

Lockwood, D. (1966) 'Sources of Variation in Working-class Images of Society', *Sociological Review* 14 (3).

Lowe, C.R. (1969) 'Industrial Bronchitis', *British Medical Journal*, February, pp. 463–86.

Lowe, S. (1986) *Urban Social Movements*, London, Macmillan.

McKee, L. and C. Bell (1986) 'His Unemployment, Her Problem: Domestic and Marital Consequences of Male Unemployment', in S. Allen, A. Waton, K. Purcell and S. Wood (eds), *The Experience of Unemployment*, London, Macmillan.

Minister of Education's Central Advisory Council (1954) *Report: Early Leaving*, London, HMSO.

McPherson, A. and J.D. Willms (1987) 'Equalisation and Improvement: Some Effects of Comprehensive Reorganisation in Scotland', *Sociology* 21 (4).

Mahowald, M.B. (1972) 'Marx's "Gemeinschaft": Another Interpretation', *Philosophy and Phenomenological Research* 33 (4).

Mann, M. (1988) *States, War and Capitalism*, Oxford, Blackwell.

Marshall, T.H. (1950) *Citizenship and Social Class*, Cambridge, Cambridge University Press.

Martin, J. and C. Roberts (1984) *Women and Employment: A Lifetime Perspective*, London, HMSO.

Mathias, P. (1969) *The First Industrial Nation, An Economic History of Britain, 1700–1914*, London, Methuen.

Meegan, R. (1989) 'Paradise Postponed: The Growth and Decline of Merseyside', in P. Cooke (ed.), *Localities: The Changing Face of Urban Britain*, London, Unwin Hyman.

Mellor, R. (1989) 'Urban Sociology: A Trend Report', *Sociology* 23 (2).

Mingione, E. (1987) 'Urban Survival Strategies, Family Structure and Informal Practices', in M. Smith and J.R. Feagin (eds) *The Capitalist City, Global Restructuring and Community Politics*, Oxford, Blackwell.

Moore, R.S. (1974) *Pit-men, Preachers and Politics, The Effects of Methodism in a Durham Mining Community*, Cambridge, Cambridge University Press.

Moore, R.S. (1975) 'Religion as a Source of Variation in Working-class Images of Society', in M. Bulmer (ed.), *Working-class Images of Society*, London, Routledge and Kegan Paul.

Morris, L.D. (1988) 'Employment, the Household and Social Networks', in D. Gallie (ed.), *Employment in Britain*, Oxford, Blackwell.

Murphy, R. (1988) *Social Closure: The Theory of Monopolisation and Exclusion*, Oxford, Clarendon.

Neuwirth, G. (1969) 'A Weberian Outline of Theory of Community: Its Application to the "Dark Ghetto"', *British Journal of Sociology* 20 (2).

Neville, R.G. (1976) 'The Yorkshire Miners and the 1893 Lockout: The Featherstone Massacre', *International Review of Social History* XXI, Part Three.

O'Donnell, K. (1988) *The Impact of Job Losses in the Coal Mining Industry on Wakefield M.D., 1981–1988*, Wakefield Metropolitan District Council.

Office of Population Censuses and Surveys (1984) *Census 1981, Key Statistics for Urban Areas: The North*, London, HMSO.

Office of Population Censuses and Surveys (1986) *General Household Survey, 1984*, London, HMSO.

Office of Population Censuses and Surveys (1987) *General Household Survey 1985*, London, HMSO.

Office of Population Censuses and Surveys (1988) *Regional Trends 1987*, London, HMSO.

Pahl, J. (1983) 'The Allocation of Money and the Structuring of Inequality in Marriage', *Sociological Review* 31.

Pahl, R.E. (1984) *Divisions of Labour*, Oxford, Blackwell.

Parker, T. (1986) *Red Hill, A Mining Community*, London, Heinemann.

Parkin, F. (ed.) (1974) *The Social Analysis of Class Structure*, London, Tavistock.

Penn, R. and D.C. Dawkins (1983) 'Structural Transformations in the British Class Structure: A Log Linear Analysis of Marital Endogamy in Rochdale 1856–1964', *Sociology* 17 (4).

Redclift, N. and E. Mingione (1985) *Beyond Unemployment, Household, Gender and Subsistence*, Oxford, Blackwell.

Registrar General, *Census of Population, 1921, County Volume: Yorkshire*, London, HMSO.

Registrar General, *Census of Population, 1951, County Volume: Yorkshire*, London, HMSO.

Rex, J. and R.S. Moore (1969) *Race, Community and Conflict: A Study of Sparkbrook*, Oxford, Oxford University Press.

Rimlinger, G.V. (1959) 'International Differences in the Strike-Propensity of Coal Miners: Experience in Four Countries', *Industrial and Labour Relations Review*, pp. 389–405.

Samuel, R., B. Bloomfield and G. Bonas (1986) *The Enemy Within, Pit Villages and the Miner's Strike of 1984–5*, London, Routledge.

Schmalenbach, H. (1961) 'The Sociological Category of Communion', in T. Parsons, E. Shils and K.D. Naegele (eds), *Theories of Society: Foundations of Modern Sociological Theory*, New York, Free Press.

Seddon, V. (ed.) (1986) *The Cutting Edge: Women and the Pit Strike*, London, Lawrence and Wishart.

Simpson, R.L. (1965) 'Sociology of the Community – Current Status and Prospects', *Rural Sociology* 30 (2).

Smith, D. (1989) *North and South: Britain's Economic, Social and Political Divide*, Harmondsworth, Penguin.

Spaven, P. (1978) 'Main Gates of Protest: Contrasts in Rank and File Activity among the South Yorkshire Miners, 1858–1894', in R. Harrison (ed.), *The Independent Collier: The Coal Miner as Archetypal Proletarian Reconsidered*, Brighton, Harvester.

Stein, M. (1964) *The Eclipse of Community*, New York, Harper Torch.

Taylor, R. (1979) 'Migration and the Residual Community', *Sociological Review* 27 (3).

Thompson, E.P. (1976) 'On History, Sociology and Historical Evidence', *British Journal of Sociology* XXVII (3).

Touraine, A. (1981) *The Voice and The Eye*, Cambridge, Cambridge University Press.

Townsend, P., N. Davidson and M. Whitehead (eds) (1988) *Inequalities in Health*, Harmondsworth, Penguin.

Trist, E.L. and K.W. Bamforth (1951) 'Some Social and Psychological Consequences of the Longwall Method of Coal Getting', *Human Relations* 4: 3–38.

Waddington, D., M. Wykes and C. Critcher with S. Hebron (1991) *Split at the Seams? Community, Continuity and Change after the 1984–5 Coal Dispute*, Milton Keynes, Open University Press.

Wild, R.A. (1981), *Australian Community Studies and Beyond*, London, Allen & Unwin.

Williams, C. (1981) *Open Cut, The Working Class in an Australian Mining Town*, London, Allen & Unwin.

Williamson, B. (1982) *Class, Culture and Community, A Biographical Study of Social Change in Mining*, London, Routledge and Kegan Paul.

Winterton, J. and R. Winterton (1985) *The Implications of NCB Restructuring Policies for West Yorkshire*, West Yorkshire Metropolitan County Council, Wakefield.

Winterton, J. and R. Winterton (1989) *Coal, Crisis and Conflict, The 1984/5 Miners' Strike in Yorkshire*, Manchester, Manchester University Press.

Wise, D. (1990) 'Grants Ease BC Losses', *Guardian*, 31 August.

Zimbalist, A. (ed.), (1979) *Case Studies in the Labour Process*, New York, Monthly Review Press.

Name index

Subject index